UNIVERSITY OF
WOLVERHAMPTON

earning
Can
Vol
Sc

Understanding Organizational
Culture

Understanding Organizational Culture

Mats Alvesson

SAGE Publications
London • Thousand Oaks • New Delhi

First published 2002

Apart from any fair dealing for the purposes of research or private
study, or criticism or review, as permitted under the Copyright,
Designs and Patents Act, 1988, this publication may be
reproduced, stored or transmitted in any form, or by any means,
only with the prior permission in writing of the publishers, or in
the case of reprographic reproduction, in accordance with the
terms of licences issued by the Copyright Licensing Agency.
Inquiries concerning reproduction outside those terms should be
sent to the publishers.

SAGE Publications Ltd
6 Bonhill Street
London EC2A 4PU

SAGE Publications Inc
2455 Teller Road
Thousand Oaks, California 91320

SAGE Publications India Pvt Ltd
32, M-Block Market
Greater Kailash - I
New Delhi 110 048

British Library Cataloguing in Publication data

A catalogue record for this book is available from
the British Library

ISBN 0-7619-7005-3
     0-7619-7006-1 (pb)

Library of Congress Control Number available

Typeset by SIVA Math Setters, Chennai, India
Printed in Great Britain by The Cromwell Press Ltd,
Trowbridge, Wiltshire

Contents

Preface

I have spent a significant part of my work time during the last 15 years developing and applying cultural perspectives on organizations. Despite considerable irritation with many uses of the culture concept in organization studies and elsewhere, I still feel that a cultural focus offers a very inspiring and potentially creative way of understanding organizations, management and working life. My interest has resulted in several books and numerous articles with theoretical and/or empirical ambitions. The present book summarizes and in particular develops and expands this work.

One of my previous books had the title *Cultural Perspectives on Organizations* and was published by Cambridge University Press in 1993. It was fairly short and condensed. The book was positively received by academics, but possibly less so by students. It was reprinted a couple of times, but when it eventually went out of print I decided to revise and expand the book, making it much more accessible. I had in mind a significant revision and expansion, but as typically happens, this moderately ambitious task soon became an entirely new and rather energy-demanding project, i.e. a new book. This increased level of ambition and the length of this text reflect the expansion of the literature on the subject, my own recent and current conceptual work and empirical studies in neighbouring areas and, more generally, my enthusiasm for the field. About a third of the present book is based on my earlier book, but also this material has been thoroughly revised and up-dated. It is primarily Chapters 2, 3 and 7 that draw upon material from the 1993 volume. In addition, there some sections which review or draw upon my earlier or parallel work. Some of this is in collaboration with Yvonne Billing and Dan Kärreman. I am grateful for their permission to incorporate joint work in this text. References are mentioned in the text.

The present book has benefited from feedback from Yvonne Billing, Mike Chumer, Simon Down, Bob Kreishner, Alan Lowe and Martin Parker, as well as from the participants of a PhD course on 'organizational culture', autumn 2000, taught by the author at Department of Business Administration, Lund University, and of a course on 'advanced organizational communication', taught by Diane Grimes, Department of Speech Communication, Syracuse University. The feedback from the students encouraged me to make the text more accessible. The cheeky comment that while journalists sometimes have the rule to not write sentences containing more than seven words, I seem to limit myself to seven subsidiary clauses per sentence, triggered some revisions. I assume that at least junior readers will appreciate these.

Lund just before Christmas 2000
Mats Alvesson

1 The Concept of Organizational Culture

Organizational culture is one of the major issues in academic research and education, in organization theory as well as in management practice. There are good reasons for this: the cultural dimension is central in all aspects of organizational life. Even in those organizations where cultural issues receive little explicit attention, how people in a company think, feel, value and act are guided by ideas, meanings and beliefs of a cultural (socially shared) nature. Whether managers think that culture is too soft or too complicated to bother about or whether there is no unique corporate culture does not reduce the significance of culture. Senior organizational members are always, in one way or another, 'managing culture' – underscoring what is important and what is less so and framing how the corporate world should be understood. Organizations practising intensive 'numbers management' may develop and reproduce a culture celebrating performance indicators and rituals around the handling of these. In most contemporary organizations, corporate culture receives a lot of attention and is seen as crucial. However, even in those cases where top managers have a strong awareness of the significance of culture, there is often a lack of a deeper understanding of how people and organizations function in terms of culture. Culture is as significant and complex as it is difficult to understand and 'use' in a thoughtful way. Awareness of and interest in culture vary between managers and companies. It is often difficult to attain a high level of cultural awareness to guide actions. The interest in quick fixes in much management writings and thinking is unhelpful. Instead a well elaborated framework and a vocabulary in which core concepts – culture, meaning, symbolism – are sorted out is necessary for understanding and for qualified organizational practice by consultants, managers and others.

It is tempting to emphasize the significance of corporate cultures for performance, growth and success. In the beginning of the 1980s books identifying characteristics of excellent companies in the USA (Peters and Waterman, 1982) and the secrets behind the at the time highly successful Japanese companies (e.g. Ouchi, 1981) highlighted corporate culture. These books, in combination with journalistic writings, created a widely spread belief of corporate cultures being perhaps the significant factor behind the performance of companies. This belief has been shaken by problems of many of the companies portrayed by Peters and Waterman as 'excellent' some years after the publication of the book as well as decreasing performances of Japanese companies during recent years. In addition, others, more 'rationalistic' business recipes, have partly replaced culture and the focus on 'people' as the latest fashion for companies and managers during the first half of the 1990s. Still, a strong case can be made for taking an interest in corporate culture in relationship to performance. Managers frequently ascribe successes such as rapid growth to their culture. 'Companies win or lose based on the cultures they create', the CEO of CompUSA, the largest retailer of personal computers, says (*Academy of Management Executive*, 1999: 34). Also many of the most influential academics agree. Pfeffer (1994: 6), for example, argues that the traditional sources of success – product and process technology, access to regulated markets, economies of scale, etc. – matter less today than in the past, 'leaving organizational culture and capabilities, derived from how people are managed, as comparatively more vital'. Knowledge is said to be the crucial factor behind sustainable advantage and success for companies and knowledge issues are closely interlinked with organizational culture (Davenport and Prusak, 1998). Knowledge management then partly becomes a matter of cultural management (Alvesson and Kärreman, 2001; McDermott, 1999). Culture is thus highly significant for how companies and other organizations function: from strategic change, to everyday leadership and how managers and employees relate to and interact with customers as well as to how knowledge is created, shared, maintained and utilized.

My major point is *not*, however, to preach culture as the principle means to corporate effectiveness, growth and success. It is, as will be elaborated in Chapter 3, difficult to establish clear and causal links between culture and something else. Trying to do so easily implicates a rather simplistic view on culture that seriously underestimates its theoretical potential and value. Nor is my interest to offer new recipes for effective management of culture. For me, organizational culture is significant as a way of understanding organizational life in all its richness and variations. The centrality of the culture concept follows from the profound importance of shared meanings for any coordinated action. As Smircich (1985) says, organizations exist as systems of meanings that are shared to various degrees. A sense of common, taken for granted ideas, beliefs and meanings are necessary for continuing organized activity. This makes interaction possible without constant confusion or intense interpretation and re-interpretation of meanings. For organizational practitioners – managers and others shaping organizational life – a developed capacity to think in terms of organizational culture facilitates acting wisely. Insights and reflections may be useful in relationship to getting people to do the 'right' things in terms of effectiveness, but also for promoting more autonomous standpoints in relationship to dominant ideologies, myths, fashions, etc. To encourage and facilitate the thinking through of various aspects of values, beliefs and assumptions in industry, occupations and organizations seem to me to be a worthwhile task. This book tries to make a contribution in this direction.

The book deals with the why and how of cultural understandings of organizations. I try to suggest novel ways of making us more alert to the possibilities of cultural analysis, showing how it can lead to insightful interpretations of organizations, management and working life. The general aims are thus to contribute to a more reflective mode of research and to more reflective corporate practitioners. Reflective then refers not only to how we relate to instrumental concerns in a more varied, thoughtful and learning-oriented way. It also includes the critical thinking through of objectives, arrangements and acts in terms of how they contribute to, or work against, the common good. It draws attention to hidden ethical and political dimensions of organizational life.

The meaning(s) of culture

A glance at just a few works that use the term 'organizational culture' will reveal enormous variation in the definitions of this term and even more in the use of the term 'culture'. 'Culture' has no fixed or broadly agreed meaning even in anthropology (Borowsky, 1994; Ortner, 1984), but variation in its use is especially noticeable in the literature on organizational culture. This is partly related to strong differences in the purpose and depth of books and articles. But also the broad variation of scientific disciplines and research orientations involved in organizational culture studies makes the field very heterogeneous.[1] The concept of culture seems to lend itself to very different uses as collectively shared forms of for example, ideas and cognition, as symbols and meanings, as values and ideologies, as rules and norms, as emotions and expressiveness, as the collective unconscious, as behaviour patterns, structures and practices, etc. all of which may be made targets to study. Of course, culture is not unique in this way. Actually, most if not all significant concepts in organization studies and social science tend to be accompanied with a variety of different meanings and definitions (Palmer and Hardy, 2000).

Culture is, however, a tricky concept as it is easily used to cover everything and consequently nothing. That certain researchers are interested in 'culture' – or at least use the term – does not mean that they have very much in common. Frequently 'culture' seems to refer to little more than a social pattern, e.g. it refers to surface phenomena rather than explores the meanings and ideas behind them. It could therefore be advocated that in many cases the term should be abandoned in favour of something like 'informal behaviour patterns', 'norm system', or simply 'social pattern'. Many people referring to culture seem to do so in a very vague way and it is important to use the concept without losing focus, direction and interpretive depth.

I use the term 'organizational culture' as an umbrella concept for a way of thinking which takes a serious interest in cultural and symbolic phenomena. This term directs the spotlight in a particular direction rather than mirroring a concrete reality for possible study. I agree with Frost *et al.*'s (1985: 17) 'definition' of organizational culture: 'Talking about organizational culture seems to mean talking about the importance for people of symbolism – of rituals, myths, stories and legends – and about the interpretation of events, ideas, and experiences that are influenced and shaped by the groups within which they live'. I will also, however, take organizational culture to include values and assumptions about social reality, but for me values are less central and less useful than meanings and symbolism in cultural analysis. This position is in line with the view broadly shared by many modern anthropologists (especially Geertz, 1973). Culture is then understood to be a system of common symbols and meanings. It provides 'the shared rules governing cognitive and affective aspects of membership in an organization, and the means whereby they are shaped and expressed' (Kunda, 1992: 8).

Culture is not primarily 'inside' people's heads, but somewhere 'between' the heads of a group of people where symbols and meanings are publicly expressed, e.g. in work group interactions, in board meetings but also in material objects.

Culture then is central in governing the understanding of behaviour, social events, institutions and processes. Culture is the setting in which these phenomena become comprehensible and meaningful.

Meaning refers to how an object or an utterance is interpreted. Meaning has a subjective referent in the sense that it appeals to an expectation, a way of relating to things. Meaning makes an object relevant and meaningful. In a cultural context, it is socially shared and not personally idiosyncratic meanings, that are of interest. I will give an example: a formal rule in a company says that factory management can only decide on investments up to £25,000, larger investments must be sanctioned by a higher authority. This can be seen as a simple, objective structural arrangement. The exact meaning of the rule, however, calls for interpretation – and here culture enters. Various meanings are possible: (a) it is under all circumstances intolerable and leads to automatic dismissal that a factory manager makes larger purchases or investments; (b) 'investment' can be interpreted or divided up in different ways and £25,000 is a rough guideline rather than a precise figure; (c) as a general principle one should consult top management before significantly or without strong reasons exceeding this level, etc. Another option is that this rule is read and applied/responded to with much variation, it may be seen as a strict guideline for younger factory managers and for managers of units seen as performing below or around average, while experienced managers heading high-performing units are not expected to obey the rule at all. A rule differs in how strictly and uniformly it is interpreted and taken seriously due to the cultural context given the rule its exact meaning. We can imagine different organizational cultures in which the same rule is given very different meanings and thus leads to different behaviours and consequences of the rule.

In a cultural context it is always socially shared meanings that are of interest, not so much highly personal meanings. Individuals may be more or less authoritarian-bound and obey with rules or they may dislike and rebel against bureaucracy – they may as individuals see rules as indicators of order and rationality or as a straitjacket and an obstacle to the exercise of judgement and responsibility. Individual meanings are certainly important and they may vary considerably within a group. But a cultural understanding concentrates *not* on individual idiosyncracies: it is the shared orientations within an organization or another group that is of interest.

A *symbol* can be defined as an object – a word or statement, a kind of action or a material phenomenon – that stands ambiguously for something else and/or something more than the object itself (Cohen, 1974). A symbol is rich in meaning – it condensates a more complex set of meanings in a particular object and thus communicates meaning in an economic way. Occasionally, the complexity of a symbol and the meaning it expresses calls for considerable interpretation and deciphering. People have private symbols, but in an organizational context it is collective symbolism that is of most interest.[2]

When thinking about culture it is important to bear in mind what culture is not, i.e. what a cultural perspective does not focus on. Making a distinction between culture and social structure is helpful here. Culture is regarded as a more or less cohesive system of meanings and symbols, in terms of which social interaction takes place. Social structure is regarded as the behavioural patterns which the social interaction itself gives rise to. In the case of culture, then, we have a frame of reference of beliefs, expressive symbols and values, by means of which individuals define their environment, express their feelings and make judgements. At the social structural level, we have a continuous process of interaction. As Geertz (1973: 145) states, culture is the creation of meaning through which human beings interpret their experiences and guide their actions, while social structure is the form which action takes or the network of social relationships which actually exists.

This means that culture and social structure represent different abstractions of the same phenomenon. Culture describes social action as depending on the meaning it has for those involved, while social structure describes social action from the point of view of its consequences on the functioning of the social system. This understanding permits treatment of the tension arising between culture and social structure. A reasonable assumption is that culture and social structure are not necessarily in a well-integrated and harmonic relationship with each other, i.e. not best defined or analysed in terms of integration and coherence. Discontinuity between social and cultural structures can occur, for example, when there is a change in formal rules or routines which is not matched by a change in cultural patterns (Fombrun, 1986). Studying the cultural therefore is not the same as studying social structure. A significant problem in much writing under the rubric of culture is that it lacks sufficient focus and depth in the exploration of meaning and symbolism; instead it drifts to a more 'superficial' study of social patterns: structures, behaviours and relations.

Despite the emphasis on culture set forth by Geertz and others as an ideational phenomenon, cultural analysis is, of course, not limited to studying the shared meanings and ideas of people or forms of communication with a strong symbolic element, such as 'exotic' rituals. Cultural analysis may be applied to all kinds of social phenomena. The point is that culture research concentrates on meanings anchored and transmitted in a symbolic form. Cultural meanings guide thinking, feeling and acting. It is thus difficult to argue that culture is not important. It may be argued that culture denotes something too vague and broad to be very useful, but cultural analysis is more delimited and precise as it is directed at specific phenomena: how people think strategically, how they interpret and respond to the acts of a superior, how they understand the customer and give meaning to a label such as 'market orientation'.

An illustrative example on the significance of cultural meaning is provided by Olie (1994) who studied mergers between Dutch and German companies. Different orientations and understandings of the decision process were profound. The German managers saw meetings as instruments for decision-making, while the Dutch managers tended to perceive them as platforms for exchanging ideas and information as a preparation for further action. In the eyes of the German managers, Dutch meetings were time-consuming and ineffective. The Germans found it even more frustrating that once a common agreement was finally reached, the Dutch tended to treat it in their own way and behave accordingly if they felt that flexibility was called for. For the German managers, a decision was seen as something one should strictly stick to. All this overlapped with an authoritarian leadership style in the German company and a preference for participative management in the Dutch camp. Here we can see how the entire decision-making process from preparation to implementation to a large extent reflects cultural beliefs and meanings about what is rational, natural and effective. This example contrasts two different sets of meanings around decision-making, but also in a 'one-culture-company' decision-making never takes place in a purely rational manner. The example thus illustrates not only problems with mergers and cross-national interaction, but also the cultural nature of decision-making.

This book treats a variety of ways of using ideas on culture in research and organizational practice. This calls for balancing between freezing a definite view on culture and letting the concept stand for anything and nothing. Most of the diverse perspectives surveyed here share the following assumptions about cultural phenomena (cf. Hofstede *et al.*, 1990; Trice and Beyer, 1993):

- they are related to history and tradition;
- have some depth, are difficult to grasp and account for, and must be interpreted;
- they are collective and shared by members of groups;
- they are primarily ideational in character, having to do with meanings, understandings, beliefs, knowledge, and other intangibles;
- they are holistic, intersubjective and emotional rather than strictly rational and analytical.

Viewing culture broadly as a shared and learned world of experiences, meanings, values, and understandings which inform people and which are expressed, reproduced, and communicated partly in symbolic form is consistent with a variety of approaches to the conduct of concrete studies. More precise ways of viewing culture and what they can reveal will be explored, compared, assessed and developed in this book.

Some comments on the contemporary interest in organizational culture

Studies on organizational culture had been conducted since the 1940s but they were sparse and scattered until the 'corporate-culture boom' of the early 1980s. During the last decade the interest in organizational culture from both academics and practitioners continue to be relatively high. Among practitioners it is to some extent connected to industry. In younger, more innovative and knowledge-intensive businesses there seems to be a stronger interest than in more mature and rationalization-oriented ones. Many IT companies, for example, are credited for developing and sustaining distinct corporate cultures.[3] The interest in identifying, developing, sharing and using knowledge in a more systematic way typically leads to a strong interest in organizational culture. But during periods of change, including in merger and acquisition situations, culture receives considerable attention also in companies where management of culture is not normally seen as a top priority.

It seems reasonable to point at a set of factors or lines of development to make sense of the increased interest in particular in the 1980s. The exaggerated view of corporate culture as a universal tool for competitiveness and 'excellence' was partly due to the fertile ground created by the boom of the Japanese companies and the corresponding difficulties for US and other Western economies at that time, and the skilful exploitation of pop-management authors and consultants. There are, however, a mix of more substantive and lasting reasons for the ongoing interest in organizational culture. For many academic writers it arises from theoretical concerns (see, e.g. Frost *et al.*, 1985). Traditional organization research, often objectivist and abstract, has proved incapable of providing deep, rich, and realistic understandings. Organizational culture differs as it addresses the lived experiences of people. The culture concept also has the advantage that it seems to provide a conceptual bridge between micro- and macro-levels of analysis and between organizational behaviour and strategic management (Smircich, 1983a: 346). It connects the organization as a whole with everyday experiences and individual action.

Changes in production technology and/or work organization during the recent decades may also have been important in bringing the cultural dimension into sharper focus. Brulin (1989) suggests that efforts to reduce storage costs by increasing the throughput speed of products in manufacturing processes call for greater flexibility and a higher degree of commitment from the workforce than in traditional forms of work organization. This sometimes leads to a reduction of the significance of distinct occupational identities and provides more space for, as well as managerial interest in, reinforcing organization-based identifications and orientations (Casey, 1996). Culture then becomes significant as a glue holding the organization together. In addition, changes in values and life-styles among employees and in society tend to make corporate control more complicated and it becomes more important to involve workers in the companies. People don't expect to be bossed, which calls for less authoritarian styles of management. These developments create a background for the interest in organizational cultures.

The expansion of high-tech and other knowledge-intensive companies employing a large number of professionals whose loyalty is crucial, also contributes to the recognition of the significance of culture in management (Alvesson, 1995; Kunda and Barley, 1988; Robertson, 1999). Weick (1987: 118) speaks of a reduction in the number of mechanistic organizations and a corresponding increase in the proportion of organic organizations 'held together by culture'. 'This is why we see more culture and judge it to be more important. There is not more culture, there simply are more organic systems'. The important trend away from mass production to service, knowledge and information in the economy makes ideational aspects – the regulation of beliefs and images – more important, for example, in service management (Alvesson, 1990). Associated with this is a change in emphasis from control of behaviour and measurement of outputs to control of employees' attitudes and commitment, the latter being crucial for the employee service-mindedness which in turn has an impact on the level of customer satisfaction.

It is also possible that organizations these days do not automatically produce 'enough' local culture – naturally emerging, distinct organization-wide cultural patterns – and it is this which accounts for the current interest in it. Van Maanen and Barley (1985: 40) remark that it is because modern management methods are antithetical to 'cultural authority' that 'the notion of "organizational culture" has attained a faddish appeal in business literature'. Cultural patterns become more diverse and less stable. As Giddens (1991: 3) writes: 'Doubt, a pervasive feature of modern critical reason, permeates into everyday life as well as philosophical consciousness, and forms a general existential dimension of the contemporary social world'. The traditional obedience to authorities has faded away. Business leaders, like other conventional authorities, are increasingly faced with an unwillingness of subordinates to be pushed around or to accept their messages at face value. Instead managers need to convince subordinates – and perhaps even themselves and their customers and partners – about the beliefs, values and ideals to strive for and accept as guidelines. A perceived need to develop or repair a cultural framework supporting authority and the orientations deemed to be appropriate may thus be a broad trend, but perhaps most salient in organic organizations, where change and instability plus frequently a rather qualified workforce make traditional sources of authority and community most vulnerable.

Cognitive interests

Any social science project should carefully reflect upon and position itself to the issue of the basic purpose or rationale. Highly valuable here is Habermas' (1972) idea of cognitive or knowledge-constitutive interests. He identifies three basic motives or interests in which any knowledge-seeking project is grounded.

The technical interest aims at developing knowledge of causal relationships in order to manipulate and control variables for the sake of accomplishing certain wanted outcomes. *The practical-hermeneutic interest* aims at achieving understanding about human existence – the creation of meaning and communication in order to produce knowledge about wo/man as a cultural being, without any particular concern for the utility of that knowledge. *The emancipatory interest* aims at liberating humans from external and internal repressive forces that prevent them from acting in accordance with their free choices. In Table 1.1 Habermas' scheme is accounted for (Willmott, 1997: 317). (For a discussion of the merits and weaknesses of this three-term framework, see Alvesson and Willmott, 1996. For applications of it to organizational culture studies, see Knights and Willmott, 1987; Stablein and Nord, 1985.)

Academic studies and practitioner thinking on organizational culture guided by *the technical interest* often proceed from the assumption that culture is in some way related to organizational performance. Advocates of this view believe that it is

Table 1.1 *Habermas' three knowledge-constitutive interests*

Cognitive interest	Type of science	Purpose	Focus	Orientation	Projected outcome
Technical	Empirical-analytic	Enhance prediction and control	Identification and manipulation of variables	Calculation	Removal of formal irrationality
Practical	Historical-hermeneutic	Improve mutual understanding	Interpretation of symbolic communication	Appreciation	Removal of misunderstanding
Emancipatory	Critical	Realize enlightenment project through development of more rational social relations	Exposure of domination and exploitation	Transformation	Removal of socially unnecessary suffering

Source: Reprinted by permission of Sage Publications Ltd from Hugh Wilmott, 'Management and organization studies as science? Methodologies of OR in critical perspective' © *Organization*, August 1997

vital to uncover linkages or causal relationships between forms of organizational culture and corporate performance and to produce knowledge that increases the chance of affecting specific cultural phenomena (symbols, rites, values, norms, etc.) or cultural systems in their totality, so that outcomes considered beneficial can be attained. This is an 'offensive' formulation of the issue, one which suggests that culture can be used as a tool or guiding concept for achieving effectiveness. A 'defensive' version of the culture-performance link sees culture more as an obstacle to economic rationality and effectiveness. It then becomes a question of controlling or bypassing culture so that 'it' does not obstruct rational plans or intentions based, for example, on strategic thinking or financial criteria. In other words, this defensive interest in culture is motivated by a desire to avoid difficulties in companies due to the 'negative' features of culture such as resistance to change and cultural conflicts, for example in the context of mergers and acquisitions. While the offensive view can be described as a *tool view* of culture, the defensive view can be called a *trap view*.

Most technically oriented writings on the subject are optimistic and want to use culture as a resource for effective managerial action. Through controlling values and subordinates' definition of reality the wanted flexible and committed orientations and effective behaviour can be produced, it is believed. I think it is important to balance this optimism by emphasizing the difficulties with managing culture. Insights about these may make it easier for managers to avoid projects or forms of communication that are likely to fail and lead to frustration, opposition and/or cynicism. Rather than to tell managers what to do, culture theory can help them know what to *not* do or to be prepared for problems following from cultural clashes in for example international business, organizational change initiatives, joint ventures or mergers and acquisitions. Of course, through illuminating difficulties and pitfalls, managers get assistance on how to think in order to use culture in a more offensive way, so the trap and tool views may be supportive rather than mutually exclusive orientations.

Culture and symbolism research guided by the *practical-hermeneutic* cognitive interest does not concern itself with what culture might accomplish or how this accomplishment might be improved but concentrates on the creation of meaning in organizational communities. The primary task is often identified as exploring organizations as a subjective or, and better, intersubjective experience. Within this cognitive interest, 'questions of interpretation and description take precedence over questions of function and causal explanations' (Sypher *et al.*, 1985: 17). A common aim is to understand 'how to achieve common interpretations of situations so that coordinated action is possible' (Smircich, 1983a: 351). From a practical-hermeneutic interest knowledge is viewed as an end in itself rather than being tied to the seemingly more useful purposes of either technical problem-solving or emancipation. This general understanding may, however, be 'used' in different ways that normally touch upon one or the other of these approaches broadly understood. Understanding – when experienced as important – may either encourage new forms of instrumental action or make people feel more enlightened. Contributions in any of these directions are not, however, the direct purpose of the researcher. The principle interest is in the understanding of the meanings, symbolism and ideas of the community being studied; in other words to find out what the 'natives' think they are up to.

The *emancipatory* approach investigates primarily the negative features of organizational life and helps to counteract the taken-for-granted beliefs and values that limit personal autonomy. From this perspective, cultural studies provide insight into organizational life that may contribute to liberating thought from its traditional patterns and the repressive aspects of culture. One example would be cultural meanings with a strong gender bias. Organizational cultures often bear strong imprints of masculine domination, leading to ideas of what is 'natural' and valuable in organizations and to emphasize instrumentality, hierarchy, toughness and denial of relations and dependence, and to downplay emotions, intuition and social relations (Alvesson and Billing, 1997). Such ideas may have a doubtful value for business, for example through allowing only a narrow set of leadership behaviour, and through excluding most women and some non-macho men to be seriously and fairly considered for promotion. These meanings and values may lead to an impoverished working life, for women as well as for many men. Within an emancipatory project it is not, however, the possible disadvantages for business results but for people in terms of constrained thinking and acting that is the primary problem. Thus, the purpose of cultural studies is liberating human potential or, more defensively, illuminating the obstacles of emancipation. The task of cultural studies, then, is to encourage critical reflection on beliefs, values, and understandings of social conditions.

There are two broad targets for emancipatory efforts. One is a critique of ideologies and sociocultural processes in organizations in which asymmetrical power relations and the exercise of power make their mark on people's consciousness. The use of the idea of 'corporate culture' may here appear as a way in which management instills favourable definitions of reality in the minds of employees, and domination through symbolism becomes the target (e.g. Knights and Willmott, 1987; Rosen, 1985; Willmott, 1993). The other emancipatory project aims at illuminating basic values and understandings with a view to counteracting ethnocentrism and broader, taken-for-granted cultural assumptions (Alvesson and Deetz, 2000; Carter and Jackson, 1987; Prasad, 1997). Whereas it is sceptical of the values typically advocated by management, its scope is broader and includes a cultural critique of ideologies and meanings that may also constrain social elites.

The three cognitive interests indicate a wide spectrum of ways to approach organizational culture (as well as other phenomena). The relationship between the three, and in particular between the technical and the emancipatory, is antagonistic. But it is also possible to see bridges between them. Contrary to the bold claims of much managerial writing, it is important to acknowledge that culture is not just something that can be actively mobilized to make people think, feel, value and behave in accordance with managerial wants, but that culture frequently works as a source of employees' resistance to managerial objectives and control. Intention behind managerial interventions and arrangements on the one hand and subordinates' reactions to these on the other, may thus differ heavily. Of course, there is always individual variation but the cultural dimension is crucial here. All managerial action then needs to consider the cultural context in which it is carried out – how subordinates, customers, etc. give meaning to, and act based on their perception of the world. Sometimes the managerial intended meaning resembles those targeted (subordinates, partners, customers, the public), sometimes the cultural meanings developed by the latter differ heavily and work as a counterforce to managerial intent. Many mergers and acquisitions for example fail or lead to less than optimal results partly due to cultural differences (e.g. Empson, 2001; Olie, 1994) or to ongoing interactions in which differences and dissension are created and reinforced (Kleppestø, 1993). Managerial work then calls for careful consideration of those interacted with and communicated to. An understanding of cultural management not as a technocratic project where managerial agents engineer the minds of their subordinate objects, but as an interactive, interpretive enterprise, may reduce – but not overcome – the gap between a technical, a practical-hermeneutic and an emancipatory approach to organizational culture.

Objectives of this book

The overall purpose of this text is to provide a qualified and broad introduction to, as well as development of, organizational culture and to strengthen it as a powerful and inspirational framework for 'deep thinking' about what goes on in organizations and in management. Cultural interpretation is, I think, one of the best ways of understanding a broad spectrum of aspects of management and organization, but its potential has only partially been utilized, despite much effort, in academic work as well as in organizational practice. We need more 'cultural imagination' in studying and practising organization. My objectives can partly be illuminated through treating the why and how of cultural interpretation.

One of this book's main objectives is to add something to the ways we think about *why* we should conduct cultural studies of organizations – specifically, what knowledge-constitutive or cognitive interests (Habermas, 1972; Alvesson and Willmott, 1996) make such studies worthwhile. In principle there are two broad answers. The first views organizational culture as a means of promoting more effective managerial action, whereas the second views culture as a point of entry for a broader understanding of and critical reflection upon organizational life and work. These two answers are not necessarily mutually exclusive (understanding and reflection may precede effective action), but the goal of promoting effectiveness tends to rule out complicated research designs and 'deep' thinking, while promotion of broad critical reflection presupposes that the project is not subordinated to managerial interests. Cultural interpretation as a knowledge resource for accomplishing managerial objectives is radically different from questioning them.

One may, however, recognize the legitimacy of managerial action based on a sophisticated understanding of culture at the same time as one is critical of forms of organizational culture that exercise socially unnecessary domination. To some extent all forms of management means domination and to some extent all social life presupposes constraint; the challenge is to identify and explore more problematic and arbitrary forms of power. The interesting aspect here is 'surplus' domination – in which a significant element of constraint to individual freedom, evaluated to do more harm than good, is targeted and/or where insight of the power element is seen to facilitate more informed and thought through considerations. The line between legitimate and illegitimate exercise of power is thin and open to debate – it therefore should not be avoided but addressed.

This book takes seriously the capacity of culture to *simultaneously* create order, meaning, cohesion and orientation, thus making collective action, indeed organizational life, possible *and* to restrict autonomy, creativity and questioning, thereby preventing novel, potentially more ethically thought through ways of organizing social life from being considered. Understanding and assessing culture calls for taking seriously what it makes possible as well as what it makes impossible. Arguably, a broadened cultural understanding which encourages problem-solving and problem-awareness – neglecting neither instrumental nor political-ethical concerns – may contribute to the social good. The trick is then to navigate between managerial technocratic consciousness and critical good-doing elitism, stimulating academic work and practical organizational acts guided by an ongoing struggle to being open for the multidimensionality of culture.

The other major objective of this book is to stimulate reflection on *how* a cultural understanding of organization can best be accomplished. This calls for an ability to vary perspectives: to consider several aspects and relate these to each other. Reflexivity and insight, not procedure and truth, then become catchwords (Alvesson and Sköldberg, 2000). This 'how' question is, of course, contingent upon the 'why' question. The overall purpose of doing organizational culture analysis is, naturally, guiding answers to questions on how such analysis is best conducted. How can we think productively about culture in academic research and education as well as in organizational practice? What does it mean to see an organization as a culture? How can we use culture in order to get a good combination of guidance/focus and openness, appreciating wholeness and depth, analytical and theoretical insight and experienced organizational life? These are challenges that the present text takes seriously.

The following topics seem vital to: (1) the role and meaning of metaphors for both organizations and culture, i.e. the basic meanings (gestalt, image) we have in mind when addressing organizational culture; (2) the significance of culture for corporate performance; (3) broadening the area of application for cultural thinking and developing it as a key dimension of management, marketing, strategy, the business concept; (4) exploring culture in relationship to leadership and understanding leadership in an organizational culture context; (5) the emancipatory potential of cultural studies as a counterweight to ethnocentrism and parochialism as well as specific forms of managerial domination and thereby as a facilitator of reflection on self-limiting forms of understanding; (6) the question of level of analysis – whether the organization is a culture, a set of subcultures, or a local reflection of societal macro-culture (a societal subculture); and (7) culture as a source of order and integration versus culture being characterized by differentiation, contradiction and ambiguity. Careful consideration of each of these themes will highlight the weaknesses and strengths of various approaches and suggest improvements that may help organizational culture thinking to produce insights about organizations and working life – in research and organizational practice.

The seven topics are addressed in Chapters 2–7, with one topic per chapter (apart from the two last topics which are treated in Chapter 7), in the same order as presented here, i.e. topic 1 is addressed in Chapter 2, topic 2 in Chapter 3 and so on.

I try to reach a broader readership and I have written the book so that it is possible to skip or skim some parts of it without too much difficulty. Practitioners may find Chapter 2 and pages 160–166 and 186–195 less significant or easy to digest. Some undergraduate students may feel the same, although those familiar with Morgan's *Images of Organization* (1986) will probably also be comfortable with these parts of the book.

Summary

Organizational culture is one of the key areas of management and organization studies as well as practice. An important task of managers is to try to manage the ideas and understandings of their subordinates. Also dealing with technical issues – budgets, information systems – call for people ascribing a positive and similar meaning for these to work well. All management takes place within culture, this includes organizational culture but also societal-level, industrial and suborganization-level culture. The expansion of the interest in culture during the 1980s reflects an increased interest in organizational life and managerial action and responds also to the development of new forms of organizations in which formal hierarchy and bureaucracy are less effective means of control and in which ideas, beliefs and values are central. This does not mean that one necessarily should adopt sweeping statements about 'new organizations' as a major rationale for an interest in organizational culture. Although 'rationalistic' modes of management control or machine-like organizations clearly still are significant, these also need to be understood in a cultural context and scrutinized in terms of the cultural orientations that they rely upon as well as trigger. In addition, we live in an increasingly international and multicultural society, making cultural issues highly salient.

This book is an effort to clarify alternative approaches to organizational culture, to contribute to an increased awareness of the phenomena that cultural studies of organizations address, to facilitate 'better' choices in the development of cultural perspectives, and to encourage attention to different aspects of traditional objects of study. In short, to contribute to a more sensitive and interpretatively sharper use of the idea of culture in organization and management studies and practice.

Culture refers to complex, inaccessible, fuzzy, holistic phenomena. Much talk about corporate culture reduces culture to a set of espoused and vague values that do not vary that much between organizations, thus conflating rather different phenomena. It is tiring to hear about values such as 'technological excellence', 'people-company' or 'market-orientation' without further exploration of what this, more precisely, is supposed to mean. Culture is best understood as referring to deep-level, partly non-conscious sets of meanings, ideas and symbolism that may be contradictory and run across different social groupings. Culture thus calls for interpretation and deciphering. Productive here is a balancing between rigour and flexibility, reductionism and consideration of a wide set of aspects, analytical sharpness and space for intuition, imagination and intelligent guesswork. Cultural interpretation cannot be pressed into a formula or a model. This kind of work calls for careful reflection and self-critique of one's own cultural bias and what different concepts of culture can reveal but also obscure.

Notes

1   Perhaps the most important aspect of this variation is the philosophical and meta-theoretical assumptions that guide approaches to organizational culture studies. The most important distinction is between an objectivist-functionalist view of social reality and an interpretive approach (Burrell and Morgan, 1979; Smircich, 1983a). There are widely differing views on whether 'culture' refers to real, objective phenomena 'out there' or if it is a framework for thinking about certain aspects of the social world. These result in very different understandings of culture that are only to a limited extent reflected in differences in its formal definition.

2   Sperber (cited by Gusfield and Michalowicz, 1984: 421) interprets as symbolic 'all activity where the means put into play seem to be clearly disproportionate to the explicit or implicit end ... that is, all activity whose rationale escapes me'. As Gusfield and Michalowicz note, what is symbolic for one person may be non-symbolic for another. Still, I think it is wise to use 'symbol' as a conceptual tool for making sense of the hidden or latent meanings of an object.

3   In management and organization studies, the terms corporate culture and organizational culture are used, sometimes interchangeably, sometimes with different meanings. Typically corporate culture refers more to the ideals, values and meanings proposed and/or embraced by senior managers and possibly other groups responsive to their messages. Sometimes authors even view corporate culture as what is espoused and what management thinks it should be, while organizational culture refers to the 'real', a more descriptive interest in cultural patterns in the organization (Anthony, 1994). I tend to downplay this distinction somewhat, while still seeing organizational culture as signalling a broader interest in cultural manifestations in the organization, and while corporate culture refers more to the business and management side. I am using the terms as overlapping but with differences in connotations.

2 Culture as a Metaphor and Metaphors for Culture

Metaphors have been the subject of increasing attention in recent years, both in social science in general and organizational analysis in particular. The writings of Gareth Morgan (1980, 1986) have been groundbreaking in rethinking how we understand organizations. Metaphors are seen as important organizing devices in thinking and talking about complex phenomena. We never relate to objective reality 'as such' but always do so through forming metaphors or images of the phenomenon we address; organizations are for example seen as if they are machines, organisms, political arenas, brains, theatres, psychic prisons, etc. The 'discovery' of culture in organization theory has contributed to this interest, as many researchers have come to see culture as a new metaphor for organization with a considerable potential for developing new ideas and new forms of understanding. Arguably, through seeing organizations as cultures we can get a 'better' or at least richer view of what goes on in organizations, of the thoughts, feelings, values and actions of people in everyday organizational life and in decision-making situations.

This is, however, not unproblematic. Culture easily becomes too general and vague to work as a good metaphor. The many meanings of culture call for clarification, going beyond the definitions and delimitations normally offered (such as the view on culture presented in Chapter 1). I argue that culture should not be seen as the 'final' image to be used when organizations (or particular organizational phenomena) are being conceptualized. Instead we have good reason to investigate and reflect upon metaphors for culture (i.e. a metaphor for the metaphor) in organizational culture thinking. Understanding organizations as cultures is thus potentially productive, but we need to go further to sharpen the perspective. Below I will discuss the distinction indicated in the title of this chapter exploring the metaphor concept and calling for more reflection upon the metaphors that are used for culture.

The metaphor concept

Earlier it was common to think, and many people still do, that whereas metaphors were useful and necessary in poetry and rhetoric, the precision of science demanded literal expressions and well-defined words. Many people even today adhere to this view (e.g. Pinder and Bourgeois, 1982), which Tsoukas (1991) calls the 'metaphors-as-dispensable literary devices' perspective. More commonly, however, metaphors are recognized as vital for understanding thinking and language use in general and as a necessary element in creativity and the development of new approaches to research objects.

A metaphor is created when a term (sometimes referred to as 'modifier') is transferred from one system or level of meaning to another (the principle subject), thereby illuminating central aspects of the latter and shadowing others (see Figure 2.1). A metaphor allows an object to be perceived and understood from the viewpoint of another object. It thus creates a departure from literal meaning: 'A word receives a metaphorical meaning in specific contexts within which they are opposed to other words taken literally; this shift in meaning results mainly from a clash between literal meanings, which excludes literal use of the word in question' (Ricoeur, 1978: 138). A good metaphor depends on an appropriate mix of similarity and difference between the transferred word and the focal one. Where there is too much or too little similarity or difference, the point may not be understood.

A frequently used metaphor for organizations in academic writings as well as everyday organizational life is the pyramid. We then have an organization as the principle subject, the 'original' pyramid is the modifier and the metaphor is the organization seen as a pyramid. An organization is viewed as in vital respects similar to the Egyptian buildings. The pyramid-like organization is characterized by its broad base, and a linear reduction in volume for every layer until the organization at the very top ends in a sharp point, at which there is (normally) only one person. This person is then seen as residing at the 'top', having a 'very high' position, being in command over those at 'the bottom'. In between there are the 'middle-level' managers. The shape of the pyramid may vary: it may be comparatively 'flat' or 'tall'. This spatial metaphor is also clearly present in most efforts to describe new work tasks: people move upwards, downwards or sidewise. Without any further knowledge of the 'reality' all this is supposed to reveal, the uninformed or the unpredjudiced listener may assume that the target of this talk must be aviationists, mountain climbers or window cleaners working in tall buildings.

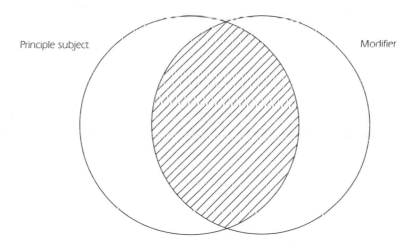

Principle subject   Modifier

Figure 2.1   **First-level metaphor (hatched area = metaphor)**
Reprinted by permission of Walter de Gruyter Inc., from Mats Alvesson,
Management of Knowledge-Intensive Companies **© Mats Alvesson, 1995.**

This illustrates a key characteristic of metaphors. They call for some goodwill, imagination and knowledge of the subject matter. A metaphor, building on the mixing of two elements, means a crossing or carrying over of a concept or idea from one field to another. It is the interaction between the two elements that are of interest and in order for this to work the metaphor user (either as a producer/ analyst or a consumer/reader) must emphasize the right elements in what is carried over as well as what is focused in the object to be illuminated. Without that the metaphor becomes pointless and frequently absurd. In the pyramid/organization case, the metaphor presupposes a neglect of some of the more robust features of a pyramid, e.g. the amount of stone and building-technical details, and many significant aspects of social relations in organizations, including fluctuations in relations, feelings, activities, language use and social variation.

In a narrow, traditional sense, a metaphor is simply an *illustrative device*; thus words which make language richer or more felicitous and formal models can both be regarded as metaphors (Brown, 1976). Metaphors in this sense are often helpful and nice, but not crucial and do not structure thinking. The researcher (or any other person) can in principle choose whether to use metaphors or not.

But metaphors may also be seen as implying something more profound. In a very broad and basic sense, in contrast to the illustrative device-view, all knowledge is metaphorical in that it emerges from or is 'constructed' from some point of view, some people argue. So, too, are our experiences, for 'our ordinary conceptual system, in terms of which we both think and act, is fundamentally metaphorical in nature' (Lakoff and Johnson, 1980: 3). Metaphor can thus be seen as *a crucial element in how people relate to reality*. Metaphors are, Morgan (1986: 12) says, 'a way of seeing and a way of thinking'. If we continue to take the pyramid metaphor as an example, it may simply be used as a literal device: high and low positions, climbing upwards, being at the top, middle layers, etc. then only represent convenient expressions. But they also indicate or create how people understand their world. The pyramid idea then means strongly asymmetrical social relations: those at the 'bottom' tend to subordinate themselves to those at the 'top'. Language then does not refer to exactly 'how it is', it also constructs or produces social relations. Language use such as top and bottom, high and low then reinforces asymmetrical relations: subordination is strengthened. Frequently in organizations, material arrangements support this image. One company that I studied had manufacturing units of two floors, divisional headquarters with three floors and then corporate headquarters with six floors, and as it also was located on a hill this meant that the term top management had not only a metaphorical but also a physical meaning – the CEO and his co-workers spent a lot of time much higher up than the rest of the company (Alvesson and Björkman, 1992).

If we address metaphor in this more profound sense and not just at the level of language use, metaphor is viewed as 'a primal, generative process that is fundamental to the creation of human understanding and meaning in all aspects of life' (Morgan, 1996: 228); this has implications for our understanding of science as well as our understanding of everyday life. Empirical 'data' do not speak directly to the researcher; they are partly determined by metaphors drawing attention to various aspects of the research object. In a similar way the manager, or any other practitioner, relates to and works within a universe that is not only filtered but also constructed through his or her images of what management and business are all about. In terms of theoretical frameworks we can talk about a *root metaphor* which is a fundamental image of the world on which one is focusing, and an *organizing metaphor* (Mangham and Overington, 1987) which frames and structures a more limited part of reality. The organization as a pyramid could exemplify what is meant by an organizing metaphor, while organization as organism frequently stands for a more fundamental, close to paradigmatic image of organization, i.e. a root metaphor. Culture is also often used in the latter way. But this varies: organism and culture are also used in other metaphorical ways: as an organizing metaphor and simply as an illustrative device. One may for example talk of the environment of a company, without necessarily proceeding from – or cognitively falling into – an organism root metaphor ordering 'all' major thinking about the subject matter. In order to understand metaphors, just noting words is insufficient; what is of interest is to assess how people relate to and think about phenomena on a 'deeper' level. This calls for interpretation of language and reasoning, not surface registration of the words used.

Brown (1976: 173) points to some of the characteristics of metaphors as follows. Metaphors involve what Aristotle called 'giving the thing a name that belongs to something else'. If a metaphor is taken literally, it usually appears absurd. The necessary ingredient of difference has a specific cognitive function: 'it makes us stop in our tracks and examine it. It offers us a new awareness'. Metaphors are intended to be understood; 'they are category errors with a purpose, linguistic madness with a method'. Metaphors must be approached and understood as if they were true at the same time that we are aware that they are fictitious – created and artificial.

Metaphors in social science – nuisance or breakthroughs?

The idea of metaphors as a central element in social science (and perhaps in all science) has created a lot of debate. Far from everybody applauds the development. From a traditional scientific point of view, the problem with metaphors is that they cannot be translated into more precise, objective language and thus elude rigorous measurement and testing. As Sennett (1980: 78) puts it, 'a metaphor creates a meaning greater than the sum of its parts, because the parts interact'. The metaphorical usage of words involves fantasy and associations that bring them generative power but limit their appropriateness for empiricists. Pinder and Bourgeois (1982: 647) admit that metaphors and tropes cannot altogether be avoided but worry about their uncontrolled, even deliberate use in formal theory:

> In short, because of the impossibility of avoiding metaphors and other tropes in everyday language, they are bound to play a role in the early stages of inquiry, guiding speculations in a heuristic manner. But the ideal of scientific precision is literal language, so,

to the extent that it is possible, administrative science must strive to control figurative terms in the development of formal hypothesis and theory. The point at which a trope loses its heuristic value and starts to mislead research and theory construction is difficult to determine. Therefore it is important to formulate concepts in literal terms that are rooted in observable organizational phenomena as soon as possible during the development of ideas into theory.

The 'free' use of metaphors means that there is no strict theoretical definition of what is being studied and that it is impossible to establish a good fit between the metaphor and the data, thus making evaluations based on empirical study impossible, critics say. This argument proceeds, however, from the assumption that 'objective reality' can be perceived and evaluated on its own terms, i.e. without a gestalt or image standing between the reality out there to be understood and the researcher (or any knowledge-seeker outside academia, e.g. a manager or a consultant) trying to make sense of what goes on. Instead, all perception is guided by conceptualization of the object through a gestalt created by metaphorical thinking; it is impossible to let the 'objective data' speak for themselves (Brown, 1976; Morgan, 1983). According to Brown (1976: 178): 'The choice for sociology is not between scientific rigor as against poetic insight. The choice is rather between more or less fruitful metaphors, and between using metaphors or being their victims.'[1]

Even though I agree with the 'metaphor-fundamentalists' such as Brown and Morgan against the advocates of 'rigor' and hypothesis-testing it is important to recognize a tension between 'scientific rigor' and 'poetic insight'. Even (we) lovers of metaphors must balance creativity and imagination with discipline and carefulness in use of metaphors. Inns and Jones (1996: 115) suggest that:

> metaphor must be used as a rational tool for exploration and be somehow 'literalized' and be made less implicit.... The distinction is that metaphor is used primarily for gestalt understanding in poetry, and essentially for rational reductionist analysis in organization theory.

They also suggest that while in poetry metaphors and what they evoke may be the *end*, in social science they are mainly *means* for exploration, theory development and empirical analysis. Inns and Jones are, however, aware of the problems of emphasizing the dichotomy between poetry and science and want to soften the clear distinctions somewhat. The ability of metaphors to explore and express experiences for example indicates a shared ground between the poets and the researchers. I would add that careful interpretative work based on the conscious use of a metaphor means awareness of and tolerance for the ambiguities and tensions involved in the project – something that rigour and rational reductionist analysis tend to suppress. I would also suggest that the development of a new metaphor may in itself be a major part of theoretical progress. Even though it needs to be explored and guided by as well as guide theoretical and empirical work, it is certainly more than just a conceptual tool to be subordinated conventional ideas of empirical inquiry.

I will in the next section explore some problems and pitfalls in using metaphors in an ambitious and offensive way, i.e. to use explicitly and fully the potentials. Before that a brief summary and extension of the advantages of a pro-fundamentalist view on metaphors.

The most frequently expressed advantage of metaphors concerns their ability to develop new ideas and guide analysis in novel ways. Mastery of the metaphors involved in thinking and research may thus encourage creativity and provide insight (Grant and Oswick, 1996; Morgan, 1980; Schön, 1979). This is, of course, not only of relevance for academics and others in high-brow work, but also managers may benefit from this. According to Palmer and Dunford (1996), managers are very positive to the idea of learning new metaphors and seeing things from different points of view.

A second advantage relates to the communicative capacities of metaphors. Metaphors can be used in communicating insight to others, for example as part of the production of scientific texts. People in organizations may also use metaphors for expressing their experiences. Metaphors thus may facilitate understanding. Within organizational culture studies there is a great interest not only in theoretical or researcher-driven metaphors but also in the metaphors used by practitioners, i.e. metaphors of the field (e.g. Dunford and Palmer, 1996; Riley, 1983).

A third advantage is that considering metaphors also draws attention to the partiality of the understanding gained by an approach built on a particular root metaphor. As Miles and Huberman (referred to in Inns and Jones, 1996) write, metaphors work as data-reducing devices. As metaphors so clearly signal – to the metaphor-user and the audience – that the intellectual operation is based on the idea that if we see the phenomenon in this way (… as if the organization is a machine/organism/madhouse …), then an awareness of the partiality and to some extent arbitrariness of the position taken facilitates openness. It may also cultivate tolerance for alternative approaches.

A fourth possible positive consequence of the popularity of metaphors and of appreciating the metaphorical level of organizational research and practice, concerns critical scrutiny. A focus on (root) metaphors may facilitate examination of the basic assumptions of a particular conceptualization of a phenomenon. This was illustrated by my brief treatment of the pyramid metaphor for organizations (even though this exemplified the organizing metaphor rather than the deeper aspects of metaphors as providers of gestalts). Occasionally the gestalt of the research object may prove to be different from what the definitions and rhetoric suggest. These relatively superficial levels may be insufficient to grasp the conceptualizations involved. Many authors writing on culture have adopted a new vocabulary which indicates a more interpretive, anthropological orientation, but the language used is often misleading. As Calás and Smircich (1987: 18) put it, commenting on mainstream organization culture studies, 'those who comprise the Corporate Culture theme have done an excellent job of staying within "positive/functionalist" assumptions while using the rhetoric of "myth", "rituals", and "qualitative methods"'. Attention to the metaphor concept might encourage a deeper, more sceptical and reflective perception of what people mean by culture. In this critical and reflective task it is not so much explicit metaphors as the 'old', implicit ones – sometimes called 'dead' metaphors – that are of interest, such as pyramid for organizational structure.[2] The idea is to remind people about the metaphorical quality, so that organizational schemes giving the impression that organizations 'are' pyramids, actually become understood as metaphors. Sceptical readings of existing texts may thus inspire rethinking the conceptual base of these. I will to some extent use this reading strategy in the latter part of this chapter.

Metaphors – some problems

Despite the benefits that the use of metaphors appears to offer the study of organizations, it also presents some problems. One of these is the risk of using 'bad' ones. An appealing metaphor – in the sense of a literal device – may stand in the way of a less elegant but more accurate and elaborate description. For example, the garbage-can metaphor for organizational decision-making (March and Olsen, 1976) may have more rhetorical appeal than theoretical value (Pinder and Bourgeois, 1982). According to the garbage-can model, decisions result from the random convergence of streams of problems, solutions, people, and situations. The degree of overlap between the type of decision-making process addressed and the garbage can is too small; key features of the garbage can – its bad smell, its containing material packed together that is considered refuse – seem of limited relevance (see Pinder and Bourgeois, 1982). This problem basically concerns the level of expression and not so much the root metaphor (and other metaphors guiding thought) itself. As Tsoukas (1991: 32) remarks, the garbage-can metaphor is 'simply a figure of speech, a literary illustration to make sense of organizational decision-making and not a metaphor intended directly to reveal formal identities between garbage cans and organisations'. The metaphor does not necessarily have to be explicitly addressed, which would avoid the problem. March and Olsen could, for example, have conducted their analysis without referring to the garbage can and kept their 'metaphor' to themselves.

A related difficulty is the 'catchiness' problem that springs partly from the current popularity of metaphors in organization studies. This can easily lead to the excessive use of seductive metaphorical expressions, rather than the development of analytically helpful metaphors that really do shed new light on things. As in the case of culture, the very popularity of metaphors can make it 'too easy' to play with them, which in turn can lead to superficiality (Oswick and Grant, 1996). 'Culture' easily refers to everything and nothing. Another example is 'empowerment', which is frequently used, often in very vague and diverse ways (Bartunek and Spreitzer, 1999). We can thus talk about a 'fashion problem' as regards metaphors in contemporary organization theory.

A third problem, once again related to the others, concerns the risk of a super-market attitude to metaphors. (I am now redirecting the focus somewhat and referring to metaphors in the sense of analytic devices or root metaphors rather than 'merely' as expressions or labels.) There is the risk that focusing on the metaphorical level will draw attention away from the deeper or more basic levels of social research, such as the paradigmatic assumptions on which metaphors rely (on these various levels, see Morgan, 1980). For example, Morgan's (1986) *Images of Organization*, despite its great value, may convey the impression that the more metaphors are employed the more comprehensive the understanding of organizational phenomena (Reed, 1990). Instead, mastery of a particular perspective demands complete understanding of its paradigmatic roots and their existential and political aspects (on the relationship between metaphors and politics, see Tinker, 1986). Attempting to employ more than a few guiding concepts in advanced analysis results in superficiality.

A fourth problem concerns the oversimplifications that can follow, if too much emphasis is put on some particular gestalt (metaphor, image) which is seen as guiding and summarizing a line of thinking. It is unlikely that the metaphors employed (espoused) will always illuminate the researchers' basic view (gestalt) of the phenomenon. Complex understanding is perhaps more often derived from a synthesis of different metaphors than from a single sharp-profile picture. This problem arises partly from the limitations of current metaphors and partly from the complexity of the phenomena we deal with. For example, it is unlikely that any researcher sees an organization exclusively as a machine or exclusively as an organism or even exclusively as a combination of the two, and the addition of further metaphors to 'capture' the framework may simply obscure and distort it; thinking and analysis are not the same as the aggregation of metaphorical bits. There is also the problem that language is restricted. The words which we have at our disposal do not always adequately signify just what we want to pinpoint. Parker (2000) suggests that organizational culture may best be formulated as 'contested local organization of generalities' – drawing attention to there being local patterns which are versions of more general cultural themes in societies and that these are often contested. This may be a good way of capturing organizations but it is not a metaphor.

We have already noted that the advantage of metaphors is that at one and the same time they illuminate and hide aspects of a particular phenomenon. The partial and reductionistic element in using metaphors not only concerns metaphors in relation to empirical objects; it also affects efforts to make sense of research and to develop frameworks. Saying that organization researchers or practitioners treat their object of study as if it were a machine or an organism certainly illuminates some important aspects of the treatment of the object, but at the same time draws attention away from others. In Morgan (1980) for example almost half of all organization theory is described as based on an organism metaphor. Rather different approaches are then indicated to be similar, meaning that some vital differences are obscured. When Morgan and others fit various authors and schools into a particular metaphor the latter does not just reflect the literature and the theories but order and shape them in a particular way.

These problems are not of course arguments against the use of metaphors. Rather, they point to the need for an approach that is self-critical and reflective, avoiding the temptation to overuse metaphors and reminding oneself and the reader that they do not tell the whole story.

Culture as critical variable versus culture as root metaphor

In a classic overview of concepts of culture in organizational analysis, Smircich (1983a) has distinguished between culture as a variable and culture as a root metaphor. Researchers who see culture as a variable draw upon a more traditional, objectivist, and functionalist view of social reality and try to improve models of organization by taking sociocultural subsystems, in addition to traditionally recognized variables, into account. In contrast, researchers who see culture as a root metaphor approach organizations as if they were cultures and draw upon anthropology in developing radically new theories or paradigms.

Researchers who treat culture as a variable recognize that organizations produce or are accompanied by more or less distinct cultural traits, such as values, norms, rituals, ceremonies, and verbal expression, and that these features affect the behaviour of managers and employees. Many writers have argued that organizational culture contributes to the systemic balance and effectiveness of an organization. The idea that a 'strong corporate culture' has a distinct and positive impact on performance was very popular at the beginning of the 1980s, but it seems to have become increasingly common to examine the relevance of culture to organizational change. The improvement of organizational performance is often viewed as a matter of achieving planned cultural change (e.g. Wilkins and Patterson, 1985). Managing organizational culture is frequently equated with changing culture. Of course, a slightly different approach is to see managing organizational culture as a matter of maintaining, strengthening or developing the meanings, ideas, values and symbolism that are seen as distinct and valuable for operations in a particular organization (e.g. Alvesson, 1995; Kunda, 1992).

The proponents of this view suggest that several positive functions are fulfilled by culture (in the sense of shared values and beliefs). These include providing a sense of identity to members of the organization, facilitating commitment to a larger whole (the organization, its purpose, or whatever), enhancing system stability, and serving as a sense-making device which can guide and shape behaviour, motivating employees to do the 'right' things. The question is 'how to mold and shape internal culture in particular ways and how to change culture, consistent with managerial purposes' (Smircich, 1983a: 346). Culture is viewed, then, as interesting in the search for suitable means of control and improved management. Ideas about causality are crucial here; getting the right culture in place is expected to have recognizable effects on important outputs such as loyalty, productivity, and perceived quality of service.

Instead of considering culture as something that an organization *has*, researchers proceeding from the root-metaphor idea stress that the organization *is* a culture or, rather, can be seen as if it is a culture: 'Culture as a root metaphor promotes a view of organizations as expressive forms, manifestations of human consciousness. Organizations are understood and analysed not mainly in economic or material terms, but in terms of their expressive, ideational, and symbolic aspects' (Smircich, 1983a: 348). According to this perspective, 'organizational culture is not just another piece of the puzzle, it is the puzzle' (Pacanowsky and O'Donnell-Trujillo, 1983: 146). Therefore, the research agenda is to explore organization as 'subjective experience' (Smircich, 1983a) or perhaps rather a socially shared – intersubjective – experience. The mode of thought that underlies the idea of culture as a root metaphor is hermeneutical or phenomenological rather than objectivist. The social world is seen not as objective, tangible, and measurable but as constructed by people and reproduced by the networks of symbols and meanings that people share and make shared action possible (Burrell and Morgan, 1979; Putnam, 1983).

Advocates of the root-metaphor view of culture are inclined to play down the pragmatic results that can help management increase effectiveness in favour of more general understanding and reflection as the major emphasis of cultural studies. In principle, for them nothing is 'not culture', and therefore culture cannot be related to anything else. (Of course, different elements of culture can be related to each other.) The culture-as-a-root-metaphor means that the cultural image guides all perception and interpretation of what goes on in organizations. Seemingly 'objective' things, such as numbers of employees, turnover, physical products, customers, etc. become of interest (almost) only in terms of their cultural meanings. The size of a company may be seen as 'small is beautiful' – it may be seen as indicating flexible, unbureaucratic and family-like orientations and relations. Limited size may, in certain organizations, signal exclusiveness and elitism. In a very successful law firm one restricted the number of employees as part of an objective to maintain extremely talented employees and partners (Starbuck, 1993). Many of the world's leading universities are medium-sized. But small may also be viewed as a temporary stage to be overcome – limited size may be associated with vulnerability and, in the longer perspective, failure, while large size is seen as standing for success and strength. In this case growth is then seen as a guiding value, perhaps at the expense of other values, e.g. profits, quality of work and legitimacy. In a science consultancy company ambition to grow in combination with limited success in doing so, led to various mystifications around the actual and predicted size. This was expressed in rather different estimations from various people in the company about the actual number of employees. The company also built more offices despite there being no shortage of space and, according to some informants, any significant expansion was not likely to take place in the nearest future (Robertson, 1999). The examples illustrate how a seemingly straightforward issue, the number of employees, is fused with cultural meaning and may even be a key symbolic issue. It is how the people being studied think and feel about financial matters, not the results in themselves in terms of abstract numbers that are of interest for the person working with a culture-root-metaphor. Not all proponents of the root-metaphor view strictly conform to this theoretical ideal, but even those who make room in their analyses for 'non-cultural' phenomena or aspects tend to avoid explicitly relating them to culture in any variable-like way. The very point is that one cannot single out something clearly 'outside' culture. Everything that is seen as meaningful for a group of people is so through being part of a cultural context.

Figures 2.2 and 2.3 illustrate the difference between a variable and a metaphor view on culture. In the first, culture refers to certain, delimited, phenomena seen as analytically distinct from other phenomena and possible to relate in external

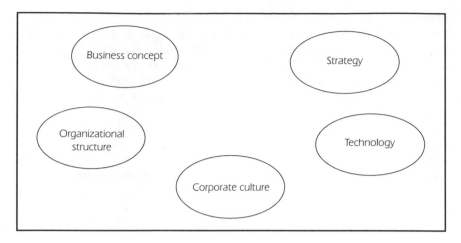

Figure 2.2   **Culture as a subsystem in an organization**
Reprinted by permission of Walter de Gruyter Inc., from Mats Alvesson,
***Management of Knowledge-Intensive Companies* © Mats Alvesson, 1995.**

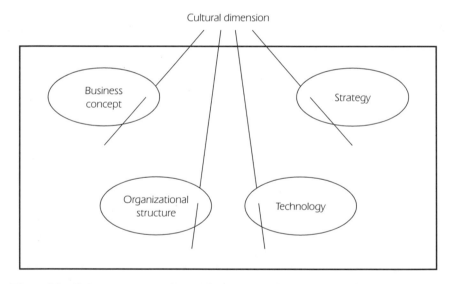

Figure 2.3   **Culture as a metaphor: a fundamental dimension which**
permeates various 'subsystems'
Reprinted by permission of Walter de Gruyter Inc., from Mats Alvesson,
***Management of Knowledge-Intensive Companies* © Mats Alvesson, 1995.**

ways to these. Culture is one of several subsystems making up the organization.
There may, for example, be a misfit between strategy and culture. In the metaphor
view, culture is not outside anything, but permeates the entire organization. There
is a cultural dimension everywhere, which then points at the shared meanings
involved. Organizational culture is, for example, expressed and reproduced in

formal organizational structures, strategic plans, administrative systems and so on. (More about this later, in particular in Chapter 4.)

Smircich's (1983a) distinction between a 'has' and 'is' view on culture points to crucial differences in basic assumptions that are not necessarily clear from a superficial reading of texts. There are, however, some problems with it, problems inherent in efforts to order messy areas. Some researchers very clearly adhere to a traditional understanding of organizations, explicitly discussing variables and try to 'measure' culture, and so on, while others proceed from a culture metaphor and focus exclusively on symbolism and meanings, but many do not easily fit into either category. Many researchers fall between the two, refraining from reducing culture to a variable without fully viewing an organization as a culture. The problem of taking a clear position is well illustrated by Smircich (1983a) herself; many of the works she cites appear in both 'variable' and 'metaphor' sections of her overview.

Part of this classification problem is that cultural concepts – meaning, symbol, values, rites, rituals, tales, etc. – do not readily lend themselves to quantification or to strict variable thinking, and consequently, even researchers not strongly oriented to the root-metaphor position often adopt a qualitative approach. This weakens the 'variable' bias, even among those interested in pragmatic results and predictions, and who believe in an 'objective reality' which we can know about through 'hard data'. At the other extreme, taking culture as a root metaphor leaves little room for aspects other than symbols and meanings; but organizations are normally economic entities in which material conditions, external environment, competition, and performance – dimensions not well captured by a cultural perspective – must be considered (Ebers, 1995). The culture-as-root-metaphor approach has interesting things to say about traditional issues such as strategy (Smircich and Stubbart, 1985), technology (Berg, 1985b), or business concept (Alvesson, 1995), phenomena which the proponents of a variable approach would typically not put in a 'culture subsystem box'. I will treat this at some length in Chapter 4. Nevertheless there are other important aspects which are difficult to include in a cultural analysis. Basics of a company's production and its financial and market situation may be informative, also in the absence of careful inquiry of the meanings and symbolism on these matters held by people in the organization. Consequently, many researchers who treat culture as a metaphor also address, although to a limited degree, 'non-cultural' aspects. Working strictly with culture as a root metaphor may lead to the reduction of everything to symbolism. Therefore many researchers combine cultural and other understandings. Of course, culture-theory-using practitioners – who are less bothered by expectations of academic rigour – also do so.

Another problem of classification is that researchers who see culture as a variable do not use cultural concepts in a literal way; here culture itself must be seen as metaphorical, although in a more narrow sense. Even if one prefers to talk about corporate culture as a variable, it still does not refer to tangible phenomena to be referred to in a straightforward, metaphor-free way. For example, 'variable metaphors' for corporate culture could be tool, obstacle (e.g. to strategic change), or control mechanism. Such metaphors are, of course, limited in scope, illuminating not a major part of an organization but a restricted set of human (managerial) functions. They may or may not be subordinated to another, more basic (root) metaphor, such as a machine, organism, or system, or no particular root metaphor – in the sense of a theoretically coherent gestalt or image – may be used. In this last case, culture and other subsystems are then seen as comprising an aggregate of components, which are treated without reference back to a particular distinct root metaphor. Here, too, the basic view of conceptualization of an organization is of course metaphorical (as is all knowledge), but my point is that the project is not guided by any particular gestalt created by the comparison of an organization with something else.

Finally, a more modest use of the culture concept that still informs a substantial part of an analysis of an organization falls between the root-metaphor and variable view. This view takes culture as an organizing metaphor which guides thinking and analysis in a more restricted way (see, e.g. Allaire and Firsirotu, 1984; Schein, 1985; Whipp *et al.*, 1989). Some parts of an organization are seen as culture, but attention is also paid to significant phenomena that are not understood in cultural terms.

Before leaving this theme I want to discuss a common critique of the culture as a metaphor for organization position, arguing that organization is, literally, culture, and that the metaphor idea is misleading. Trice and Beyer (1993: 21), for example, say that culture is 'not merely a metaphor', and continue: 'Cultures exist; they are naturally occurring, real systems of thought, feeling, and behavior that inevitably result from sustained human interaction'. One could also say that culture is too broad in itself and too similar to organization to be able to function as a good metaphor. If we compare it with Brown's criteria for good metaphors as summarized earlier in this chapter, one could say that culture is not up to standard as it covers 'too much' of organization. The criteria for a good metaphor of providing the right balance of similarity and difference between the two elements involved in the creation of the metaphor is not met.

Both critiques of the culture as metaphor are relevant, but do not rule out the possibility of applying culture as a productive root metaphor in organization studies. It certainly makes sense to say that cultural phenomena exist in contemporary companies as much as in mountain villages in France or in a nomad tribe in North Africa. However, the point of seeing all sorts of corporate phenomena in a cultural perspective means that a certain understanding is privileged and other aspects are neglected. This becomes clearer if we don't just talk about organizations as cultures in general, but concentrate on specific cultural manifestations. Optimally, the culture metaphor illuminates phenomena in a novel way. Business meetings, from a non-cultural perspective, held by most management researchers and presumably most practitioners, are typically seen as instrumental and task-oriented for the benefit of corporate performance. From a culture metaphor they may appear as heavily symbolically loaded, expressing ritualistic and mythical qualities. Such a cultural interpretation does not just reflect simply and objectively what exists, but relies on the ability and interest in seeing things in a particular way. Culture concepts as ritual and myth have a metaphorical quality, permitting the 'seeing as …' mode of approaching, thus making inspired interpretation possible.

The concept of organizational culture may then be applied so that it works as a metaphor through hitting the right balance between similarity and difference between the elements of culture and organization. The productive ability of the metaphor – its ability to illuminate something in a novel, insightful way – is then related to applying it on organizational phenomena that are not obviously 'cultural'. Seemingly more instrumental, 'result-oriented' activities should then be examined in addition to events and actions that are characterized by obvious symbolism, such as corporate anniverseries or physical status markers.

There is a problem with the broadness and to some extent vagueness of the culture metaphor. Even with the view suggested in Chapter 1 – and this is much more distinct than more all-embracing concepts covering 'ways of life' and behaviour patterns – culture covers a lot. In order to work as a helpful interpretive device, it must be reduced in scope and allow for more interpretive depth. As metaphor it needs to be sharpened. Most advanced users of culture theory tend to use the culture metaphor in a way that makes it more distinct and thus more clearly metaphorical than what is indicated by most formal definitions of organizational culture. People working with a cultural approach are not always explicit about this. One way of illuminating how the culture idea is used and also to suggest new ways of thinking about the organizational culture metaphor (or rather metaphors) is to address a metaphorical level behind the metaphor.

Metaphors for culture

The use of culture as a metaphor in fact implies 'metaphorization' at many levels. Not only does organizational culture, i.e. the combination and juxtaposition of organization and culture, create a metaphor, but the word culture is also metaphorical in itself. Culture is not a literal word; it draws in turn on another metaphor. Thus, we can go even further and look at the metaphor behind the metaphor, e.g. second-level metaphors (Alvesson, 1993c). When people talk about culture in organization studies, for example, what do they think of? What are their gestalts? Is culture seen as 'personality writ large', 'an overall control mechanism', 'a community' or what? Culture defined as a set of meanings and values shared by a group of people, for example, can be used in all these senses. Further definitions of 'meanings and values' do not necessarily restrict the possibilities that much. If proponents of culture as a metaphor have got it right, not only the conceptualization of organization but also the conceptualization of culture is metaphorical.

The idea then is to determine which metaphor structures culture, and produce an image of it (see Figure 2.4 for a graphical illustration of the idea of the metaphor for the metaphor). The first-level metaphor is now targeted by another modifier and thus a new metaphor is produced.[3] The first-level metaphor becomes a new principle subject in the interaction with the modifier in the production of a new, second-level metaphor. For example culture (first-level metaphor) is combined with lighthouse (modifier) and the metaphor culture as lighthouse (second-level metaphor) is produced.

Interpreting the metaphor behind the metaphor is an uncertain and difficult business. It is seldom self-evident how the former should be conceptualized. It is

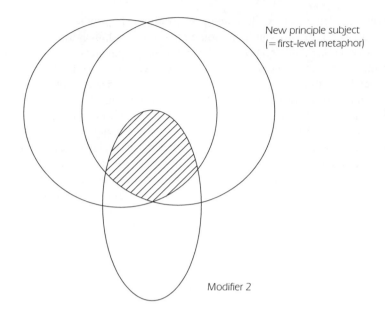

New principle subject
(= first-level metaphor)

Modifier 2

Figure 2.4   **Second-level metaphor**
               Reprinted by permission of Sage Publications Ltd from
               John Hassard and Martin Parker (eds.), *Postmodernism*
               and Organizations, **© Mats Alvesson, 1993**

by no means always possible to find a particular gestalt or image created by the juxtaposition of culture and something else. The multidimensionality of what 'culture' refers to often prevents us from seeing it as a gestalt, or from using a single phrase or meaning (combination of words) to capture the metaphor involved. The problem is partly linguistic: the capacity of language to signify is limited. We cannot use words to describe phenomena in a true, objective and precise way. This restriction should remind us that the full complexity involved is seldom illuminated by invoking a metaphor. Rather, the metaphor draws attention to certain central features in thinking about the phenomenon. Metaphors are simplifications, not only of 'external' reality but also of research and thinking about 'reality'. So not only when we say something about organizations, but also when we address people's theoretical frameworks for organizational phenomena, a metaphor helps in reducing complexity and focusing some vital aspects at the expense of others. Saying that certain researchers proceed from for example an organism, machine or brain metaphor give only a partial and simplistic picture of how they think about their subject matter.

    That the conceptualization of culture is itself metaphorical has received very little attention in the organizational culture literature. Very few researchers have examined the metaphors they draw upon or create when they use culture as a theoretical concept. One exception is Nord (1985), who discusses social glue and magnet as metaphors for culture. As mentioned above, one could say that organizations, like societies, actually 'are' cultures, i.e. organizations or collectives in organizations literally include or contain values, meanings, and symbols. It is not clear that it makes sense to view organizations 'as if' they were cultures. But, as mentioned, qualified researchers and other analysts structure culture in a particular way, and actually produce the necessary 'as if qualities' and thus make possible the metaphor of organizational culture. In using a metaphor for culture, the culture concept is narrowed down and a clearer distance is created between it and organization. Thinking about culture may thus be sharpened as the metaphor becomes more distinct. In order to clarify this idea it is necessary to extend the focus beyond organization and culture as the only elements creating the metaphor. The way in which culture is modified so that it also becomes a metaphor must be investigated. By looking at the metaphors used for (organizational) culture, we can better understand the guiding frameworks for organizational culture research (and, by implication, for culture recreation in organizational practice).

Consideration of eight metaphors for culture drawn from the contemporary literature will reveal their differences and indicate some potential problems with particular uses of the culture concept in organization research. The eight metaphors do not represent a comprehensive list of ways of using the metaphor of culture, but cover many of the most common modes of thinking culturally.

Culture as exchange-regulator

One metaphor for culture is exchange-regulator. Culture is seen here as a control mechanism that can handle complex exchange relations. Wilkins and Ouchi (1983: 469) 'take the paradigmatic view on culture and call it a clan' and define culture as 'shared social knowledge'. Culture/clan is: (1) a general paradigm that helps participants determine what is in the best interest of the collective; and (2) the perception of goal congruence (the belief in a general or long-term equity) (p. 475). Their analysis suggests that complex exchange situations, characterized by ambiguity and difficulty in monitoring employees' performances, increase the risk of opportunistic behaviour. Culture (clan) is for Wilkins and Ouchi a variable that can replace the need for close monitoring and direct control. It does so by socializing employees into believing that their objectives in the exchange process are congruent with those of the employed and by providing a general paradigm which facilitates the determination of what is best for the relationship. Culture provides members of the organization with intellectual tools and a 'long memory' which facilitate the perception and evaluation of fair rewards in the long run and thus discourages them from short-term opportunistic behaviour.

The culture variable, then, is viewed as a form of control that operates upon people's shared views on the utilitarian exchange relationship to reduce transaction costs. Organizations in which a culture of the 'right kind' has been developed – by selective recruitment, socialization, and 'ceremonial control' (Ouchi, 1980) – will achieve high performance. Aspects of 'shared social knowledge' which are not directly relevant to exchange relations are neglected. For Wilkins and Ouchi culture has a specific and positive function.

Culture as compass

Another metaphor for culture in organizational research is the compass. This image of culture is common in talk about organizational culture. Wiener (1988: 536), for example, draws attention to the direction-pointing capacity of the shared value system that he sees as the core of organizational culture:

> By definition, individual values serve as a guide to a person's intentions and actions. Similarly, organizational value systems provide guides for organizational goals, policies, and strategies. Thus, the nature of the values is a crucial factor in the impact that culture will have on organizational effectiveness. If the prevailing values support appropriate goals and strategies, the culture is an important asset. Conversely, the wrong values can make the culture a major liability.

'Wrong' values are thus like a defective compass: they indicate the 'wrong' direction, and consequently people will not get where they want to go (or, perhaps, where management wants them to go). 'Right' values are associated with a well-functioning device. Wiener (1988: 537) makes distinctions between functional and elitist values and between traditions and charismatic leaders as sources of values. Functional values concern 'modes of conduct' and are useful for operations, while elitist values concern 'the status, superiority, and importance of the organization itself'. In relation to the compass, these values parallel technical functionality and the image of the brand. Traditional values are anchored in history and are persistent, while leader-induced values are less stable. An idea of product durability and reliability apparently governs the argument, and the compass metaphor seems to throw some light on this. Wiener (1988: 538) crosses types and sources of values and concludes, hardly surprisingly, that functional-traditional ones 'are most likely to contribute to the development of proper values and, consequently, to organizational effectiveness'. These values are those which are long-lasting, reliable, relevant, and capable of keeping people on the right course.

Culture as social glue

Besides culture as compass, the social glue metaphor is perhaps the most common view of culture. The idea here is that organizations are integrated and controlled through informal, non-structural means – shared values, beliefs, understandings, and norms. Culture in this sense contributes to the avoidance of fragmentation, conflict, tension, and other miseries; organizational life is seen as characterized by consensus, harmony and community.

There seem to be two major versions of the social-glue metaphor. One is more pragmatic and assumes that consensus and harmony are not only possible but also 'natural', i.e. people interacting over time construct some level of consensus on how to relate to the world. This can be called the integration approach (Martin and Meyerson, 1988). Another version emphasizes the control aspect and, rather than postulating consensus as something organically produced, talks about corporate culture as a strategy for achieving social-glue-like effects. Ray (1986: 294) views corporate culture as the last frontier of control: 'the top management team aims to have individuals possess direct ties to the values and goals of the dominant elites in order to activate the emotion and sentiment which might lead to devotion, loyalty, and commitment to the company'. In this second version the glue is viewed as fragile, in need of maintenance work, and not always capable of holding the organization together. In certain companies, where different people and operations are loosely coupled, for example many professional business service firms, tendencies to fragmentation are inherent in the structure and here top management frequently tries to develop a corporate culture functioning as a social-integrative force (Alvesson, 1995).

Culture as sacred cow

Many researchers stress the deeper levels of culture and members' internalization of certain ideals and values, and the image of the sacred cow appears to capture significant dimensions of their approach. Gagliardi (1986: 123), for example, speaks of the 'sacred' as significant for the core of culture. Crucial here are organizational values, which 'can be seen as the idealization of a collective experience of success in the use of a skill and the emotional transfiguration of previous beliefs'. These values are the result of a historical process in which people gradually accept and internalize beliefs and values based on a leader's (often the founder's) 'vision' once it has been shown to be successful (see Schein, 1985). Through the idealization process, 'the rational acceptance of beliefs gives way to the emotional identification with values', which in due course become sacred. Gagliardi suggests that every organization has a primary strategy, the maintenance of its cultural identity, as distinct from a series of secondary strategies, derivative from the primary one, which are more explicit and tied to concrete objectives. This primary strategy is tightly coupled to the sacred values, and it places firm limits on change. Thus core values are seen as almost impossible to change because of their taken-for-granted character and the deep commitment to them of organizational members.

The sacred-cow metaphor for organizational culture thus stresses the limits of instrumental reason and focuses on deeper value commitments and the stability of the cultural core. The metaphor gives 'shared basic values' a different meaning from the compass or social glue even though the definitions of culture are sometimes similar. The sacred-cow view of course can also be seen as referring to similar functions as the compass or the social-glue idea – the metaphors are in no way contradictory – but it does not clearly show the direction of concrete behaviour, nor can it be regarded as a control strategy. Rather, what the sacred-cow metaphor refers to is value commitments that control strategies. It differs from other metaphors in referring to much deeper and more affective aspects of culture.

Culture as affect-regulator

A quite different approach to culture concentrates on its affective and expressive dimensions. Organizational cultures can then be seen as 'emotional arenas' (Fineman, 1993). Van Maanen and Kunda (1989: 52) emphasize that 'attempts to build, strengthen, deepen or thicken organizational culture often involve the subtle (or not so subtle) control of employee emotions – or at least those emotions expressed in the workplace' – and see culture as a 'control device' to 'inform, guide, and discipline the emotions of organizational members' (p. 56). A core dimension of organizational life and what unites members and ties them to the organization is corporate socioaffective bonds. But occasionally organizational culture is more a management-induced set of rules for the expression of emotions, for example in service industries. Disney World cultivates the appearance of the sold personnel-commodity 'as a cheerful lad or lassie whose enthusiasm and dedication is obvious to all' (Van Maanen, 1991: 72). The Body Shop not only allows but also exercises pressure to express emotions in a particular way (Martin *et al.*, 1998).

Attention may concentrate on broader patterns of feelings – whether visible mainly in encounters with customers or also in 'back-stage settings' – or be focused on emotions of a more restricted nature, involving self-control and the reduction of tensions through socialization and certain types of symbols (see Dandridge *et al.*, 1980).

Culture as disorder

The metaphor of non-order proceeds from the assumption that modern societies and organizations are characterized by ambiguity – uncertainty, contradiction, confusion – and that a cultural perspective on organizations must take this into account. This approach might even be seen as a negation of many common definitions of culture:

> Cultural manifestations are not clearly consistent or clearly inconsistent with each other. Instead, the relationships between manifestations are characterized by a lack of clarity. Differences in interpretation are seen as incommensurable, irreconcilable, and unavoidable ... consensus, dissensus, and confusion coexist, making it difficult to draw cultural and subcultural boundaries. (Martin and Meyerson, 1988: 115, 117)

Some might object that this kind of situation suggests that no culture has yet been developed, but, as Martin (1987) remarks, a modern, complex society or organization does not become 'non-cultural' because of fragmentation and differences in its social and cultural patterns.

Martin and Meyerson (1988) propose that rather than providing clarity and lucidity in a dark, formless jungle, culture can be seen as the jungle itself. This metaphor seems to me not very illuminating – most people probably associate it with lack of civilization. Fragmentation is an alternative, used by Martin in her later work (Martin, 1992; Martin and Frost, 1996). The concept of disorder may be the best choice to mark the non-systematic, fluid and contradictory character of cultural manifestations in organizations to which Martin and Meyerson draw attention. It contrasts nicely with prevailing ideas about the ordering and organizing functions of culture, even though it can be argued that it moves on the border of where a culture concept is meaningful: one may consider alternative languages to culture vocabulary for illuminating what Martin and co-workers have in mind. More about the ambiguity and disorder aspects on culture in Chapter 8.

Culture as blinders

Morgan (1986) has compared the organization to a 'psychic prison', and Krefting and Frost (1985: 156) appeal to the same idea in speaking of 'blinders'. They argue that organizational culture is funnelled through the unconscious' and therefore differs from what is indicated by the organization, which is a metaphor for order and orderliness.[4] Their understanding of organizational culture is inspired by Jungian ideas, which, although originally developed to explain individual development, have been extended to organizations. According to Krefting and Frost (1985: 165):

> Effective cultures need a balance, which requires the incorporation of shadows or other less dominant elements. Such cultures must also deal with 'problems posed by life-situations' (Turner) in complex and realistic ways rather than at the idealized, archetypal level. When organizational culture goes awry, blockage may well result from unincorporated shadows or unresolved archetypal conflicts; hence, exploring the problem in terms of shadows or archetypes may well be the way to approach it.

Viewing culture as being to a significant degree rooted in the unconscious leads to an emphasis on its deeper aspects: members have only limited access to it and easily become victims of shadows, archetypes, and fantasies. Any knowledge of it is likely to be somewhat uncertain and speculative (perhaps even more than other versions of culture thinking). The blinder metaphor may, however, also be expressed in other ways than aided by Jungian ideas.

Anthony (1994) also emphasizes that culture may protect leaders from the expression of values and opinions that may challenge their own worldviews. Corporate culture, used as a vehicle for the control of subordinates, brings about conformism and compliance, and thus deprives managers of the potential increase in cognitive rationality following from the communicating of alternative and deviate ideas of what exists, what is good and what can be accomplished. Because the cultural control apparatus 'incorporates self-validating techniques designed for the comfort and security of those it encloses, the techniques function so successfully that there can be no intrusion and no correction of error' (Anthony, 1994: 88).

Culture as world-closure

Another metaphor for culture that suggests that it prevents people from understanding social reality stresses sociological rather than psychological elements or specific arrangements leading to blind spots and may be called world-closure. The basic idea is that social reality is in principle open and negotiable; culture makes it appear given, natural, and, when it comes to basic premises, impossible (or at least very difficult) to question. This effect may be produced by traditions or other impersonal forces or by the more or less conscious influence of powerful actors using cultural and ideological means. Knights and Willmott (1987: 51–2), studying a British insurance company, interpret the chief executive's frequent use of the 'team' metaphor as follows:

The use of the team metaphor involves activation of a number of interpretive schemes, facilities, and norms.... The notion of a team does not describe the situation – here, the assembly of Pensco's management. Rather, if successful, its articulation has the effect of defining the situation. In this case, its usage becomes symbolic and ideological in the sense that it draws upon this interpretive scheme to constitute the identity of Pensco middle management in a way that naturalizes, legitimizes, and thus reproduces prevailing asymmetries of power within (and beyond) the company.... The (widespread) appeal to the idea of a team conveys the image of a 'community' in which norms are shared, the objective of the 'game' is well established, the captain/leader speaks for the group, and the players are under a moral obligation to follow his instructions as they engage in the play.

Knights and Willmott see organizational culture as a management strategy that aims to implant management's favourable perceptions and definitions of social reality in the interpretive schemes of employees. If this strategy is successful, these perceptions and definitions come to constitute a selective and biased worldview that reproduces a particular social order and the asymmetrical representation of interests that characterizes it. As do some of the other metaphors examined here, this one places managers above cultural conditions, manipulating cultural elements rather than being shaped and/or restricted by culture.

Other metaphors for culture

These eight metaphors of course in no way exhaust the ways in which culture is used in organization research. The same guiding concept or framework can often be denoted in different ways, and beyond this there are many other approaches to culture that I will not attempt to illustrate. Additional examples of metaphors for culture in organizational analysis include contract (Jones, 1983), magnet (Nord, 1985), paradigm (Pfeffer, 1981a), power game (Frost, 1987), neurosis (Kets de Vries and Miller, 1986), hologram (Pondy, 1983, cited by Martin and Meyerson, 1988), social energy (Trice and Beyer, 1993), island of clarity (Martin and Meyerson, 1988), and founder writ large (Martin, Sitkin and Boehm, 1985) – the last two used somewhat sceptically, by the authors referred to. Many of the mentioned metaphors overlap the ones that I have reviewed above.

Dimensions of contrast

There are many dimensions in which these various metaphors for organizational culture can be compared. I will indicate five of them here, and in doing so I have been to some extent inspired by Burrell and Morgan's (1979) distinction between objectivism and subjectivism and between regulative/consensual and radical/conflict assumptions.

The first dimension is *functionalism versus non-functionalism*. The functionalist position is that culture normally serves the common good – it promotes the effectiveness of the organization and the well-being of all its stakeholders. Opposition to this view may take several forms. The background and reproduction of culture is a complex affair, and cultural manifestations may include (non-functional) conflicts as well as consensus. Cultural manifestations can exist without fulfilling any positive function (being reproduced, for instance, by the autonomous powers of tradition). This position may be called the agnostic. Another position is that cultural manifestations serve the interests of the status quo and the ruling elite – they may be 'functional' for the elite but hardly for members in general. This view, held by Marxists and other proponents of critical theory, may be labelled the sectional functionalist. Yet another position is that culture is rooted in the unconscious, in traditions, and in other sources outside or in opposition to rational thought and decision-making – in other words, it makes it difficult for people to control their situations and achieve their objectives. This position may be called the dysfunctionalist. Of the metaphors treated above, culture as exchange-regulator and as compass have a clear functionalist bias. Culture as affect-regulator and as non-order is agnostic, culture as world-closure sectional functionalist, and culture as blinders dysfunctionalist.

Another dimension is *objectivism versus subjectivism*,[5] and it has two slightly different aspects: (1) social reality viewed as anchored in systems, structures, and other objective features as opposed to the minds and consciousness of actors in society; and (2) social phenomena understood as objective, robust, real, and capable of being studied as natural phenomena (imitating the methodology of natural science) rather than as expressions of the subjectivity and consciousness of researchers (Burrell and Morgan, 1979). Here I concentrate on the first aspect. The exchange-regulator, compass and social-glue metaphors are typically objectivist and the blinders metaphor subjectivist, with the rest of the metaphors falling in between.

A third important dimension is *cognition versus emotion*. The exchange regulator metaphor is highly cognitively oriented – relying on instrumentalism and self-interest as the only important motives – while the sacred-cow, affect-regulator, and blinders metaphors give priority to emotional aspects of culture. The rest of the metaphors occupy a less clear-cut position, in which the cognitive and emotional elements are fused.

A fourth dimension is *free will versus determinism*. To what extent can people control culture and to what extent are they controlled by it? Some authors, typically those with a strong managerial interest, adopt a dualistic position. The affect-regulator and blinders metaphors portray managers as (potentially) in control of culture while employees respond passively to their dictates. The world-closure metaphor points to differences between participants in asymmetrical power relations but recognizes that subordinates have the chance of opposing power, and the social-glue metaphor (as Ray uses it) seems to represent a similar stand. The compass and exchange-regulator metaphors both represent a more traditional determinist position: the active engagement of participants is not visible, and 'variables' of other kinds explain outcomes.

One final dimension worth mentioning is *pro-management versus anti-management*. The exchange-regulator, compass and social-glue metaphors must be read as pro-management, while the idea of culture as world-closure is critical and anti-management, and the rest are relatively neutral.

All metaphors – including the culture metaphors mentioned here – are necessarily partial, i.e. one-sided and neglect certain aspects. The pro-management ones, for example, stress the positive effects of culture, the anti-management ones the ways in which culture, through manipulation by elite actors or through tradition and socialization, contributes to the fixing and freezing of the sociocultural order. Evaluation of organizational culture studies is therefore to a large extent a matter of discussing the benefits and drawbacks of different forms of reductionism: reductionism which aims at equipping managers with the means for increased effectiveness and reductionism which aims at highlighting how the open and nego-tiable character of the social world is obscured by various forms of domination.

Summary

This chapter has aimed at developing further an understanding of the variety of ways in which the culture concept can be used by pointing at crucial dimensions – implying choices in organizational culture thinking. The concept of organiza-tional culture may be used as a variable or as a metaphor for organization. The latter use represents a theoretically informed approach with rich interpretative potential. It indicates the possibility of achieving an understanding of the below sur-face aspects of organizational life and a wide set of aspects of corporations. Using culture as a variable or as root metaphor are not the only two possibilities, but rather represent extremes along a continuum. Many people take more or less consciously a middle position. Organizational culture can then be seen as an organizing metaphor. It is not uncommon, however, to be confused and indecisive in terms of how to relate to the metaphorical quality of culture – contradictions easily enter the picture in efforts to think culturally about management and organizations.

In this chapter I have argued the need for, and helpfulness of, looking at the image or gestalt behind the idea of organizational culture. The point is that also a metaphor comes from somewhere and the metaphorical nature of the thinking and framework behind any definition and surface-level use of the culture concept in organization studies could be made more explicit. Looking at the metaphor for the metaphor in social research is potentially rewarding through encouraging critical rethinking of established ideas, which may rely on un- or half-conscious metaphors, and provid-ing inspiration for new ideas. In cultural studies and culturally aware organizational practice this may be particularly helpful in avoiding vague and sweeping culture talk and analysis. In order to use the culture concept with an analytical bite it must be given a distinct meaning. Being conscious about a second-order metaphor behind the gestalt informing one's thinking, together with the definitions applied, is one way of sharpening culture as an interpretive framework and tool.

The chapter has explored eight metaphors, culture as:

- exchange-regulator; functioning as a control mechanism in which the infor-mal contract and the long-term rewards are regulated, aided by a common value and reference system and a corporate memory;

- compass, in which culture gives a sense of direction and guidelines for priorities;
- social glues, where common ideas, symbols and values are sources of identification with the group/organization and counteracts fragmentation;
- sacred cow, where basic assumptions and values point at a core of the organization which people are strongly committed to;
- affect-regulator, where culture provides guidelines and scripts for emotions and affections and how they should be expressed;
- disorder, ambiguity and fragmentation as key aspects of organizational culture;
- blinders, un- or non-conscious aspects of culture, culture as taken-for-granted ideas leading to blind spots;
- world closure, cultural ideas and meanings creating a fixed world within which people adjust, unable to critically explore and transcend existing social constructions.

Thinking culturally about organizational phenomena also calls for consideration of some other basic dimensions. One is ideas regarding whether organizational culture generally supports some broad socially shared values, or whether organizational cultures typically reflect only an elite group's interest or conviction, or if culture typically stands for frozen, non-conscious ideas that constrain free thought, creativity and open-minded problem-solving. A second is objectivism versus interpretation. Is it possible to objectively define and measure culture, through for example identifying, isolating and getting data on how people relate to a specific value? Or is culture best understood as subtle, not fully conscious ideas, meanings and symbols that call for careful interpretation, reasoning and sometimes guessing on how to make sense of the 'deeper' aspects of how people create their worlds? Is culture a matter of systematic, integrated sets of rather robust phenomena structuring the social world in a clear way; or is culture fragmented, ambiguous, and anchored in the more or less unstructured subjectivities and traffic of symbolism in various social settings? A third dimension is cognition versus emotions. While most conceptions of culture take both into account, emphasis may be either on how people think, process information and intellectually construct their worlds, or how people feel, value and use symbols in an expressive manner. A fourth dimension concerns the agents of culture creation and reproduction. One may argue that culture is a force-like mechanism that operates beyond the backs and controls of individuals and groups: cultural traditions and taken-for-granted meanings rule the lives of people, who only rarely may rethink and create new meanings and guidelines, breaking with earlier dominating ones. One may also proceed from the assumption that culture is an ongoing creation of social reality and the individuals, through their interactions and communications shape and re-shape their worlds, sometimes habitually so, sometimes in a more conscious and active way. This dimension boils down to determinism – culture creates individuals – versus agency – individuals create culture. A fifth dimension concerns the role of management. Here sometimes management authors and practitioners assume a mixed view on determinism versus free will. Managers may be assumed to create or engineer culture, which then creates the minds and hearts of the subordinates. One may work with the assumption that culture is extremely difficult to mould by managers, or see it as at least potentially manager-driven and thus an effective management control tool. In addition to giving more or less option for managerial cultural engineering, such a project may be perceived positively or negatively. Management cultural control may be seen as necessary and laudable – a vital element behind organizational performance – or a morally and political deficit project, involving mind control and potentially leading to organizational totalitarianism. Most of the five dimensions are related to various cognitive interests: a technical interest, for example, typically goes hand in hand with the idea of culture being anchored in shared values, it being objective, functioning as a force and to some extent, at least, driven by management.

Of course, there are many other dimensions of the use of culture theory in organization and management studies. Arguably, those mentioned capture significant issues and show the need for thinking reflexively about how to use organizational culture theory, i.e. carefully consider what is focused and what is downplayed in cultural analysis and what should be attended to in organizational practice.

To some extent all the basic aspects treated here are paradigmatically grounded, i.e. they are part of one's world view (Burrell and Morgan, 1979). But they are not immune to empirical variation. Even though one may tend to think about culture in a particular way – for example seeing organizational culture as impregnated with patriarchical ideas and values or bringing order and harmony into chaos and conflict – empirical material can lead the researcher to certain ideas and to adopt a particular metaphor. The open-minded researcher is influenced by theoretical ideas and convictions as well as fieldwork impressions and personal experiences. Such impressions and experiences are certainly influenced by the root metaphor the researcher starts with, but are not entirely dominated by this. A grasp of the variation of interpretive possibilities associated with a cultural framework – suggested here through pointing at a number of second-level metaphors for culture – may facilitate a sensitive interaction between theory and empirical material.

Notes

1   The two views of metaphor are incommensurable in Kuhn's (1970) terms; their arguments cannot really be evaluated independently of their respective paradigmatic assumptions. Although various suggestions have been made for achieving partial understanding across paradigms through dialogue and debate, the communication difficulties of scholars involved in different 'language games' should not be underestimated (see Bernstein, 1983; Jackson and Willmott, 1987).

2   The distinction is not as clear as it might appear, however, because focusing on the implicit and not clearly recognized metaphors in research may mean that these appear new, thus functioning in a creative way. By signifying the implicit, new ideas may be encouraged.

3   I will not distinguish here between root metaphors and the more modest forms of organizing metaphor, but will treat them together. A particular metaphor or metaphorical

expression can be used in different ways as organizing or root metaphors. For example, organizational culture understood as a paradigm shared by organizational members can refer either to a subsystem of cognition (a 'soft' variable) which can facilitate or obstruct strategic change (another 'soft' variable), or to an all-embracing view of an organizational reality (root metaphor), which could mean, for example, that strategic change is seen as paradigmatic change and not as something 'outside' the paradigm. In either case paradigm is a metaphor for culture.

4   Many researchers of organizational culture in fact stress 'organization' more than 'culture', and for them organizational culture is as organized, systemic, and order-creating as 'organization' itself.

5   For a critique of this distinction and the vocabulary employed, briefly mentioned in Chapter 1, see Deetz (1996).

3 Organizational Culture and Performance

The concept of organizational culture has drawn attention to the long-neglected, subjective or 'soft' side of organizational life. However, many aspects of organizational culture have not received much attention. Instead, emphasis has been placed primarily on the cultural and symbolic aspects that are relevant in an instrumental/pragmatic context. The technical cognitive interest prevails. Culture then is treated as an object of management action. In this regard, Ouchi and Wilkins (1985: 462) note that 'the contemporary student of organizational culture often takes the organization not as a natural solution to deep and universal forces but rather as a rational instrument designed by top management to shape the behavior of the employees in purposive ways'. Accordingly, much research on corporate culture and organizational symbolism is dominated by a preoccupation with a limited set of meanings, symbols, values, and ideas presumed to be manageable and directly related to effectiveness and performance. This is in many ways understandable, but there are two major problems following from this emphasis. One is that many aspects of organizational culture are simply disregarded. It seems strange that the (major part of the) literature should generally disregard such values as bureaucratic-'meritocratic' hierarchy, unequal distribution of privileges and rewards, a mixture of individualism and conformity, male domination, emphasis on money, economic growth, consumerism, advanced technology, exploitation of nature, and the equation of economic criteria with rationality. Instrumental reason dominates; quantifiable values and the optimization of means for the attainment of pre-given ends define rationality (Horkheimer and Adorno, 1947; Marcuse, 1964). Mainstream organizational culture thinking – in organizations but also in academia – tend to take this for granted. The values and ideas to which organizational culture research pays attention are primarily connected with the means and operations employed to achieve pre-defined and unquestioned goals. A second problem is that subordinating organizational culture thinking to narrowly defined instrumental concerns also reduces the potential of culture to aid managerial action. Organizational culture calls for considerations that break with some of the assumptions characterizing technical thinking, i.e. the idea that a particular input leads to a predictable effect. This chapter thus shows some problems associated with the use of the term culture that does not take the idea of culture seriously enough and presses the concept into a limited version of the technical cognitive interest. It argues for a 'softer' version of this interest as well as for thinking following the other two cognitive interests (as sketched in Chapter 1).

The dominance of instrumental values

A basic problem in much management thinking and writing is an impatience in showing the great potential of organizational culture. Associated with this is a bias for a premature distinction between the good and the bad values and ideas, trivialization of culture, overstressing the role of management and the employment of causal thinking.

Premature normativity: the idea of good culture

Associated with the technical interest of optimizing means for accomplishment of goals is an underdeveloped capacity to reflect upon normative matters. Viewing cultures as means leads to evaluations of them as more or less 'good', i.e. as useful, without consideration whether this goodness is the same as usefulness or if usefulness may be very multidimensional. The more popular literature argues that 'good' or 'valuable' cultures – often equated with 'strong' cultures – are characterized by norms beneficial to the company, to customers, and to mankind and by 'good' performance in general:

> Good cultures are characterized by norms and values supportive of excellence, teamwork, profitability, honesty, a customer service orientation, pride in one's work, and commitment to the organization. Most of all, they are supportive of adaptability – the capacity to thrive over the long run despite new competition, new regulations, new technological developments, and the strains of growth. (Baker, 1980: 10)

Good cultures are, according to this author, cultures that incorporate all good things in peaceful co-existence. Also many other authors eager to appeal to practitioners focus on highly positive-sounding virtues, attitudes, and behaviour claimed to be useful to the achievement of corporate goals as defined by management (e.g. Deal and Kennedy, 1982; Trice and Beyer, 1985). They are largely instrumental in character, without considering any ambiguity of the virtue of culture or what it supposedly accomplished in terms of goal realization. The assumption that culture can be simply evaluated in terms of right and wrong come through in embarrassing statements such as that 'the wrong values make the culture a major liability' (Wiener, 1988: 536) has already been mentioned. Similarly, Kilmann *et al* (1985: 4) argue that 'a culture has a positive impact on an organization when it points behavior in the right direction.... Alternatively, a culture has negative impact when it points behaviour in the wrong direction'. According to Wilkins and Patterson (1985: 272): 'The ideal culture ... is characterized by a clear assumption of equity ... a clear sense of collective competence ... and an ability to continually apply the collective competence to new situations as well as to alter it when necessary.' Kanter (1983) talks about 'cultures of pride', which are good, and 'cultures of inferiority', which any sane person will avoid. This type of functionalist, normative, and instrumentally biased thinking is also found in Schein's (1985) book, in which culture is seen as a pattern of basic assumptions that has 'proved' to be valid for a group coping with problems of external adaptation and internal integration. Basically, culture in this literature is instrumental in relation to the formal goals of an organization and to the management objectives or tasks associated with these goals (i.e. external and internal effectiveness). It is assumed to exist because it works – or at least used to work. Of course, changed circumstances can make a culture dysfunctional – calling for planned, intentional change – but the approach assumes that culture is or can be 'good' for some worthwhile purpose. As will be shown later 'good' and 'bad' are not, however, self-evident, especially when it comes to complex phenomena such as culture.

A bias towards the 'positive' functions of culture and its close relation to issues such as harmony, consensus, clarity, and meaningfulness is also implicit in many of these studies (see Martin and Meyerson, 1988). Symbols and cultural aspects are often seen as functional (or dysfunctional) for the organization in terms of goal attainment, meeting the emotional-expressive needs of members, reducing tension in communication, and so on. Instrumental/functional dimensions are often emphasized, for instance, in studies of rites and ceremonies (e.g. Dandridge, 1986; Trice and Beyer, 1984). The typical research focus is on social integration (Alvesson, 1987). Culture is understood as (usually or potentially) useful – and those aspects of culture that are not easily or directly seen as useful remain out of sight, e.g. on gender and ethics. The most common ideas guiding organizational analysis draw upon such metaphors for culture as tool, social glue, need satisfier, or regulator of social relations.

Problems include the premature use of moral judgement, in a way hidden behind technical understanding in which culture is viewed as a tool and presumably as easy to evaluate in terms of its goodness as a hammer. But few issues are simply good or bad, functional or dysfunctional. Some things that may be seen as good may be less positive from another angle. A 'clear sense of collective competence' – to connect to the citation above – does in itself sound positive and is good for self-esteem and commitment, but a high level of self-confidence may be a mixed blessing as it easily forms a part of, or leads to, fantasies of omnipotence, and may obstruct openness, reflection, willingness to listen to critique and take new external ideas seriously (Brown and Starkey, 2000).

Cultural themes thus call for careful consideration, where normative judgement should be applied with great caution. Normative talk easily prevents more nuanced interpretation.

Trivialization of culture

As argued above, the consequence of the functionalist/pragmatic approach is that culture tends to be reduced to those limited aspects of this complex phenomenon that are perceived to be directly related to organizational efficiency and competitive advantage (see, e.g. Barney, 1986; Kilmann *et al.*, 1985). This means a rather selected interest in organizational culture. But much worse is a tendency to emphasize mainly the superficial aspects of these selected parts of organizational culture. These superficial aspects have the advantage that they are compatible with technical thinking, presumably accessible to managerial interventions. Culture may even be equated with certain behavioural norms viewed as 'an excellent vehicle for helping people understand and manage the cultural aspects of organizational life' (Allen, 1985: 334). In marketing, market-oriented culture is frequently defined as the key to strong performances (Harris and Ogbonna, 1999), culture here implying certain behaviours. The problem, of course, is that norms are not the best vehicle for understanding culture. Whereas norms tell people how to behave, culture has a much broader and more complex influence on thinking, feeling, and sense-making (Schneider, 1976). Again, Barney (1986), Pfeffer (1994) and others argue that to serve as a source of sustained competitive advantage culture must be 'valuable, rare, and imperfectly imitable'. If this statement is to make any sense at all, culture must be interpreted as highly normative, accessible to evaluation in terms of frequency (i.e. quantifiable), and capable of being copied at will. This conception deprives culture of the richness that is normally seen as its strength. At the same time, any culture may be seen as vital for competitive advantage (or as disadvantage), as it is arguably, highly significant and not easy to imitate. As Pfeffer (1994), among others, notes, many of the earlier identified sources of competitive advantage, such as economies of scale, products or process technology, access to financial resources and protected or regulated markets, become of diminishing significance as a consequence of more fragmented markets with an increasing need for flexibility in production, shorter product life cycle, internationalizations and de-regulations. A company's competence and ability to manage people – to a considerable degree overlapping organizational culture – are not easy to imitate. Even to describe and analyse culture is difficult, as indicated by all the management texts providing only superficial and trivial descriptions of culture, such as norms about 'market-oriented' behaviour.

The trivialization of organizational culture is not, however, solely restricted to writings promising the quick fix. Despite an effort to define organizational culture on a deeper level, emphasizing basic assumptions, Schein (1985) in most of his empirical examples tends to address the more superficial aspects. One example concerns the acquisition of a franchised business:

> The lack of understanding of the cultural risks of buying a franchised business was brought out even more clearly in another case, where a very stuffy, traditional, moralistic company whose management prided itself on its high ethical standards bought a chain of fast-food restaurants that were locally franchised around the country. The company's managers discovered, much to their chagrin, that one of the biggest of these restaurants in a nearby state had become the local brothel. The activities of the town were so well integrated around this restaurant that the alternative of closing it down posed the risk of drawing precisely the kind of attention this company wanted at all costs to avoid. The managers asked themselves, after the fact, 'Should we have known what our acquisition involved on this more subtle level? Should we have understood our own value system better, to ensure compatibility?' (Schein, 1985: 34–5)

Here the problem seems to be lack of knowledge on a very specific point – what the company was buying – rather than lack of understanding of the company's own value system. Most ordinary, 'respectable' corporations, whatever their organizational culture, would probably wish to avoid becoming owners of brothels. Prostitution is broadly seen as illegitimate, not only by those who

Schein views as 'very stuffy, traditional, moralistic' people. Apart from the moral issue, there is of course the risk that bad publicity would follow and harm the company.

Managerialization of culture

Another aspect of adapting culture to technical concerns, and the reduction of complexity and depth contingent upon such concerns, is the confusion of organizational culture with the firm's management ideology. Frequently what is referred to as organizational or corporate culture really stands for the ideals and visions prescribed by top management (Alvesson, 1987; Westley and Jaeger, 1985). It is sometimes held that the best way to investigate 'corporate culture' is through interviews with top managers, but the outcome of this approach tends to be a description of the espoused ideology of those managers that 'only skim the culture that surrounds the top executives' (Czarniawska-Joerges, 1992: 174). Denison (1984) in a survey claiming to study corporate culture, for example asked one manager per company in a large number of companies to fill in a questionnaire.

Organizational culture and managerial ideology are in most cases not the same, partly due to the lack of depth of ideology compared to culture, partly due to variation within organizations and discrepancies between top management and other groups. To differentiate between corporate culture as prescribed and manager-led and organizational culture as 'real culture' and more or less emergent from below is one possibility (Anthony, 1994). However, management ideology is not necessarily very different from organizational culture – there are cases where management ideology powerfully impregnates cultural patterns (Alvesson, 1995; Kunda, 1992). But this needs to be empirically investigated and shown, and cannot be assumed. Management ideology is but one of several expressions of organizational culture. In most discussions of the relationship between culture and performance, authors focus on values espoused by senior managers, to a higher or lower degree shared by larger groups, while the complexity and variety of culture is neglected.[1]

From a management point of view, the managerialization of organizational culture immediately appears appealing; but arguably deeper, less conscious aspects of cultural patterns than those managers are already aware of and promote are more valuable, at least in the long run, to focus on. Rather than smoothing over differences and variations in meanings, ideas and values within organizations, highlighting the latter is significant as a basis of informed management thinking and action.

Loosening the grip of premature practicality

The three weaknesses of much organizational culture thinking reviewed above are related to the wish to make culture appear as of immediate interest to practitioners, and to fit into a predominantly technical cognitive interest in which culture is reduced to a tool. Cultural studies should be permitted to develop unrestricted by, or at least more loosely connected to, concerns for practicality. It is important here is to recognize the contradiction between sophisticated thinking and easily applicable practical concerns:

The more rigorously (anthropologically) the term (culture) is applied, the more the concept of organizational culture gains in theoretical interpretative power and the more it loses in practicality. In the effort to overcome this contradiction the danger is that theoretical rigour will be lost in the interest of practicality. (Westley and Jaeger, 1985: 15)

Even if one wants to contribute to practicality, rather than to anthropology, this still calls for another kind of intellectual approach than most of the authors cited above exemplify. Oversimplification and promises of 'quick fixes' do not necessarily serve narrow pragmatic interests, neither those of managers nor of others. Making things look clear-cut and simple may mislead. Practitioners might benefit much more from the pro-managerial and pragmatic organizational culture literature if it stopped promising recipes for how to manage and control culture and instead discussed other phenomena which managers might, with luck and skill, be able to influence – for example, specific cultural manifestations, workplace spirit and behavioural norms. Learning to 'think culturally' about organizational reality might inspire enlightened managerial everyday action rather than unrealistic programmes for culture change or bending patterns of meaning, ideas and values to managerial will.

Before assuming that culture is functional or good for organizational or managerial purposes, it makes sense to distinguish among possible consequences and to recognize that they may conflict. Critical reflection and learning may be a good thing, consensus facilitating control and coordinated action another, and reduction of anxiety a third; but not all these good things may be attainable at the same time and they may contradict each other. Perhaps more important, contradictory interests – those of professions, divisions, classes, consumers, environmentalists, the state, owners, top management, etc. – may produce different views on what is good, important, and appropriate. Also within complex organizations, corporate goal-attainment may presuppose considerable variation in cultural orientations. Most aspects of culture are difficult to designate as clearly good or bad. To simplify these relationships runs the risk of producing misleading pictures of cultural manifestations. Instead, the focus must become the tensions between the creative and destructive possibilities of culture formation (Jeffcutt, 1993).

Approaches to the culture–performance relationship

There are different ideas regarding to what extent organizational culture can be used as a managerial tool. I will point at and discuss three versions of how managers can work with culture. These represent the relative significance of management versus culture: can management control culture or must management adapt to culture?

Cultural engineering: corporate culture as managerial design

In the most instrumentally oriented of these formulations, culture is conceived as a *building block* in organizational design – a subsystem, well-demarcated from other parts of the organization, which includes norms, values, beliefs, and behavioural styles of employees. Even though it may be difficult to master, it is in principle no different from other parts of the organization in terms of management and control. The term 'cultural engineering' captures the spirit of this position, which is sometimes called the 'corporate-culture school' (Alvesson and Berg, 1992).

Kilmann (1985: 354) recognizes that there is considerable disagreement about what culture is but concludes that 'it is still important to consider what makes a culture good or bad, adaptive or dysfunctional'. He describes culture almost as a physical force: 'Culture provides meaning, direction, and mobilization – it is the social energy that moves the corporation into allocation … the energy that flows from shared commitments among group members' (p. 352) and 'the force controlling behaviour at every level in the organization' (p. 358). He believes that every firm has a distinctive culture that can develop and change quickly and must be managed and controlled: 'If left alone, a culture eventually becomes dysfunctional' (p. 354). The underlying metaphor then clearly comes from technical science.

The crucial dimension of culture, according to Kilmann, is norms; it is here that culture is 'most easily controlled'. More precisely, it is the norms that guide the behaviour and attitudes of the people in the company that are of greatest interest and significance, because they have a powerful effect on the requirements for its success – quality, efficiency, product reliability, customer service, innovation, hard work, loyalty, etc. This is the core of most (American) texts on corporate culture (e.g. Deal and Kennedy, 1982; Peters and Waterman, 1982; Sathe, 1985; Wiener, 1988). There are many difficulties with this model. Norms refer to a too superficial and behaviour-near aspect to really capture culture, at least as defined in this book. Norms and behaviours are affected by many dimensions other than culture. Within a culture there are a number of norms related to the enormous variety of different behaviours. The point with culture is that it indicates the meaning dimension, i.e. what is behind and informs norms.

A related problem with this behaviour-near view on culture is the tendency to see culture as more or less forcefully affecting behaviour. For example, Sathe (1985: 236) argues that 'the strength of a culture influences the intensity of behavior', and the 'strength' of a culture is determined by 'how many important shared assumptions there are', how widely they are shared, and how clearly they are ranked. A 'strong' culture is thus characterized by homogeneity, simplicity, and clearly ordered assumptions. In a 'complex' culture – by definition any culture – assumptions will probably be very difficult to identify and rank, and it can even be argued that such a measurement approach distorts the phenomena it is supposed to study. As Fitzgerald (1988: 9–10) has put it:

> Values do not exist as isolated, independent, or incremental entities. Beliefs and assumptions, tastes and inclinations, hopes and purposes, values and principles are not modular packages stored on warehouse shelves, waiting for inventory. They have no separate existence, as do spark plugs in an engine; they cannot be examined one at a time and replaced when burned out…. They have their own inner dynamic: Patriotism, dignity, order, progress, equality, security – each implies other values, as well as their opposites. Patriotism implies homeland, duty, and honor, but also takes its strength from its contrast to disloyalty; dignity requires the possibility of humiliation and shame.

Values form a knotted (if unsymmetrical) net that we cannot unravel without altering their reciprocity, harmonies, and synergy.

Moreover, to suggest that cultures can be measured on the single dimension of 'strength' deprives the concept of analytic and interpretive capacity: culture is a complex web of meanings, not a bundle of muscles.

Another problem with this approach is the tendency to view norms and values as capable of being abstracted from other things in an organization. 'Corporate-culture' writers propose that, other things being equal, a company-wide set of norms and values can be affected by the same external forces, and be the cause of behaviour and performance. This is problematic because, among other things, work norms are probably closely tied to a variety of circumstances in the work-place rather than being organization-wide. The kind of job and organization, the reward structure, and the employee's age, gender, qualifications, and interests are probably more significant in determining these norms. Hofstede *et al.* (1990), for example, found age, educational level, and hierarchical position to predict work values. To try to isolate norms and values shared throughout the organization (or any other large unit) as a separate causal factor in work performance is not easy. This is not to say that norms do not matter. Rather, to a large extent they are probably associated with different groups to different degrees and have different content. For example, on the shopfloor, output restriction is reported to be a common norm, and it is probably seldom shared by management.

It would in fact be odd if CEOs, typists, factory workers, salesmen, engineers, and product designers shared norms and acted upon them in similar ways. Division of labour is a cornerstone of the modern corporation, and norms that opposed rather than reflected diversity would not necessarily make it more efficient. It might be – and sometimes is – argued that 'corporate culture' counteracts the disintegration fostered by the vertical and horizontal differentiation of modern organizations. But to the extent that this is the case, probably less is achieved through organization-wide norms that directly affect behaviour in a homogeneous way than through shared feelings of identification and community. Therefore it is important to distinguish between common culture as a source of shared understanding and culture as something that directly affects behaviour through norms. The social-glue metaphor thus makes more sense than culture as energizer and/or blueprint for specific behaviours. The conclusion suggested here is that the values and norms that comprise 'corporate culture' have a limited direct impact on organizational effectiveness in terms of work behaviour and willingness to work. Still, the relevance of cultural patterns for what goes on in organizations and different kinds of outcomes is great, but in much more indirect ways than assumed by the authors here reviewed.

Management as symbolic action: shared understandings as managerial accomplishment

A second approach linking organizational culture with performance emphasizes the reality-defining powers of management action. It is assumed that the leaders of an organization exercise more or less far-reaching influence on the way in which employees perceive and understand their tasks and on the workplace by creating and maintaining metaphors and myths. One result of this type of influence, from management's point of view, might be the sharing of a 'favourable' definition of organizational reality and work by the whole organization or a part of it (Berg, 1986; Pfeffer, 1981a; Smircich and Morgan, 1982).

Pfeffer (1981a) distinguishes between internal, management control and external, environmental control (such as market conditions and other forms of external resource dependencies (cf. Pfeffer and Salancik, 1978) and between substantive outcomes (actions and activities which lead to tangible, measurable results and have physical referents, such as budgets, salary allocations, sales, and profits) and symbolic outcomes (attitudes, sentiments, values, and perceptions). He suggests that while constraints beyond managerial control basically determine the substantive outcomes, management does have far-reaching influence on employees' attitudes to social reality. The symbolic outcomes of managerial action increase the probability of the development of a common set of understandings about organizational affairs among members.[2] Managerial action – and 'culture' (although Pfeffer does not explicitly use this concept) – involves the development of consensus around the definition of workplace activity (p. 21).[3]

Pfeffer is careful to point out that this consensus is not necessarily about values, interests and goals, but rather about means and technology. He here differs from most other writers on organizational culture that put emphasis on values and norms rather than on meanings (cf., e.g. Kilmann, 1985).

Pfeffer considers any linkage between symbolic and substantive outcomes weak and indirect. Perception and understanding are less a cause than a consequence of behaviour and outcomes. The most important behaviour patterns are basically determined by external constraints. The cultural dimension is more a stabilizing force: 'Shared understandings are likely to emerge to rationalize the patterns of behavior that develop, and in the absence of such rationalization and meaning creation, the structured patterns of behavior are likely to be less stable and persistent' (p. 14). Some possible consequences of symbolic action include mobilization/motivation, satisfaction of demands, implementation of change, and, most important, attitudes and feelings of satisfaction. Clever symbolic action may partly replace 'substance' in an ambiguous situation and thus increase the satisfaction felt by a group without any 'real', substantive change: 'Symbolic actions may serve to mollify groups that are dissatisfied with the organization, thereby ensuring their continued support of the organization and the lessening of opposition and conflict' (p. 35). Symbolic action may also produce commitment and identification with the company. Pfeffer is more careful, then, than most writers on 'corporate culture' about postulating causal relations between culture and corporate performance, instead stressing the avoidance of problems which might negatively affect organizational performance such as conflict, resistance, widespread frustration, high turnover, and absenteeism.

With regard to the effects he talks about as a product of (managerial) action, whereas it is true that social processes intervene in the perception of as well as the creation of social reality, these social processes are themselves governed by (socially constructed and material) 'reality'. In other words, the substantive aspects of a job situation have symbolic consequences. Although Pfeffer refers to Berger and Luckmann's (1966) concept of the social construction of social reality, he overlooks the historical dimension of this process. Our world view and patterns of social perception are historically anchored, and this may make perceptions, attitudes, and sentiments difficult to alter. Furthermore, he tends to underestimate the multiplicity of sources of socially governed perceptions and understandings of organizational affairs. Van Maanen and Barley (1984, 1985) suggest that the great variety of professions and occupations in most complex organizations may create social conflict and competitive definitions of reality and that this tendency may be reinforced by new technology. This means that consensus over technology may frequently be less prevalent than Pfeffer seems to indicate. This is not to deny that managerial action may affect how social reality is perceived in a way that leads to shared beliefs and understandings – or at least reduced diversity in these regards. The outcome of this may be stabilizing, serving to reduce conflict about technologies and negative evaluations of ambiguous situations and conditions. At the same time, the extent to which this action can produce an organizational paradigm (roughly corresponding to organizational culture) remains an open question.

Organizational culture as a constraint of management rationality: awareness of culture as a navigation aid

A third position in using the idea of organizational culture in relation to corporate performance is to treat culture as a diagnostic instrument, as an aid in making wise decisions and avoiding traps. It stresses the deep values and basic assumptions of organizations – unconscious or half-conscious beliefs and ideals about objectives, relationships to the external world, and the internal relations that underlie behavioural norms and other 'artefacts'. Culture is viewed as relatively resistant to attempts to control and change and only occasionally manageable. This approach is not much concerned about giving advice on how culture can be controlled, but it does attempt to be of practical relevance by informing managers of what may be difficult or impossible to accomplish and providing ideas for constructive action in the light of culture. Mapping cultural terrain produces a guide for how to orient oneself and reduce making mistakes. Understanding the 'holy cows' of a group is for example crucial in order to avoid highly negative reactions. There are other, less dramatic traps involved, such as an unwillingness/inability to change priorities or work style due to ingrained habits and cultural competence.

The focus here is not on the effects of managerial action but rather on the consequences of organizational cultures on how initiatives and change efforts are reacted upon. Cultures are anchored in the organizational collective and exercise influence without the direct involvement of particular key actors. For Schein (1985: 9) culture is 'a pattern of basic assumptions invented, discovered, or developed by a given group as it learns to cope with its problems of external adaptation and internal integration – that has worked well enough to be considered valid and therefore, to be taught to new members as the correct way to perceive, think, and feel in relation to those problems'. Indeed, members will find behaviour based on any other premise inconceivable. Artefacts are the visible and audible patterns of culture, existing on a surface level, and values, on the intermediary level, concern what 'ought' to be done and are more or less understood and consciously grasped by the organizational community.

Schein suggests that cultural phenomena have far-reaching effects on organizational effectiveness and individual satisfaction. As examples he points to the effects of culture on strategy, mergers, acquisitions, and diversifications, the integration of new technologies, intergroup conflicts within the organization, the effectiveness of communication, socialization, and the level of productivity.

One example concerns a company that had become successful by marketing a very complex product to sophisticated consumers:

> When the company later developed a smaller, simpler, less expensive version of this product, which could be sold to less sophisticated customers, its product designers and its marketing and sales divisions could not deal with the new customer type. The sales and marketing people could not imagine what the concerns of the new, less knowledgeable customer might be, and the product designers continued to be convinced that they could judge product attractiveness themselves. Neither group was motivated to understand the new customer type because, unconsciously, they tended to look down on such customers. (Schein, 1985: 32)

He suggests that this problem was not merely one of inadequate training but 'cultural' in nature: 'the perceptions and resulting behaviour patterns were built on deeply held, long-standing assumptions that were taken-for-granted because they had led to prior success'. The 'deeply held, long-standing assumption' in question is presumably that the company would manufacture and sell a complex product to sophisticated customers. This example illustrates the difficulties of accomplishing a re-orientation of the ideas and understandings of people. Competence has a strong cultural undertone and technical skills are far from sufficient. If top management had understood this better, perhaps they would have refrained from developing this product that its personnel were not good at selling or perhaps undertaken other measures to address the problems, e.g. employing new people with more suitable orientations. The example does not seem to be about sacred values, but more about how the personnel have developed blind spots in their ideas about their customers – relating to these without understanding their situation and knowledge.[4]

This example can, however, be utilized also for other lessons. Apparently, much of the organization no longer shared the disdain for the new type of customers, and in fact a simpler version of the product for a less sophisticated consumer group was developed, produced and marketed. Those who took the former situation for granted might resist change, have a low opinion of it, or be less skilled in dealing with a certain type of customer; but this does not really touch upon the deep level which Schein sees as the crucial one (basic assumptions). Schein's cases give us some hints about cultural meanings and values of two groups within the company being a problem for expansion of the market, but the analysis is insufficient to tell us that much about the nature of the problem.

From Schein's description, it seems that the company was unable to understand and judge the concerns and tastes of its customers; it may be speculative to bring basic assumptions in to the discussion. Working for some time with a particular object will produce competence, not only in the strictly technical sense but also in a somewhat wider social or cultural one, in line with the demands of that object. Dealing with a new customer group will require the development of new capacities for understanding their concerns and tastes. An inability to understand and communicate with new customers may be the result of a lack of the required social and cultural skills. Negative attitudes and traditional values may of course be of some significance here, but a simpler explanation than Schein's would appear to be sufficient.

Comment

The three proposed standpoints can be summarized as a contest between management and culture. They reflect different assumptions of senior managers' possibilities of moulding organizational members' ideas, meanings, values and norms after their business goals. In the first, management wins; in the second, management and culture are intertwined and carry similar weight; in the third, culture is the stronger force to which managers must adapt. Management's possibilities to shape culture vary with circumstances – in a young company in a fast-growing market the chances are much better than in a situation of managing a highly experienced workforce on a mature market. Generally, some care about assuming too much ability of management to control and intentionally change culture is recommended. Stressing management as symbolic action indicates the spheres in which a significant cultural impact is possible – a shared definition of a particular sphere of organizational reality seems more achievable than getting everybody to adopt the same values and work according to the same norms. Using culture as a source of insights about what is difficult to accomplish may often have a strong pragmatic value – as indicated by, for example, the high failure rate of mergers and acquisitions.

The culture–performance relationship

The discussion so far has been dealing primarily with identifying various ways of thinking about the relevance of the culture concept for corporate performances. Critique against promises of using culture as a means for corporate goals have been raised. Much interest has nevertheless been given to effects on performance of the 'right' or strong enough corporate culture. There is a lot of writing and talk about this but also a few systematic empirical studies. Let us now turn to empirical investigations of culture–performance relationships.

The effects of organizational culture on performance

There are four views on the relationship between organizational culture on performance:

1 Perhaps the most common one is the so-called strong-culture thesis. It has often been assumed that commitment of an organization's employees and

managers to the same set of values, beliefs and norms will have positive results – that the 'strength' of 'corporate culture' is directly correlated with the level of profits in a company (e.g. Denison, 1984). Researchers adopting this hypothesis tend to place new kinds of human relations (involving employees in decision-making, allowing them some discretion, developing holistic relations, etc.) at the core of organizational culture (e.g. Peters and Waterman, 1982; Ouchi, 1981). It is frequently argued that a distinct organizational culture contributes to performance through facilitating goal alignment – a common culture makes it easier to agree upon goals as well as appropriate means for attaining them. There are also positive effects on motivation – a shared culture encourages people to identify with the organization and feel belongingness and responsibility for it, it is assumed (Brown, 1995).

2   There are also, however, researchers that suggest the reverse relationship between culture and performance: that high performance leads to the creation of a 'strong' corporate culture (cultural homogeneity). It is possible that success brings about a common set of orientations, beliefs and values. A particular workplace spirit may develop and there may be little incentive or encouragement to question 'ways of doing things', thus forming broad consensus and possibly conformism. This culture may be more than just a by-product of high performances: values and meanings may reproduce a successful organization and thus contribute to performances. It may also be a source of conservatism and a liability in situations calling for radical change.

3   Another idea draws upon contingency thinking to suggest that under certain conditions a particular type of culture is appropriate, even necessary, and contributes to efficiency. Wilkins and Ouchi (1983), for example, consider culture an important regulatory mechanism in organizational settings too complex and ambiguous to be controlled by traditional means (bureaucracy and the market). In corporate situations where these means of regulation function well, corporate control as a distinct form is less significant.

4   Still another version says that 'adaptive cultures' are the key to good performance, i.e. cultures that are able to respond to changes in the environment. Such cultures are characterized by people willing to take risk, trust each other, are proactive, work together to identify problems and opportunities, etc. It may be tempting to say that 'adaptive cultures' are self-evidently superior. There easily enters an element of tautology here: 'adaptive' implying successful adaption and this is per definition good for business. But as Brown (1995) remarks, there are organizations that are relatively stable and fit with a relatively stable environment, and risk-taking and innovation are not necessarily successful. Too much change can lead to instability, low cost-efficiency, risky projects and a loss of sense of direction.

It is very difficult to investigate and test these diverse ideas. The relatively few systematic empirical studies on the culture–performance link lead us to conclude that none of these four ideas have received much empirical support (Brown, 1995; Calori and Sarnin, 1991; Siehl and Martin, 1990). Siehl and Martin find important methodological deficiencies in all these studies and suggest that the idea of a corporate culture concept cannot be linked simply and tightly to corporate results.

Is it meaningful to try to investigate any causal link between culture and performance?

Of course failure to establish an empirical link does not mean that no such link exists. Empirical study in the area is very difficult to carry out. Not only is culture difficult to capture but so is performance (Sköldberg, 1990). It is common sense that something that we can call 'corporate culture' will have an impact on many types of actions in organizations and consequently also on corporate financial results. Any such influence may, however, be lost among all the factors and inter-action patterns that have something to do with these results. Bhaskar's distinction between 'the domain of the empirical', experiences created by direct and indirect observation, and 'the domain of the real', events which take place whether or not we observe them, is useful here (Outhwaite, 1983). The empirical is distinct from the real partly because not everything is observed and partly because not everything is observable. This view strongly warns against an empiricist approach. In the absence of opportunities to 'observe' culture and its role, we can of course specu-late about it. As we have seen, however, such speculation is also problematic.

Instead of giving up the idea of finding clear-cut empirical answers to the ques-tion of 'corporate culture's' effect on performance, some researchers have argued that a more refined approach which takes into account the complexity of culture should guide empirical studies. Saffold (1988: 546), for example, argues that it is reasonable to expect that 'a phenomenon as pervasive as organizational culture affects organizational performance' but current models oversimplify the relation-ship. He points to five important shortcomings of empirical studies: (1) 'strong-culture' studies tend to emphasize a single, unitary organizational culture even though multiple subcultures rather than unitary cultures seem to be the rule; (2) measures of the 'strength' of culture are ambiguous partly because in the study of culture 'meanings are central, not frequencies' (Van Maanen and Barley, 1984: 307); (3) there is a preference for broad-brush cultural profiles, focusing on very general values and norms, which fail to do justice to the complexity of culture; (4) there is insufficient attention to the variety of possible culture–performance links. A particular cultural feature may affect different performance-related organi-zational processes in different directions. Development of shared meanings may, for example, have a positive effect on organizational control but at the same time create conformism and reduce the organization's capacity to learn and change; (5) there are many methodological problems in existing studies, ranging from overreliance on top management views to the absence of control groups.

Saffold goes on to suggest an enriched framework which involves the 'use of appropriate measures of culture's impact', the use of contextual rather than modal analysis (i.e. avoidance of static and abstract categorizations), and attention to multiple interactions. This framework involves: (1) measures of cultural dis-persion, the degree to which cultural characteristics are dispersed throughout an organization (sociologically, psychologically, historically and artefactually);

(2) measures of cultural potency (the power of the culture itself to influence behaviour); (3) studies of 'how specific culturally conditioned processes contribute to outcomes'; and (4) the recognition of multiple, mutually causal interactions. Hardly surprisingly, he notes that 'if it all sounds complex, it is – unavoidably so', but believes that his framework 'reflects the true richness of culture–performance relationships'. In this observation he is probably correct.

Saffold's 'three correctives' will probably discourage researchers from attempting the task of studying culture–performance relationships. Siehl and Martin (1990) suggest that there are more worthwhile projects. I agree. The four propositions about the connection between culture and performance treated in the previous section all presumably offer some input to thinking and are worth taking seriously also in the absence of a firm answer to the possibly naive question of which is the correct one. Even if research should converge in finding support for one of these as being more frequently valid than the others, there are still reasons for practitioners to think through their own organizational situation in relationship to various views on culture. Even if studies of large samples of organizations should indicate no or only a weak general correlation between e.g. 'strong' cultures and performance, a specific organization may still benefit from efforts to develop more shared values and orientations.

Does culture cause anything? The problems of separating culture and other phenomena

The technical cognitive interest and the metaphors based upon it typically rest upon and favour separating corporate phenomena into variables and then seek correlations and causal relations. Through manipulating a certain variable – e.g. the organizational reward system or the design of the product – certain outcomes are promoted, e.g. employees paying more attention to costs or increased consumers' curiosity. I will here try to show that this logic works less well in the case of organizational culture. Again, I will proceed from a brief review of how respected organizational culture researchers have difficulties dealing with the issue of separating culture from other phenomena and establishing causal relationships. My purpose is of course not to engage in faultfinding for its own sake, but to show some traps and difficulties in cultural thinking that we can learn from.

In an overview article on the investigation of workplace cultures, Louis characterizes culture as:

> a set of understandings or meanings shared by a group of people. The meanings are largely tacit among members, are clearly relevant to the particular group, and are distinctive to the group. Meanings are passed on to new group members … [culture's content is] the totality of socially transmitted behavior patterns, a style of social and artistic expression, a set of common understandings. (1985: 74)

She cites four examples of the effects of workplace culture: increase in the safety and meaningfulness of work through team-oriented work in coal mines (Trist and Bamforth, 1951); increase in workers' commitment to and identification with a group and organization; elimination of the need for structural controls to induce desired attitudes and behaviour; and facilitation of the socialization of new members.

Given Louis' definition of culture, it is difficult to see how culture and the outcomes of culture can be separated. If culture *is* meanings and socially transmitted behaviour patterns, how can it then *induce* attitudes and behaviours and replace structural controls? Organizational culture then becomes both cause and effect. The teamwork in the coalmines is not necessarily an effect of the culture there; the work situation and its teamwork orientation may produce a certain culture. Even better, one might say that the workplace culture cannot be separated from the way the job is performed and therefore no causal relationship can be established. Workplace culture is a way (a set of aspects) of doing a job – the shared meanings and understandings is the cognitive basis of a certain kind of work as a social practice. Formulated like this, culture is intrinsically related to behaviour, rather than standing in an external relationship. It is an aspect on behaviour, rather than a force that causes behaviour.

The same holds for the statement that 'the socialization of new members is facilitated by work group cultures' (Louis, 1985: 85); without culture, socialization is impossible, and without socialization there would be no one to 'carry' culture. Furthermore, if there were no specific work group culture, there would be no need for socialization: people would fit in anyway as a result of a shared broader culture associated with nation, class, profession, etc. In for example organization dominated by a strong profession, newcomers belonging to the profession are typically not going through a particular workplace socialization process. In other organizations, not characterized by distinct work group cultures or cultures associated with occupations or other macro groups, the workplace would be characterized by very different individuals, with very idiosyncratic ideas and orientations, thus making cooperation difficult; but here there would not be any need or possibilities for socialization. (Similar remarks can be made against Schein (1985) who also argues that culture and socialization are externally related rather than logically hanging together.) Rather than saying that work group culture facilitates socialization, it makes more sense to say that work group culture is the prerequisite for socialization. Without a distinct culture, no distinct socialization is needed or possible.

I do, however, agree with Louis that workplace culture is important to understanding the nature of workers' commitment and identification with the workplace. Improved work safety in the coal mine and attention to the welfare of the families of work group members could also be interpreted as outcomes of workplace culture. Coping with accidents and health problems typically involves cultural changes at the workplace level, e.g. reconstructing meanings and values associated with masculinity and risk-taking. Generally, it is often difficult to separate clearly what is culture and what is its outcomes; Louis' definition of culture seems to include much of what is generally presented as partly 'outside' culture, to some extent outcomes of culture.

Louis' study is a fairly typical example of the difficulty in separating 'culture' from 'non-culture'. Another author speculating about the implications of culture for organizational performance and other outcomes is Gagliardi (1986: 124). He claims that 'a common culture strengthens cohesion, improves the ability to communicate, allowing that the spirit, rather than the letter, of the organization's rules are observed'. It is hard to imagine that cohesion, ability to communicate, and a spirit of organizational rules would be possible without a common culture. These presumed outcomes exist to a greater or lesser extent in most definitions of culture (including those by Gagliardi and Louis). But as mentioned, there is a possibility that a culture might include anti-communal, individualistic and/or bureaucratic values which could produce outcomes other than those suggested by Gagliardi, but this possibility is not included in his view of culture as inherently 'good' or functional. Thus this kind of statement appears either as tautological/ trivial or in many cases – if the culture concept is stripped of a strong functional-istic bias and the possibility of anti-communal or bureaucratic values and ideals is acknowledged – as unfounded. More generally, Pennings and Gresov (1986: 323) also refer to the difficulty of isolating values and norms and estimating their causal importance: 'the deterministic weight to be assigned to cultural factors is highly problematic. In assessing, for instance, the extent to which values deter-mine behaviour, the best evidence of what values exist often lies in norms. But the existence of a norm is usually evidenced by regularities of behaviour and hence the whole explanation becomes tautological': culture explains what it is – it is 'cause' and 'effect' at the same time. The culture literature share this unfortu-nate bias with many other fields of management, eager to point at what leads to effectiveness, e.g. large parts of the research on leadership (Alvesson and Deetz, 2000) and strategy (Levy *et al.*, 2001).

Before ending this section, I want to emphasize that I am not saying that it is impossible to identify outcomes of culture such as financial results or absence patterns. Tautological reasoning can be avoided. It frequently makes sense to try to point at how the shared meanings may affect action and possible outcomes. But one needs to be careful about how culture is conceptualized and realize that culture is also an aspect of the outcome. Culture affects results in subtle, complex ways and cause–effect thinking can seldom appreciate this. One way of reducing the problem is to avoid sweeping statements about cultures as wholes and instead look at specific cultural manifestations and study their consequences, e.g. out-comes more 'close' to the manifestations than financial results.

Positive and less positive outcomes of corporate culture: a case study

The organizational culture of a computer consultancy company

Having delivered all this critique against the efforts of others to relate organiza-tional culture to performances and other valued outputs, the simplistic evaluation of cultures in terms of good or bad as well as the overemphasis on the positive function of culture, I will try to manoevre a bit more carefully. (I still suspect that the observant reader will find contradictions and problems also in my text.) Some years ago I did a case study of a Swedish computer consultancy company and I will refer to it in terms of possible connections between culture and performance (Alvesson, 1993b; 1995).

The company, called Enator, was founded ten years prior to my study and employed 500 people. Rapid growth, high profits, low personnel turnover and very favourable market ratings plus considerable positive public attention (including media interest) meant that the company performed well at the time. Managers and other employees attributed a great deal of the success to the corporate culture.

Important values and norms in the company were openness, friendship, to have fun, informality, communicative and social orientations and skills, a downplayed sense of hierarchy, personal support, working hard for the company, being prepared to spend some leisure time taking part in activities orchestrated by the company, etc. Some devaluation of technical skills compared to social, communicative aspects of project management and customer interaction could also be part of the values and ideas in the company. An important part of the maintenance of these values was the recruitment of people who shared these values and orientations (cf. Sathe, 1985; Wilkins and Ouchi, 1983, etc.). These cultural orientations seemed to be rather well anchored among the majority of the employees.

The creation and reproduction of a culture and its impact on people can take place through specific activities, various types of behaviours from key actors and other 'cultural agents', through language and through material arrangements. Action, verbal and material symbolism thus shape and express culture (Dandridge *et al.*, 1980). I'll use these three categories to produce an overview of corporate culture.

A large number of events were institutionalized in order to strengthen the social relations in the company. Every third month the various units (subsidiaries employing up to 50 persons) did something special, which was financed by the company: combining a conference or a training session with walking in the mountains, sailing, diving, etc. Large parties also took place every year. A number of company-supported activities regularly took place in the corporate building outside Stockholm: a chorus, art club, navigation course and so on. The management tried to make the employees consider the company as a family.

Major identity-facilitating activities took place when the company celebrated various events. Enator's tenth anniversary, for example, was celebrated during three days on the island of Rhodes in Greece. All the 500 employees, the board and some other people were flown to the island and faced with a programme including a variety of social activities.

Language use in the company was also intended to shape ideas and meanings. A slogan was 'fun and profit', illuminating the significance of having a good workplace climate as well as being profitable. The term 'giant directors' were sometimes used in order to signal distance from excessive respect for hierarchy and formal positions. Sometimes senior managers said things like 'as I am the only person here whose time is not debitable, I'll fix the coffee'. This was intended to express relatively egalitarian social relations.

The design and interior of the main corporate building also had some meaning and identity-reinforcing qualities. One was to support the view that the company should be seen as a home. The house was laid out in a way that supports the idea. Half of the top floor was designed in such a way that a homely feeling was created. There was a kitchen, sauna, pool, television, cosy furniture, a piano bar, etc. People were working in office landscapes. They sat tightly together. There was very little area per individual. The 'public' spaces were rather large.

The building was quite original and received much attention from the mass-media in Sweden. The architecture included a number of other cultural artefacts, expressing the management 'philosophy' of the company. Contrary to the common mode, top management was located on the first floor. The internal walls and the office of the top managers were made from transparent glass. This was intended to symbolize openness and to facilitate interaction. The design also reflected a view of how work should be conducted. Very few straight lines existed. There were no long corridors. The middle of the building was dominated by a triangular open square. Some of the strengths of Enator in project work, according to interviewees, were also said to be symbolized in the architecture: an ability to communicate and handle social relations with clients. In order to be understood and have an impact physical material intended as communication must often be complemented by a conversation or explanation indicating the meaning of the design (Berg and Kreiner, 1990). In the company the employees were encouraged to accept and embrace the ideas and values of the company mentioned above, and in this light the architecture and interiors were relevant and conducive to its philosophy and make sense for the employees. Corporate talk and the materia then supported each other.

One key aspect of all this was that management considered itself to be very competent in dealing with personnel and the social side of business and the organization. According to the CEO, 'If there is anything we are good at, it is this. We are damned good at this'.

In this company, comparatively distinct and broadly shared patterns of meanings, ideas, values and beliefs, communicated through actions, language and materia were developed. Corporate culture guided managers and other personnel in their way of relating to the company, to each other, to customers, etc. The meaning of being an organizational member – being part of a social community, viewing work and organizational belonging partly in non-instrumental terms – was for example then a salient cultural expression.

Some possible positive outcomes

The management style and the corporate culture led to people being knitted more closely to each other and to the company. A feeling of loyalty was fostered. There are indications of this from statements made by interviewed consultants such as 'one feels more inclined to work a bit harder for this company'. The work groups, sometimes assembled with people who did not know each other in advance, tended to run smoother from the start and cooperation was improved. People felt that they primarily belonged to Enator and worked with this in their mind. The corporate culture also functioned as a resource for managers to make people do the job even in situations when it did not feel pleasant or stimulating. As one consultant said:

The managers are drawing heavily on loyalty. The culture's purpose is to build a sense of belongingness, a loyalty with the company. If we hadn't that, people would quit all the time. The reasons from the company are egoistic. But this is not necessarily negative. It is fun also. But you don't say 'I don't give a damn in this. I will not do it. I am not going to that place again'. You don't do that. Of course, you do the job.

Personnel turnover was very low. Many consultancy companies risk that key people leave the company to start businesses of their own. Enator seemed to be very successful in avoiding this, although a successful foreign subsidiary departed led by the manager, which was a big blow for the company.

There are thus indications on a high level of corporate loyalty and identification as well as a broadly shared understanding of work principles, and good social relations were associated with corporate culture. All this was likely to affect work cooperation, efforts and client interactions in positive ways. Low turnover meant reduced costs for hiring, but even more significantly that the company safeguarded its human capital in a labour market in which there was much demand for IT people. Culture could then be seen as a *social glue* contributing to keeping the organization together.

The problem of separating culture and specific outcomes of culture is worth considering here. When cultural values include belongingness and loyalty, which almost per definition means a dis-inclination to leave the organization, and these go hand in hand with low turnover, it is not particular revealing to say that the culture has an effect on turnover. On the other hand, a focus on culture as ideas, meanings and values means that any behavioural implication is not automatic or self-evident.⁵ The interview quotation above gives a good hint on how cultural meanings and values work: there are ideas and values frequently expressed and drawn upon in the company, e.g. by managers when they want to persuade employees, which then guide and inform people in specific situations.

Complexities 1

Even though organizational culture seems to be a central dimension in or behind the company's rapid growth and good results, factors other than the corporate culture as an abstract, isolated entity must be acknowledged here. These concern both management control efforts and contingency and demographic factors. A young, expanding company in a growing market with a relatively homogeneous workforce – many of them between 30 and 40 years old – in professional jobs, certainly made the development of this climate and commitment easier. These structural factors do not, however, automatically produce these effects. Many companies in a fast-growing market fail. Only a few really succeed. A homogeneous group – in terms of professionality and age – is not a guarantee for a good atmosphere. It can be said, however, that the preconditions for the development of a corporate culture were very favourable for Enator. It is difficult to separate a corporate culture from the external conditions of its shaping and reproduction. The border between cultural aspects – meanings, ideas, values – and the somewhat more superficial organizational climate – the experienced spirit, the attitudes and emotions – makes it also difficult to evaluate the exact role of the culture.

One should also add that developing and nurturing these cultural orientations are not for free. Costs involve investments, not so much of money as of managerial time and energy. But costs involve also that other virtues than those prioritized to some extent must be sacrificed. For example, people who are not perceived to fit in this company in terms of personal style cannot be recruited or promoted without problems and/or weakening of the dominant cultural meanings and values: this may have meant that Enator employed fewer technically excellent managers and personnel than the competitors. Another potential problem was that the emphasis on having fun and being positive means that critique and complaints were discouraged. Only bring up problems if you have a constructive alternative, was one norm. The other side of a positive workplace climate may then be low awareness of problems and thus limited learning possibilities. Almost deliberately, i.e. directly connected to the values and norms espoused, parts of the culture then functioned as a blinder, reducing problem awareness.

Complexities 2

Nevertheless, despite the mentioned complexities and uncertainties there are good reasons to believe that Enator's financial results at the end of the day probably benefited from the particular meanings, ideas, beliefs and values that characterized the organization, at least for a number of years.

Here, however, context must be borne in mind. At the time, the market was growing and there was a scarcity of computer people. In this situation, a culture functioning as a social glue is a strong benefit. In a less positive market situation and with plenty of computer people available, an emphasis on organizational membership as highly positive and as a source of self-identity may be less of an advantage. Strong feelings of community and downplayed hierarchy may make managerial work more difficult when tough decisions are to be made, in terms of deteriorating working conditions or tasks or even making people redundant. In such situations, a less committed, more instrumentally oriented workforce may be easier to deal with. Managers that sincerely believe in strong bonds between the company and the personnel may even be prepared to take some losses rather than dismiss personnel. It is, to make things even a bit more complicated, not possible to say something very certain about the pros and cons of meanings and values as those expressed in the Enator case even under circumstances less favourable than when the culture was formed. Outcomes – or aspects – of culture such as corporate commitment, social bonds, loyalty, and the emphasis on fun activities may still be a resource in times of recession. Companies need loyal employees also in difficult times and after downsizing. This can be maintained if the contradictions between the ideal and practices going in different directions are not perceived as too strong or the reasons for deviation from the espoused ideals are accepted.

A stronger problem, however, followed from the earlier emphasis on being positive and optimistic and nurturing a happy workplace climate. This was related to the success of the company during the first 10–15 years and made it difficult to adapt thinking, decision-making and communication to less fortunate conditions:

A part of Enator's way of dealing with things in the 80'ies was to pump positive information into the organization, but not to work with negative information in the same way, i.e. one did not balance positive and negative information in the success culture that was emerging. In times of radical change this was a negative factor that the managers were not that capable of sitting down with the employees, saying 'guys, there are problems piling up around the corner'. Instead they said: 'this is a storm, it will disappear in due course, it is only temporary'. This is something that successful organizations easily run into, and it was precisely what happened in this case. (Manager, interviewed some years after the original study)

We can here make connections to several of the second-level metaphors for culture treated in Chapter 2. In the company culture can be said to have worked as an *affect-regulator* – prescribing certain emotions and their expression. Being positive, optimistic and friendly were celebrated, while critique, negativity and a focus on difficulties were discouraged. This led to some limitations of problem-awareness and cooperation difficulties with a new CEO who had the assignment to turn losses into profits mainly through cutting costs, i.e. dismissing employees. Values around and norms for expressing emotions also interact with and overlap selective perception and blind spots in how one creates the organizational reality. Culture as *blinder* meant a de-emphasis on severe signs on problems, sometimes bordering on denial. This aspect becomes salient and problematic in times of difficulties, in particular before these are obvious. Feelings – guided by cultural rules – affect our observations and are important in how we construct our reality (Jaggar, 1989). Of course, a deep recession and a shrinking market gradually leads to people in the company rethinking the situation, but the collective emotional orientations make this slower and perhaps more painful at times. It should, however, be added at the same time that a preference for optimism may be an advantage in keeping up the spirit also in a time of crisis.

Of course, from a managerial point of view, the good culture is adaptable and will change with circumstances. The problem is that such a chameleon-like culture does not really exist. An organization ingrained with positive and warm feelings in an expansion situation cannot immediately switch to embrace a neutral, detached and cold mentality. Culture means a certain level of commitment, depth and inertia. It guides and constrains. It changes relatively slowly and painfully, and seldom in full accordance with managerial intentions.

This case illustrates the potential significance of cultural meanings and values for corporate results, but also that the relationship is not causal, linear, external or stable. Better than to make simplistic evaluations of a set of meanings and values in terms of 'good', 'functional' or 'profitable' is to try to evaluate the complexities and uncertainties involved and realize that cultural manifestations call for more sophisticated understandings and evaluations. Dealing with cultural issues in a way that contributes to corporate results calls for an ongoing struggle in which culture as a tool and as a trap is carefully considered with frequent intervals.

The case also illustrates the three standpoints on management versus culture reviewed earlier (see pp. 47–53). The development of the company according to my interpretations above indicates a transition from management being fairly successful in shaping culture to culture almost controlling managers. I will return to this case company in Chapter 5, addressing leadership during different stages in the company's development, and here the second position – management as symbolic action – will also be illustrated.

The ambiguity of performance: blame time and milking

Most interest in culture and performance focus on the organizational level: ideas on corporate culture are linked to corporate results. For the large majority of organizational participants, even up to fairly senior levels, company-wide cultural patterns and aggregated results are of less concern than the meanings, values and ideas in the work units they work in and/or are responsible for and their results. Also, in order to understand organizational culture in relationship to performance, it is often wise to focus on the cultural nature of performance issues in relationship to individual actors and smaller units.

An interesting question then is how performances on the unit level are evaluated and what matters for the rewards/sanctions, reputation and career prospects of individual managers in charge. This has, of course, a presumably 'rational' side tied to reliability of different performance measurements and human resource management systems. There are, however, significant cultural dimensions involved here. What are the beliefs and governing ideas behind the forming of opinions of the performances of organizational actors? Are these rationalistic and measurement oriented, or do mainly impressions and indicators on 'qualitative' dimensions matter? Is there a short-term or a long-term perspective in the evaluation of performance? Is there an 'organizational memory' so that performances are put into the context of history, development and connections over time; or are there only vague notions of what has happened earlier in a unit and what a particular individual has accomplished over time and not just only recently? Is there an 'intellectual' orientation and an engagement in careful analysis before concluding who or what bear different kinds of responsibilities for a particular result or a failure? Or is there a strong 'action-orientation' where judgements and decisions are arrived at relatively quickly and thus based on simple models and unsophisticated ways of reasoning – meaning that a result is ascribed to the person at present in charge rather than to a complex mix of internal and external circumstances for which nobody in particular can be blamed?

Another set of issues concern the consequences for people of particular results, such as the relative role of a particular track record (irrespective of its unreliability) for the career of a person. Are people promoted based on indications of results? Or on seniority? Or do connections and nepotism matter more? Arguably, some cultures (national, organizational, professional) give priority to social relations and supportive relationships with regards to promotion; others view these as immoral (nepotistic, corrupted) and/or bad for business. One may talk about meritocratic versus political-nepotistic cultures. Another issue regards the significance of historical results in relationship to people's 'potential' based on their capacity to give favourable impressions of themselves. In many cases how people manage in 'high-visibility' situations such as presentations for senior managers may mean more for promotion than what they actually have accomplished (Jackall, 1988).

In Chapter 2, organizational culture as an *exchange-regulator* was addressed. In this light culture means the framework for how to deal with the company–employee relationship in terms of mutual expectations on the relationship performances–rewards, including how one responds to the questions just raised. In certain cultures the values and meanings around performance-evaluations and rewards encourage a long-term perspective and bear in mind the various contributions that people make over time. In others, ideas and expectations around the exchange is more focused, narrow and 'performance-oriented', frequently meaning a strong attention to what can be measured in the short time period.

Arguably, the cultural analysis of how different kind of ideas, meanings and ways of reasoning about performance matters is an interesting and important topic. There are a few writings addressing the issue on a conceptual level (e.g. Wilkins and Ouchi, 1983) but very few empirical studies. The topic is, on the whole, neglected by most of the literature on organizational culture and performance. An excellent, but – as a cynic might have predicted – in the management literature neglected exception is Jackall (1988), who studied the world of managers in big US corporations. He puts performance in the centre of cultural analysis, not outside it.

Jackall emphasizes the ambiguity and arbitrariness of performance evaluations in the companies he investigated. He also stresses the politics, suboptimizations and short-sightedness of people involved. Of course, there are positions and organizational situations in which fairly reliable performance indicators exist. But in many cases, it is not easy to say how well or how badly a particular unit and its manager perform. Coincidence, chance and complexities matter. These circumstances do not put any strong imprints on how senior managers relate to the situation – they disregard the complications and look at the short-term rather than the long run. Several conditions contribute to this orientation on time. The expansion of MBAs with little interest in production and with managerial tools reflecting the short-term mentality characterizing business education, the pressure from the financial markets for rapid results as well as the fragmentation of consciousness that follows from the structure and pace of managerial work all contribute to this. Managers think in short terms because they are evaluated by their superiors and their peers on their short-term results in most US and many other companies. Jackall quotes one manager saying that 'our horizon is today's lunch' as well as the old joke 'I know what you did for me yesterday, but what have you done for me lately' as fairly illustrative for how many people feel about the time horizon in at least parts of US business (Jackall, 1988: 84).

This short-term mentality means that little of a strong sense of responsibility is developed and a specific outcome easily is linked to the wrong person.

> Big corporations implicitly encourage scapegoating by their complete lack of any tracking system to trace responsibility. Whoever is currently and directly in charge of an area is responsible – that is, potentially blamable – for whatever goes wrong there, even if he has inherited other's mistakes. (Jackall, 1988: 87)

Sometimes things go wrong and a negative result or a growing awareness of a problem emerges which means that 'blame-time' comes. Blame-time does not typically mean the in-depth exploration and careful sorting out who is truly responsible for a bad result, but bear the imprints of limited accountability and political processes.

The shortcomings of rationality in ascribing results to particular individuals are sometimes also strong in cases where the financial results are more 'positive'. Good short-term results may follow from harsh cost-cutting, that may lead to difficulties and bad results after some time. This is called milking and may be more less systematically used and be more or less tolerated in different organizations.

> Some managers become very adept at milking businesses and showing a consistent record of high returns. They move from one job to another in a company, always upward, rarely staying more than two years in any post. They may leave behind them detoriating plants and unsafe working conditions or, say, in marketing areas where fixed assets are not an issue, depleted lines of credit and neglected lists of customers, but they know that if they move quickly enough, the blame will fall on others. The ideal situation, of course, is to end up in a position where one can fire one's successor for one's own previous mistakes. (Jackall, 1988: 94)

In a management consultancy company that I studied project managers that understaffed assignments and pushed their team members very hard – with negative effects on personal development, job satisfaction, and turnover – were often appreciated by senior management, as they frequently were able to produce a very high margin in their projects. Due to limited transparency the substantial unfortunate 'side effects', were not always obvious to senior management.

Milking is of great interest from a cultural perspective partly because it stresses the limits of rationalistic ideas about 'numbers' and 'results'. It emphasizes the importance of the time perspective, of how evaluations are made and what kind of judgement and communication permeates an organization. Is milking more or less accepted, i.e. is it part of organizational culture? Is it on the border or the grey zone between what is viewed as, when conducted in a moderate way, normal and sensible ('rules of the game') and what is dangerous for business? Or are performance evaluations and career moves long-term, corporate memory of high quality and – probably contingent thereupon – opportunism hampered, meaning that milking would, if detected, be very negative for a person's future.

There is much variation between different companies in this respect. In many Japanese companies the long-term and more collective orientations presumably reduce the substantive and moral space for milking. In one of the companies studied by Jackall milking, although sometimes recognized as a problem and disapproved of, was used regularly and an element in every successful career. One manager, Noll, had a reputation for aggressive milking in the plants he had headed. At one occasion, a vice-president who was his superior accused him of this. Noll responded with great boldness: 'Joe, how in hell do you think you got to where you are and how do you think you stay there?' The effect of this was that 'the matter was dropped because everyone present, including the vice-president, knew that Noll was right, that is, he was simply pointing out the institutional logic that they all live by' (Jackall, 1988: 96).

In the management consultancy case the situation was slightly different. There were considerable concerns for retaining the personnel and milking though running projects very tight was not part of a 'cultural normality' in the same way as in Noll's company. Managers could run into problems if they were identified as repeatedly understaffing projects. One may say that the cultural exchange-regulating system here was somewhat less 'milking-accepting' than in the case of Noll and his colleagues.

Another interesting aspect concerns the cultural rules for addressing the milking issue openly in a company. Jackall treats some important constraints for this. One is the importance ascribed to being loyal with one's boss. People pointing at problematic or immoral behaviour of superiors can easily be seen as unreliable and disloyal in superior–subordinate relationship, which leads effectively to marginalization. Another is certain rules against raising moral issues: there is a code against playing the 'holier than thou game'. One may say that the exchange-regulating relationship between superiors and subordinates – building upon mutual support and reliability – worked against the optimality of the exchange-regulating relationship between employee and the company, as it tended to conceal opportunism.

In my management consultancy case, the victims of the understaffing of projects were mainly junior consultants, uncertain about their self-esteem, eager to perform well and get accepted and, over time, promoted. In the company the general expectation was that people worked hard and showed themselves to be of the 'right stuff'. To raise complaints could easily be turned against themselves and perceived as indicating an unwillingness to work as much that is 'needed' (to some extent masked as 'client orientation') or inability to 'deliver'.

A problem is, of course, is that it is frequently difficult to clearly identify milking or understaffing motivated by a one sided objective of creating a high margin and a disregard of personnel concerns. The situation is often ambiguous. Pressure from above to produce strong short-term results, problems of separating milking from tough but financially sound rationalizations and the difficulties in predicting the amount of resources needed for a particular project all help to make the picture difficult to see through. As we will return to in particular in Chapter 7, ambiguity is a central feature in companies and this contributes to the usefulness of a cultural approach to organizational performances.

Conclusion

Organizational culture is highly relevant for understanding the things that characterize organizations, including financial and other forms of performance.

In the chapter I have identified three positions on this topic:

- Culture as building block – corporate culture is assumed to be designed by management and having a strong impact on results.
- Management as symbolic action – culture is seen as mediated in actions, language use and arrangements primarily affecting beliefs and understandings, thus having mainly consequences on attitudes and orientations, and less directly so for 'substantive outcomes' (such as profits).

- Culture as a terrain of possibilities and pitfalls – understanding culture is important for managers' possibilities in navigating in and with the organization.

The predominant thought model among practitioners as well as academics seem to be the building block. Many people using it unfortunately assume that corporate culture stands in a simple causal relationship to corporate results, can easily be evaluated in terms of 'good' or 'bad' (functional or dysfunctional), and may be controlled by management. The other two positions are more realistic and more useful, as an inspiration for ongoing management action in relationship to subordinates and, respectively, as a source of informed decisions and manoevring.

It is not possible to say that corporate culture – in general or a specific type of culture – has a clear and simple effect on performance. This does not mean that there is no connection between culture (however defined) and performance; on a general level there certainly is. I agree with Whipp *et al.* (1989: 582) that 'elements of culture … may supply vital links between the rational aspects of policy and the subjective, less tangible features of employees' behaviour exactly because of the way values pervade an enterprise'. Propositions of how culture brings about distinct outcomes, however, often seem problematic. Either the causal link is speculative and uncertain or it is difficult to separate culture from outcome. Some of the authors treated in some depth above (Schein and Louis), run into problems when they claim causal relations or correlations between organizational culture and what they treat as other elements. This is to some extent a matter of using too broad-brushed concepts of culture. If one takes an interest in specific cultural manifestations they can be tentatively related to other manifestations or outcomes, e.g. actions symbolizing equality through avoidance of salient hierarchy, and status symbols may facilitate feelings of community, which then may reduce turnover. In the case company treated in the chapter, Enator, under certain conditions this was most likely positive for the company, but it is difficult, even misleading, to say that the culture as a whole was a significant cause of profits.

The managerially oriented technical cognitive interest, modelled after engineering sciences and practices, dominates much organizational culture, but is misplaced. So is also the inclination to go for quick fixes in management popular writings and training. Organizational culture is best conceptualized as complex patterns of meanings, ideas and symbolism. To evaluate their implications in terms of guidance and constraints of relevance for managerial decision-making and action calls for the postponement of normative judgements until a qualified understanding of the subject matter has been accomplished. Such understanding frequently prevents catchy labels signalling ideals such as 'culture of pride' or 'marketing-oriented culture' presumed to bring about profits.

The practical applications in organizational life are rather a matter of aspiring for insights, understandings, and then, in a second step, aim for slow fixes. Sometimes organizational culture is very useful for trap-avoiding – it facilitates insights about how depth dimensions may lead to serious problems for rationalistic projects that take the human side of business insufficiently into account.

All this is not to deny that leading actors, and to some extent also people in less salient positions, may have a strong impact on cultural meanings in organizations, as illustrated by the Enator case, where the preconditions for a rather far-reaching impact was quite good. Managers, often more than other people, contribute in the shaping or reshaping of meanings and ideas held by the people they interact with. However, context must be borne in mind in understanding when and how managers affect the orientations of their subordinates. There are no recipes for success that just can be copied and applied without consideration of time and space. Impact on meaning formation is actually what leadership is about, from a cultural point of view. As will be explored in Chapters 5 and 8, this is not (normally) about large-scale engineering projects controlling and intentionally changing corporate culture, but is typically better understood in more incremental, everyday life, and culturally constrained ways. Culturally informed local action then typically concentrates on the everyday life and how to deal with its mundane character.

The difficulties in establishing results and the linking of results to particular actors contribute to the need for paying attention to how performance evaluation, credit and blame exist in a cultural context. Of interest here are cultural themes such as time perspective, intellectual versus action orientations in relationship to tracking responsibility and cultural rules for pointing versus tabooing milking strategies for improving performances. Obviously, there is considerable national and industry-level variation. Japanese companies have a reputation for being long-term oriented and thus having a richer coverage of individuals' contributions than for example US companies. Organizations with complex R & D work, where individual contributions may be impossible to measure even in a medium long perspective, have a completely different evaluation situation than for example sales organizations.

One view of organizational cultures in this respect thus concerns their qualities as *exchange-regulators*. These may be summarized as being about: (1) the span of dimensions incorporated (core performances or consideration of a mixture of relevant qualities); (2) the time perspective employed (including what kind of organizational memory that exists); (3) the degree of openness and transparency in and around evaluation procedures in reward and promotion situations; and (4) the experienced quality of evaluations made (including perceptions of the energy and skills devoted to the assessment process). Exchange-regulating aspects of culture also include orientations around trust, scepticism and opportunism in relationship to equity in the employer/employee relationship.

In the next chapter the relevance and significance of a cultural approach to a wide spectrum of corporate dimensions will be further explored. Through indicating the richness in ways in which cultural patterns in organizations affect all kinds of actions and relations, both internally and externally, it is made clear that understanding culture is crucial for managerial and other organizational actions, without this being so simple that a causal link between organizational culture and performance can be established.

Notes

1 Often, especially in large organizations, it is difficult to study more than a limited part of the organization. One possibility is to concentrate on a particular unit. One possible avenue is to investigate 'what happens between floors, in the middle management level, the "thick waist" of complex organizations' (Czarniawska-Joerges, 1992: 87).

2 As many authors emphasize, all phenomena are symbolic in the sense that they must be put into a cultural framework in order to be understood (Sköldberg, 1990; Tompkins, 1987). Tangible things such as products and money are therefore also symbolic. In order to separate symbols with strong physical referents from other ('pure') symbols, Sköldberg (1990) talks about the latter as 'meta-symbolic'. Meta-symbolism refers to other more tangible forms of symbolism: a story or myth might symbolize certain social relations, which in themselves are symbolic. In order to separate the two forms of symbols (à la Pfeffer), as well as to remind ourselves that even 'substantive' phenomena are symbolic, we could refer to these as 'substantive-symbolic' as opposed to 'meta-symbolic'. A distinction such as Pfeffer makes between the substantive versus the symbolic could then be read as the substantive-symbolic versus the meta-symbolic. However, in our present context we have no need to call attention to the symbolic nature of substantive phenomena. The recognition of the basically symbolic character of management action makes Pfeffer's position different from that of a variable approach, and he relies rather heavily on culture as an organizing metaphor, but without using it as a root metaphor, as the dualism of his approach makes clear.

3 Pfeffer uses the metaphor 'paradigm' in referring to the overall patterns of an organization in these regards, but it is not any of the 'paradigms' of Kuhn (1970). Kuhn's metaphors for 'paradigm' are world view, community, and key exemplar; in using various metaphors he is probably not atypical of scholars working with complex concepts and frameworks.

4 Making a connection to the second-level metaphors addressed in Chapter 2, the blinder metaphor seems more relevant here than the sacred cow metaphor to explore the problem.

5 People may feel a high level of loyalty in the company, but may still leave if they receive a very good offer or for family reasons, while keeping a positive feeling about the ex-employer (Alvesson, 2000). There is no very tight or coherent relationship between the cultural and behavioural levels, although meanings and ideas tend to guide action.

4 Organizational Culture and Business Administration

This chapter addresses the relevance of a cultural approach to a wide set of business concerns. Rather than treating culture as of relevance solely for organizational issues, this kind of thinking is highly useful for understanding most aspects of management and corporations, including the business concept, strategy, rationalizations, management control and marketing. The idea is then to go beyond relating organizational culture as a variable to other variables, e.g. correlating organizational culture with customer orientation or seeing organizational culture as an obstacle to strategic change, but to emphasize the cultural meanings of the various phenomena, i.e. the meaning and understanding of the customer and the cultural change involved in strategic change. Given the presence and significance of cultural meanings 'everywhere' in an organization, as in social life in general, it makes little sense in seeing culture as a causal factor behind results. At the same time as culture is of great relevance for actions and arrangements preceding performances, it is also for how performances are defined and read, as treated in Chapter 3.

These examples do not offer any radically new insight for those well acquainted with cultural thinking, but most efforts to relate a concept of organizational culture to business themes have been somewhat superficial, treated culture as a variable and not penetrated in depth the cultural meaning and symbolism dimensions of virtually all aspects of management and business. This chapter tries to move the understanding a bit further than is common and encourage more ambitious cultural thinking in various subareas of business administration.

It is, of course, impossible and not necessary to go through all or even most areas of business and show the relevance of cultural thinking. This chapter instead targets a few significant and representative themes: primarily the business concept and marketing, and to a lesser extent strategy, rationalizations and performance control.

Organizational culture and the business concept

An influential way of capturing the totality of a corporation, and providing a starting point for strategies is the idea of the business concept. This is normally seen as mainly an analytic concept. It can also, as will be shown in a case study, be viewed from a cultural point of view, which then throws a rather different light on it.

The notion of the business concept

It is broadly agreed that there is a need for defining and conceptualizing the core idea or basic nature of a particular company or other type of organization. This is sometimes labelled the mission statement or business concept. The notion of the business concept has had and continues to have a considerable impact on management studies and corporate practice. A seminal source, at least in the Swedish context, is Normann (1977). His concern was the complicated and hard to pin down know-how that is built into the organization and that can give the company superior capability in relation to its environment (the market). According to Normann, the term 'business concept' is perhaps not really ideal partly because the interest is with concrete relationships as well as ideas, and partly because it references a complex system and therefore cannot be reduced solely to a single concept or an idea. Normann defined the business concept as a 'system for dominance' in a given market segment.

The business concept combines and weaves together a number of factors within and outside the company: the niche/market segment, the company's product system, and the company's organizational structure, competence and management style. The business concept thus represents a harmony between the market, the product and the organization.

Compared to many mission statements – which sometimes are not much more than slogans (Swales and Rogers, 1995) – business concepts often are somewhat more informative and elaborated. In some cases, however, the terms are used synonymously.

The business concept of a computer consultancy company

In Chapter 3, the reader got acquainted with the computer consultancy company Enator. According to interviews with managers and written documents, the company's business concept was a matter of 'combining management know-how with technical computer know-how, so that clients become more competitive and efficient' (Annual report, cited in Alvesson, 1995).

Enator pushes its business concept hard. The business concept has a crucial role in the training and socialization of new recruits. During a week-long introduction course, the managers serving as teachers repeatedly emphasize the business concept. It is often mentioned in corporate publications and often cropped up spontaneously in my interviews. The message is frequently hammered out by managers in interactions with subordinates.

Like Normann (1977), we could assume that a company's business concept is a decisive factor in its success and that the degree of agreement and harmony between the various parts of the company determines whether the business concept works – or fails to work. Perhaps we should conclude that the concept has been implemented and has a powerful impact in view of Enator's splendid successes in the form of high profits, rapid growth, good market reputation and a high degree of personnel satisfaction. However, the question is whether matters really are as simple as this.

The ten or so people that I interviewed about Enator's business concept gave me what can only be described as highly divergent responses when questioned about the concept – despite the fact that all my interviewees should have had a good insight into the company. Some of my interviewees considered that the official business concept described actual conditions rather well and that Enator's successes were largely a result of close adherence to the concept. Here are some typical responses:

> Linking the development of a new system to the customer's business concept and area of operations is our basic philosophy.

> I don't believe we are any better [than other companies] from a purely technical point of view. We are better at some things. And that is precisely the fundamental business concept: management and computer development. But we are no better at computer development, perhaps worse in some cases. But on the management side – our way of handling customers – that's where we are better. Our target group is corporate managements, not data-processing departments.

Other interviewees give a different picture about the company. A consultant that had worked for Enator almost since the start said:

> We are supposed to be computer consultants, combined with management consulting, and this has been part of our business concept for several years. But Christer, Hasse and John (i.e. Enator's founders) represented the management side. They didn't recruit people at a lower level with that orientation, they wanted computer consultants – programmers and systems analysts.

Another person interpreted 'management' to having contact with the management of client companies and also said that:

> Management is not just running the company, it's also project management. I don't think we can say that we have smarter technical people than our customers. But nonetheless we work much better in projects than they do. That's because we bring in some project management. It permeates our whole approach. Push things forward until you achieve objectives. This has been expressed in the project philosophy course, and this is an approach which characterizes Enator's whole method of working.

Through somewhat unconventional interpretations like this, the 'management' dimension of the business is rescued. I interviewed some (ex-) subsidiary managers several years after having conducted this study. They had then left the company. One person expressed the following opinion about the espoused business concept:

> It was a myth. A sales trick.

> We did not have that type of competence among the consultants. We did not have that type of management consultants.... It was a skillfully phantasised and carefully nurtured myth, I claim somewhat maliciously. But I think it it is true, also. I still don't think there is anything wrong to do so, because it worked during the 80's. That is not a bad character. If the consultants feel that we are good in combining management and IT – fine. Than they were happy about it, worked in their project and earned money through programming, for that is what it was all about.

Another interviewee, in retrospect, talked in somewhat more nuanced terms, saying that the ambition was to connect to management issues, but said that only a few of the projects succeeded in this respect.

Still, at the time of my study there were shared understandings about the company being skilled in coping with customer relations (the social, communicative dimension) so that the business concept indicates an ideal for project work going beyond a strict technical focus and relating more to the organizational context of IT. The business concept then represents an endeavour, the ideal ambition being to

> enhance the focus on computer questions so that it is no longer purely the computer departments which are concerned with data processing, but instead it becomes an aspect of the company's operations which is just as important as personnel questions and other product resources. (Manager)

In this light, the perception that ambition is not always realized is not that significant as a blow to the credibility of the business concept. The company comforts itself with the thought that there is a chance of achieving this objective, even if there may be projects which do not fully achieve Enator's business concept, managers and others said. Such projects may be used as a springboard to establish contact with corporate management and thus coming closer to strategic issues. This is how people in the company bridge over the contradiction between ideals and (perceived) reality. (Abravanel 1983, would here talk about mediating myths.) Of course, the ambiguity and fluidity of the vocabularies used facilitate such contradiction-bridging operations. They do not, however, succeed in avoiding experiences of contradictions between ideal and reality, between claims of what one is doing and direct work-related experiences.

It may be tempting to say that the business concept is simply misleading, a smoke-screen for what really was going on. I would not go quite that far. After all, there are varied opinions on the subject matter and the concept of management can be interpreted in different ways. It makes sense, however, to say that the relationship between the business concept and what people in the company actually do is ambiguous. The ambiguity involved supports the idea of looking at the business concept as a cultural manifestation.

It makes much more sense to see the business concept as a symbol used for *ideological* purposes, rather than reflecting the company's way of doing business, fulfilling an analytical function. It evokes positive attitudes to the company, both internally and/or externally. The concept is then designed 'in order to ensure maximum employee buy-in' (Swales and Rogers, 1995: 223).

The need for a broad anchoring of the business concept within the company is related to the professional service company's marketing situation, the knowledge-intensive work and the organization's ad-hocratic features. The importance of the business concept as a cohesive force seems to be much greater in knowledge-intensive service companies than in several other types of operations.

> [S]omething which I think is characteristic of knowledge companies is that there has to be a fantastically powerful business concept which holds things together, irrespective of objectives and strategies. I think a business concept is even more important in a knowledge company than in any other type of company. It is a major parameter to hang things on. There is no product which you can rely on if you land up in a tricky situation, when you have to explain what you're doing. There's just a business concept. (Enator executive)

The intention behind the frequent communication of the business concept within the organization is thus partly to use it as a symbol fulfilling a social glue-function.

In a study of a US computer specialist unit, Deetz (1997) also observed the significance of the business concept to support how people relate to their operations. When it was redefined from an internal support unit to a consultancy organization, people revised their views on themselves and their work significantly and identified themselves more strongly with the unit. The identity as being a part of a consultancy organization was more powerful than as a member of an internal service unit. This happened even though the organizational change in itself was less drastic, as it operated as part of a corporate group with more or less the same internal clients as before.

As should now be apparent, the business concept as a symbol has quite varied meanings for the entire collective working at Enator. Variation occurs not only between different people, but also in different contexts. For those in the company who consider that the business concept does not cover core operations, the formulation of the business concept tends to be a historical by-product or some kind of notation of a ceremony, something to know about and perhaps to feel some respect for, but of no great concern in daily and concrete actions. For some people, the business concept is hardly more than a publicity stunt and then indicates managerial cynicism. For other people – and this seems to include the majority of corporate management and other organizational members – the business concept says something important about the company's way of working, at any rate its ambitions for its work, but it is treated as an ideal to which one has a rather relaxed attitude in practical sales and project work situations.

Thus, the business concept may be regarded as a (positive) symbol for the major part of the organization, expressing the company and its qualities. A great deal of the corporate pride centred on the business concept. One person said: 'This is what we are good at. This is Enator's strength'. The business concept spotlights the areas where Enator is better than other companies and is not merely a dispassionate description of the 'company's way of making money'. For certain personnel groups, the business concept has an expressive-affective loading and thus has 'institutional' qualities – that is, it signals the quality and worth of the company, it is viewed as being of value in itself (Selznick, 1957). For them, the business concept expresses the organizational identity of Enator and this becomes a source of identity also for parts of the personnel.

As Ashforth and Mael (1996: 20) put it, 'as the bureaucratic structure dissolves, it becomes increasingly important to have a clear "cognitive structure", a sense of the whole: what the organization stands for and where it is going'. Specific actions in order to create and strengthen a feeling of organizational identity are important here. The intensive communication of the business concept offering an attractive formulation of what the company stands for is one option. This formulation is not necessarily intended to hold for reality tests, although a discrepancy between how it is interpreted and reality perceived by those supposed to accept the concept may backfire.

The dynamics and flexibility of the business concept must, however, be emphasized. The meaning is contingent upon if the concept is invoked in strategic analysis, in sales talk, in project management or in PR work. As a symbol the meaning is not fixed.

Even though the meaning of the business concept or the mission statement varies considerably between different organizations and within these – from PR stunt to a mirror of what the company does or wants to accomplish – it makes sense to draw attention to its symbolic qualities. Enator is not unique in this sense (cf. Deetz, 1997; Swales and Rogers, 1995), even though the reasons for seeing the business concept as an organizational symbol is exceptionally strong in this company. In many if not all cases there is sufficient ambiguity and space for the use of different languages in illuminating the company's activities, to make cultural meanings and symbolism crucial for the role and effects of the business concept. This is, of course, not to say that a cultural-symbolic perspective is necessarily more appropriate than functionalist-rationalist ideas, only that the former perspective may contribute with vital aspects.

This example of course also illustrates the difficulties in finding mechanical relationship between cultural manifestations and corporate performances. The business concept of Enator was seen by many senior organizational participants as very important for the company's success on the market. It may, at least during certain periods, have been more important as an organizational identity strengthening symbol and may also have influenced a greater part of the assignments. But it was also a source of confusion and some mistakes – some managers that tried to work according to it faced problems as the customers frequently were more interested in more mundane programming tasks than a combination of IT and management knowledge. The relevance of the business concept for operational matters was thus frequently questionable.

This example can illustrate the usefulness of several of the second-level metaphors for culture treated in Chapter 2 – and these are implicitly drawn upon in the interpretations above. The variations and contradictions around the meaning and relevance of the business concept are focused by the *disorder* metaphor for culture – emphasizing the ambiguity of significant organizational symbols. However, for many in the company the business concept seemed to work as an integrating symbol – a *social glue*. It was felt to express the nature and spirit of the company and as such contributed to holding 'things together' as an executive, quoted above, expressed it. For many of the employees the business concept also was a focus of attention for the expression of positive feelings about the company. As mentioned, the technical competence of the company was to some extent downplayed, while the ability to consider broader aspects, interacting with client management and putting IT in a strategic context, was felt to symbolize the progressiveness of the company. Here the *affect-regulating* capacity of a key symbol is illustrated: it influenced more how many people felt than thought about the company and its virtues. The persuasive powers of the formulated business concept in combination with the pride over the progressiveness of the company encouraged many people to emphasize the business concept as a key feature of the company and a neglect of the contradictions between the business concept and what people actually did in their assignments – in this sense the *blinder* metaphor is relevant, underscoring selective perceptions and denial of contradictions.

Corporate strategy

A cultural approach to strategy

A cultural view of strategy rejects objectivistic ideas about the company's external 'environment' and instead emphasizes reality as a social construction, i.e. what is defined as reality is 'real' in the context of human action. The consequences of the environment for the organization and the actions of organizational participants are revealed in the interpretations, frames of reference, perceptions and forms of understanding which characterize the strategic actors as a collective. Ideas about the market and the environment in general determine organizational operations, not external circumstances *per se* (Chaffee, 1985; Smircich and Stubbart, 1985). This means that the realization of a strategy requires carefully taking into account the manner in which the collective involved gives meaning and content to different aspects of the environment. Conceptualizing strategic change as cultural change implies the re-orientations of the corporate collectivity's values, ideas and understandings. Such shared meanings are the basis of collective action, including the overall direction indicated by the concept of strategy. One definition of strategy based on this approach might read as follows:

> Strategy in the interpretative model might be defined as orienting metaphors or frames of reference that allow the organization and its environment to be understood by organizational stakeholders. On this basis, stakeholders are motivated to believe and to act in ways that are expected to produce favourable results for the organization. 'Metaphors' is plural in this definition because the maintenance of social ties in the organization precludes enforcing agreement on a single interpretation. (Chaffee, 1985: 93)

Berg (1985a: 289) also proposes a cultural-symbolic perspective on strategy and organizational change, although a more unitary version than the one suggested by Chaffee. Berg considers that strategy should be regarded as a more or less synthesized abstraction of the aspects of the company's identity which are to be developed. He considers that organizational and strategic change is primarily a question of transforming the underlying organizational symbolism holding the organization together and providing points of reference for social action. Seen in a symbolic perspective, the explicit strategy is reduced to a conscious formulation of aspects of 'the corporate myth', that is to say emotionally-loaded ideas with a historical basis about the fundamental character of operations (cf. Hedberg and Jönsson, 1977; Jönsson and Lundin, 1977). In common with these authors, Berg (1985a: 295) rejects the planning approach, suggesting that 'a strategy is not regarded as a plan, but as a collective image that can be acted upon'. This approach means that strategic planning is regarded as a renewal rite, in which the collective process links with fundamental values and ideas and the plan/rite as a manifestation of the corporate mission and vision are emphasized. Similar views have been expressed, for example, by Broms and Gahmberg (1983, 1987).

Weick (1985) goes further than many other researchers interested in both culture and strategy when he suggests that the two terms describe the same type of organizational phenomena. Culture as well as strategy guide expression and interpretation; they concern acts of judging, creating, justifying, affirming and sanctioning; they provide direction, suggest a way of ordering the world, and they provide continuity and identity. For these reasons culture and strategy are more or less synonymous. Weick cites one definition of strategy that uses the same words that are common in definitions of organizational culture. Replacing strategy with culture has some appeal. It may counteract some of the masculine connotations and top management-centredness associated with the strategy concept (Alvesson and Willmott, 1996; Knights and Morgan, 1991) and it may encourage rethinking the subject matter in a novel way. Still, I agree with Brown (1995: 168) when he suggests that:

> Certainly, strategic planning documents may be thought of as cultural artifacts, but there seems little point in expanding our already inclusive definitions of culture to include long-term plans or patterns of competitive activities.

There is a fine line between emphasizing and investigating the cultural dimensions of plans and competitive activities and to solely use culture vocabulary. But strategy also involves rationalistic and autocratic elements, sometimes a new CEO may be in a situation to impose a certain direction that is not a direct manifestation of organizational culture, but breaks with the earlier patterns and/or is at odds with the identity and values of large part of the organization, etc. There are also elements in strategies that are not very sensitive in terms of cultural values and identity, as they don't involve the experienced 'core' or 'essence' of the company. I am thinking of strategies that do not involve the rethinking and redirecting of the efforts of the entire collective, but mostly concern delimited parts of the company, e.g. certain financial arrangements or starting production in new countries with locally recruited personnel.

Even though strategy sometimes needs to be understood through perspectives and vocabularies other than organizational culture, culture and strategy are often intertwined and a cultural understanding of strategy is productive. In the same way as one views organization as culture, strategy, at least when involving a large part of the collective, can be seen as culture: the metaphor means that one is not replacing strategy with culture but sees it as a cultural manifestation. Brown (1995: 197) points at the following ways in which culture directly affects or guides strategy formulation:

> Culture acts as a perception filter, affects the interpretation of information, sets moral and ethical standards, provides rules, norms and heuristics for action, and influences how power and authority are wielded in reaching decisions regarding what action to pursue. The formulated strategy is a cultural artifact which helps employees understand their role in the organisation, is a focus for identification and loyalty, encourages motivation, and provides a framework for ideas that enables individuals to comprehend their environment and the place of their organisation within it.

A cultural perspective on strategy and the re-interpretation of many elements of strategic work, analysis, decision-making, implementation and change aided by the culture metaphor is thus an interesting possibility. In particular, in the contemporary context in which resources and competence is viewed as the key element of competitive advantage (Barney, 1986; Pralahed and Hamel, 1990), the culture metaphor on strategy may provide valuable insights.

Strategy talk as cultural manifestation

Not only specific theoretical ideas on strategy but also ideas and talk about the notion of strategy in itself can be seen as cultural manifestations. An anthropologist approaching the organizational world for the first time may be struck by all the talk about strategy and the significance attached to this talk and the rituals in which it is celebrated. Talk and text about strategy in the business world and management text are of relatively recent origin and have expanded rapidly and increasingly spread in the organizational world (Knights and Morgan, 1991; Sveningsson, 2000). Also organizations such as universities are now engaged in making strategic plans, taken more or less seriously by others than the plan-makers: the inclination to express more and more concerns as 'strategic' can be seen as elevating status. 'Strategic human resource management' and 'strategic marketing' are examples of functions trying to beef up their roles. That something is of 'strategic significance' frequently seems to mean that it is 'very significant'. Less and less then is not 'strategic'. Being strategic then becomes a symbol for what counts, what is rational and superior to the mundanity of everyday life and pure practical matters.

Many aspects of corporate strategies as conventionally defined – in academia and in the corporate world – may also be interpreted as expressing a somewhat macho view holding a firm grip over management thinking. Arguably, this is also the case with the premise that 'strategy formation should be a controlled, conscious process of thought', being in the hands of the chief executive officer, 'that person is THE strategist' (Mintzberg, 1990: 176). Another example is the idea that full-blown and explicit strategies should first be thought out and formulated before they are implemented. Mintzberg criticizes this kind of approach for overemphasizing strategy, viewing it as something that can control organizational resources (rather than being affected by these in simultaneous interaction and mutual influence), promoting inflexibility and separating thinking from acting. He also suggests that people in a company differ in evaluations of strengths and weaknesses; such assessments may be bound up with feelings: aspirations, biases and hopes. Expressed here is a critique of the notion of the lonely, strong, analytically superior corporate leader, being in command of an organizational hierarchy that obeys. This critique is well in tune with the idea on strategy expressed by Chaffee in the citation above. The ideal of proceeding through the sequence diagnosis, prescription, and then action is consistent with the classical notion of rationality, but stands in opposition to a more gradual and flexible approach, in which trial and error and learning are more significant than thinking out the major steps and routes in advance, assuming that the plan is correct and the world stands still for it to be implemented. This kind of highly rationalistic, detached, commander-oriented thinking fits military notions well and the masculine nature of it is worth expressing (Knights and Morgan, 1991). Perhaps the school's assumptions, as well as its success, are rooted in the appeal of strong cultural masculinity? Perhaps masculinistic orientations among the corporate actors responsible for what is called 'strategy' may encourage them to act in specific ways in terms of organizational development and change?

In the proposed reconceptualizations by Berg, Chaffee and others a more collectively oriented view, in which cognition and feelings, analysis and action are taken into account are proposed, involving a de-masculinization of strategy.

Organizational culture and marketing

Organizational culture is a concept of great relevance also for marketing. Some themes within marketing are well illuminated through a culture concept, for example market orientation, service marketing and internal marketing.

Marketing orientation is often defined as comprising three elements: market information generation, intra-organizational dissemination of such information, and responsiveness to generated and disseminated market intelligence (Harris and Ogbonna, 1999). According to Narver and Slater (1990) a 'market oriented culture' comprises three main behaviours: an orientation towards the customer, a focus on competitors, and coordination between functions.

In efforts to capture the orientations to markets and customers in companies most authors within marketing have problems getting beyond rather superficial and positive-sounding descriptions. Standard slogans about being 'quality-oriented', 'market-driven' or focused on the 'customer's needs' do not say very much. Abstract conceptions such as market orientation or a market oriented culture are often based on broad-brushed and shallow descriptions of 'culture'. In addition, there is a tendency to sweep over vital distinctions. Take customer-orientation as an example. It is assumed that this is closely related to effectiveness. But Hofstede *et al.* (1990) found no correlation between customer- and result-orientation. Being highly concerned about the needs and the situation of the customer may distract from optimizing economic results from the interaction with him or her. Deetz (1997) found for example that computer specialists underreported the time they worked for clients to their managers, perhaps when they had worked less effectively, partly because they did not want the client to be charged too much. The precise meaning of customer-orientation, as held by a particular group of people, needs to be investigated, which calls for exploration also of similar or overlapping terms: does 'customer-orientation' mean that the espoused wishes of customers are taken at face value or that the worker considers what may be best for the customer in a long-term perspective; how are conflicts between concerns for the customer and for profits perceived and coped with, etc.? What does it mean in terms of balance between trying to satisfy customers' individual preferences through flexible manufacturing and having rationalized production processes that are cost-efficient and reliable?

Common thinking on 'marketing orientation' and 'market orientated culture' makes a number of assumptions about culture that can be questioned (Harris and Ogbonna, 1999). It claims a clear link between marketing oriented culture and performance. It assumes an integrated and unitary organizational culture in which market orientation is broadly accepted. It also relies on the idea that a particular subculture and subfunction, that of marketing, promoted not only by this function but by top management as well, is imposed on and dominates other groups and functions in the company. An organization-wide market-oriented culture is not only desirable and attainable but also controllable, it is assumed. The idea is that such a culture is characterized by considerable 'strength'. The marketing literature thus echoes the more objectivist and functionalist versions of organizational culture literature, reflecting a dominance of a 'neo-positivist' conception of knowledge within the marketing tradition. These assumptions are, as should be clear from reviews and discussions in other parts of this book, problematic (see also Harris and Ogbonna [1999] for a review of the critique).

Just focusing on a few manifestations of 'marketing orientation' as quantifiably measurable organizational artefacts means that the understanding of the subject matter is limited in terms of cultural depth and breadth. Of interest is whether a particular dominant notion, such as market orientation, broadly exists on the level of meaning and sense-making and is thus a crucial aspect of everyday work, or it is a matter of behaviour compliance or surface acting, governed by external control mechanisms more than 'genuinely' shared ideas, beliefs and values. This theme seems to be seriously under-focused and under-researched in efforts to apply the organizational culture framework on marketing issues, but also on many other issues.

In order to be able to describe a set of values and orientations, it is important also to consider what is *not* given priority and what receives *less* attention as a consequence of a particular culture. Market orientation may mean that production gets a low priority. More resources, status and power may then be allocated to marketing and sales, while those responsible for production are downgraded both substantially and symbolically. In an industrial firm I studied manufacturing people felt that they had clearly lower status than marketing. People promoted to senior positions regularly came from marketing and an annual prize was given to the best person in sales, while a similar prize never had been honoured to a production person. Interviewees from manufacturing complained, and when I communicated this to a senior manager he responded that 'he had never thought about so being the case', indicating the taken-for-grantedness of a culture more focused on marketing than production (Alvesson and Björkman, 1992).

A more detailed study should take the constructed nature of the market and the customer seriously. Frequently, it is assumed that the market and the customers are so and so as a matter of fact. But, as du Gay and Salaman (1992: 618) write:

That demand is now highly differentiated, with consumers being both knowledgeable, and demanding is not simply an important *fact* of modern economic life, it is, more significantly, an important *idea* in modern economic life which plays a critical role in attempts to restructure organizations.

From a cultural point of view it is the specific collectively shared ideas and actions based on these that are developed in a particular company that is of interest to study. The development of shared meanings of for example consumer sovereignty, perhaps reflected in slogans as 'the customer as king', is then a vital part of organizational culture, which then more or less guide marketing efforts and interactions with consumers. Particular constructions of the consumers also are invoked for purposes of control of the workers.

... the language of the paradigmatic customer is focused and applied in work restructuring ... when customers – as constructed by management through customer survey technologies – are made to exert control over employees. (Ibid.: 621)

The important task is then to investigate how the 'paradigmatic customer' looks like, and how various groups overlap or differ in their understandings of this subject. A very common move in talk of marketing issues, but hardly limited to these, is to favour and constrain the effort to capture an overall and coherent orientation through an account that seems to cover everything but reveals very little, such as a unitary 'customer orientation' or 'high-quality'.

Let me just give one example of superficiality in the treatment of marketing themes. In his well-known book, *Organizational Culture and Leadership*, Schein (1985) devotes one chapter on 'how organization founders shape culture'. One of the examples concerns Jones, the founder of a large chain of supermarkets, department stores, and related businesses. We learn that Jones 'assumed that his primary mission was to supply a high-quality, reliable product to customers in clean, attractive surroundings, that his customers' needs were the primary consideration in all major decisions' (p. 213), that he employed and favoured family members in his business, and that he believed in cleanliness, personal example (visible management), innovation, measuring results, problem solving, competition within the company (except for family members), and centralized power and authority. (I will here concentrate on the themes of particular interest in a marketing context and have only mentioned the others in order to present the broader set of 'assumptions' held by Jones.)

Schein's account provides little space for different interpretations of the case. Whether Jones' assumptions and convictions were accepted and internalized by broader groups in the company is unclear. But irrespective of this, the description is too vague to say something interesting about the meanings, understandings and ideas of the market, the product and the customer that the company was characterized by, apart from it being located in the upper quality and, presumably, price segment. The described 'culture' was clearly contingent upon the general nature of the business and the work. His 'primary mission' seems to be the standard formula for relating to the customers, shared broadly in the quality oriented department store business. These 'assumptions' and 'mission' probably depended upon customers' non-negotiable demands in a few simple respects and other market factors than any distinct values and orientations. Given a want to locate the business in high-quality/high-price category, is hardly possible that he could have 'assumed' that he was to supply low-quality, unreliable products to customers in filthy, unattractive surroundings and that customers' needs should be disregarded in major decisions? There is of course the possibility of free (strategic) choice in certain regards, and low-price business is an option, but once one aims for, or is in a certain kind of business segment certain sociomaterial restrictions and priorities to some extent follow automatically. In a mine or a heavy industry, cleanliness and attractive surroundings are probably not of any particular importance; in an expensive shop, you can't avoid to take them seriously. Hardly surprisingly, many of Jones' values in relation to the customers are also mentioned in an account of management philosophy in a Danish supermarket chain (Grant, cited in Bakka and Fivelsdal, 1988), where cleanliness, consideration of customers (who are 'always right'), and visible management were also central. Mentioning these standard features of the business as 'assumptions' or 'values' is rather unhelpful. The broad 'musts' of the business don't say anything about the distinctive and more nuanced ideas, meanings and values characterizing a particular company (or a group within it). The example then illustrates the use of cultural jargon, rather than of cultural analysis.

'Cleanliness' may, however, be used as a starting point for inquiry. The more precise ideas, beliefs and meanings of 'cleanliness' are of interest from a cultural point of view. What people mean by 'cleanliness' in various work contexts, how the topic is expressed in various communicative settings, the variation and consistency between groups and also within them in terms of such meanings, how various acts and arrangements are guided by particular understandings of cleanliness, must be explored in order to say anything of interest. Similarly, the meaning of 'a high-quality, reliable product', 'attractive surroundings', the idea that 'customers' needs were the primary consideration' cries out for exploration, clarification and distinct interpretations.

A good example of how one may move closer to appreciate the cultural meaning of the customer is provided by Dougherty and Kunda (1990) who analysed photos of customers to some big US computer manufacturers that appeared in their annual reports. IBM portrayed its customers as service providers – librarians, secretaries, sales people. The customers appeared in a fairly personal way, focused on the pictures. Digital portrayed its customers as complex networks and engineering oriented problem solvers, active, hardworking technicians and professionals. The situation is focused, while the people appear rather impersonal, e.g. behind masks in a surgical operation. Burroughs portrayed its customers as relatively isolated processors of information in technological settings such as control rooms. The equipment is central in their photographs. These understandings of the customers and their situations indicate how the respective company ascribe meaning to the customer and thus offer cultural clues to the marketing.

Service management and the involvement of the personnel

In service marketing and service management, the theme of organizational culture appears to be of particular relevance. Since the late 1970s, service management and marketing has appeared as a big subject of marketing theory and practice, calling for a re-orientation of marketing in the context of the service economy. Service marketing is based on three fundamental assumptions. The first is that services have certain unique characteristics that distinguish them from physical products. The second assumption is that these unique characteristics result in certain specific problems for service companies which manufacturing enterprises avoid. The third assumption is that the marketing of services requires a special type of activity and a theoretical basis which take the special features of service activities fully into account (Zeithaml *et al.*, 1985).

Despite the fact that 'the service sector' is extremely heterogeneous and broadranging – including everything from hairdressing to insurance and from air-travel to consultancy services – some authors claim that it is possible to observe certain common characteristics (Normann, 1983). One such common feature is that services are non-tangible. They are not goods. Amongst other things, this means that they cannot be stored, that they are hard to demonstrate and that customers are forced to buy 'a pig in a poke' to a greater extent than in the case of physical goods. Another special feature is that most services consist of actions and inter-actions between the seller and the buyer. Social processes are thus significant. Keeping a tap on and controlling the interplay between company personnel and customers demands special management and organizational features. In addition, the production and consumption of a service are not clearly separated, since both take place simultaneously and at the same location. In other words, the manufac-turing process takes place 'in the field'. This means, for example, that differenti-ation between various functions – e.g. production and sales – becomes blurred at the company level.

Authors on service marketing emphasize that there is a broad area of contact and interaction between the company and its customers in a service company. A considerable proportion of the activities conducted involve contacts and inter-action between personnel/customers. The marketing function is not restricted to a special marketing and sales department, but also permeates the area of the com-pany which produces the services. Normann (1983) expresses this by saying that the company is 'personality-intensive' in the daily production of quality. In this context the management of 'human resources' becomes particularly important (Schneider and Bowen, 1993).

All this means that organizational culture becomes of high relevance as a theme for management control and as an entrance for understanding this kind of business and the management of it. A concept of culture is less productive – for practitioners, but also harder to apply for academics – in robot-like settings than in those where the human dimension is central. People are always central in organi-zations, but sometimes their features as people become even more significant and a broader set of orientations become involved in work. So is in particular the case in long-term, complex interactions. In many forms of service work, the nurturing of the right mindset is an important managerial task and here the culture concept becomes useful.

An important part of service marketing – although often prevalent also in mar-keting of physical products – is *internal marketing*. Internal marketing may be seen as a method of ensuring that 'external' marketing actually works – that is to say that the customer is satisfied, that additional sales are achieved and that a last-ing and satisfactory relationship with the customer is established. It is thought that satisfactory internal marketing is a prerequisite for external marketing, in particular in service businesses (Filipo, 1986; Grönroos, 1983). The idea here is to sell the image and the service of the company to its own employees in the first instance, who then adapt an orientation making them effective marketers of what they believe in. Managerial efforts to engineer or, to express it more softly, to shape, maintain and strengthen a set of meanings, ideas and values around what a company stands for and the products/services it offers can sometimes be seen as simultaneously affecting organizational culture and conducting internal marketing. A former manager of the computer consultancy company Enator presents the initial course for new employees in which the newcomers should learn about the company and how it operates, thus transmitting organizational culture, in terms of internal marketing:

> It was a week of selling, you sold to the consultants. You sold a perspective.

One metaphor for management of organizational culture could then be internal marketing. For at least conscious, perhaps manipulative work with those aspects of meaning patterns relating to customers, products and markets, the internal marketing 'metaphor' is relevant.

So far some examples have been offered on a relatively explicit, easily recognized level of how organizational culture is relevant for marketing themes. Of perhaps even greater interest and potential relevance is to explore cultural assumptions and ideas on how elements in the marketing world are constructed, i.e. not so much address objects of interest for normative control (such as marketing orientation, service culture or internal marketing), but the taken-for-granted level of ideas, beliefs and meanings. This will be illustrated in the next section.

Organizational culture and constructions of the customer: a case study

I will illustrate how a cultural approach may give a deeper and more 'realistic' view on how people in a company may engage in cultural construction of the vital themes of marketing. The case presented concerns how customers are being constructed in marketing practice.

The case is based on an ethnographic study of the editorial wing of a Swedish evening newspaper (Kärreman and Alvesson, 2001). The study focused on a cultural understanding of the newspaper and of the journalists and editors working there. The empirical basis for the case reported here primarily consists of an account of a meeting being studied in a highly intense way, but supplemented with a wider understanding of the organization (Kärreman, 1996). Arguably, combining a focus on a specific situation and a broader, ethnography-based knowledge of the larger site in which the situation is 'hosted' is potentially productive (Alvesson and Deetz, 2000).

During the situation, various statements and interactions mean that a particular understanding of the customer is (re-)produced. The customer is not explicitly on the agenda and a lot of what is expressed about him/her may be non-conscious or not directly recorded by the participants, but nevertheless in various ways surfaces in the talk. Almost all statements on the nature of the customers (readers) are openly or tacitly confirmed and there are no disputes on these matters. It therefore seems as if the participants are establishing certain 'truths' during the meeting.

The espoused purpose of the meeting, gathering around 15 people mostly working as editors (in charge of different sections or shifts of the newspaper) is to review and discuss the news bills of the previous month, and their assumed effects on daily sales. A premise of the meeting is that the quality of each news bill directly affects sales. During the meeting there are a few explicit references to the behaviours, life situations and characters of the people that they hope will buy the newspaper. I will present a few excerpts of this meeting. (The entire situation is presented in Kärreman and Alvesson [2001].)

The meeting starts with a brief review of the general situation of the industry, which is gloomy as sales are going down. One of the participants wants to change the atmosphere and encourages the person chairing the session:

'Tell us something enjoyable, Hans'.

Without further delay, Hans fulfils this wish:

'Yes, sales are increasing on holidays in May. And we have some holidays in June too that looks good, as long as people don't get too pissed and forget to buy the paper on Midsummer.'

Later on in the meeting, the potential sales effect of having the TV-guide in the journal and promoting this on the first page is discussed.

'When the bitches', Love says – the colorful language used perhaps being more colorful than what is typical, but not so colorful that it would be considered out of line – 'are lining up in the grocery store, with their hands full of stuff and grumpy kids at their side, looking at three news bills, do not you think they would take the paper with the TV-guide? I think they would. Don't you?' 'Just to silence the kids?', Hannes, the other morning editor, asks with a smile.

At one point in the meeting, somebody airs the opinion that the news bills may not influence sales, suggesting that there are so many issues that matter. An intensive debate starts. One participant, Bert, unimpressed by the argument against the significance of the news bill produces this argument:

'I mean, damn it, this thing with Borg and Loredana [refer to the in Sweden at that time widely publicized romantic affair between former tennis star Björn Borg and Italian singer Loredana Berte], why should sales suddenly go up [when news bills are headlined by Borg and Loredana] if it weren't for people seeing the news bill?'

A heated debate bursts out. Almost everybody starts to talk, making it impossible to hear a single voice. Breaking free from the noise, Bert's voice calls for attention:

'I want to say, Hans, that one thing is for sure. From all these meetings, we know for a fact that if we has good celebrity gossip on the news bills, it sells. Stenmark, Borg, eh…'.
    Bert stops for a moment. Jonas fills in: 'Christer Sjögren [A crooner, world famous in Sweden]'. Love nods and repeats: 'Christer Sjögren, perhaps, but that's the way it is. Hans, you simply can't say that news bills doesn't sell'.
    'No, no, no', Hans – who never claimed that news bills don't sell newspapers – replies. 'But the question is whether they care about TV', Love continues, 'that's where we started'. 'I think that there are certain signals', Tommy argues, 'that plays an important part. Holidays rises expectations, a holiday mood. So when the news bill announce "Holiday TV-guide" instead of "43 dead", that'll make a difference. Also, the colors on the front page are some kind of hidden signs. Whether it is colorful and fun or not, that it distinguishes itself'.

Having finally agreed upon, or at least marginalized any deviant opinion about, the sales potential of the news bill and commented upon all the news bills that were posted during days when sales were above, and respectively, below average, the participants end the meeting through addressing the newspaper itself.

'If you grab Mondays issues, there isn't that much weight in them. They feel danger-ously light in your hand', Wally remarks.
'Yes, it's thin'.
'Mondays are thin', Wally repeats.
'But I think that we have been good on putting content in that tiny format', Tommy says, and continues in what becomes the meeting's final word, 'the paper contains pretty much despite its tiny format. There is a lot of short articles and notes, and so on, well, there have been a few days with little content. But when we have this tiny format, we have to have many things to read. People mustn't feel that the paper is something you browse in seconds'.
Tommy's argument is well received, with nods and a humming from the participants.

Even though the people at the meeting – comprising the majority of the editors who through their individual daily decisions form the newspaper and enact social reality – about never directly raises the question who is our customer or what is our market segment and what kind of attitude and values should we develop toward them, they nevertheless provide answers to these questions.

During the meeting, the customer is *constructed* as mainly interested in tele-vision and celebrity gossip. The public – at least the public that potentially read evening newspapers – is described in rather degrading terms. They have unglamo-rous lives and may even be seen as a bit tragic, but hardly deserving much sympathy. Typical consumers may be 'a bitch with three grumpy kids' in a supermarket line or people that during holidays may 'get too pissed and forget to buy the paper'. The significance attached to pay days – when sales are unexpect-edly low the participants sometimes attribute it to the fact that the previous month's earnings are running out – suggests that readers are believed to be rela-tively poor and/or a bit careless about their financial situation. The reader wants some joy in life: they want to read the television section and not news about '43 dead', according to the meeting participants. The reader wants short articles and notes.

These ideas about the (potential) customer are cultural constructions and not just simple reflections about how things are. Actually, all the statements about the readers seem to be more or less informed guesses. Even if sometimes females being accompanied by children in a bad mood in a supermarket are more inclined to buy newspapers including a promoting a TV-guide, there is a particular mean-ing and value attached to the version 'a bitch with three grumpy kids', clearly dif-ferent from 'a female with small children'. The participants develop a certain shared meaning pattern and a particular mentality through their interaction and their use of language.

Within this set of meaning, jokes and sarcasm are central. The group communi-cates to itself: We who work here like to joke, do not take things too seriously, but have a distance to ourselves, to the profession and to the world. Our cultural rules and orientations are communicated during the meeting. The newsmakers present themselves as ironists, even cynics. They turn Mr Unknown into a Famous Robber, to quote their own vocabulary, through reporting about an event in which a fairly unknown actor was referred to as a famous actor. Their readers do not want 'news about famous people' but 'celebrity gossip'. Again the specific language reflects as well (as re-)constructs a particular shared orientation and a common mentality.

The constructions provide a momentary shared universe to act upon. They imply a cultural understanding shared by those present – and presumably larger parts of the organization. A person viewing a good product as full of brief articles so that 'people have plenty to read' may feel that an intellectual orientation – perhaps calling for background information, in-depth analysis and acknowledgement of complexity – is out of touch with an appropriate work identity. Being a newsmaker, at least in this organization, equals being brief, punchy and witty. Ultimately, it is rather about being entertaining (gossip, television sections) than important (43 dead). Even though these cultural meanings and values prevail in the meeting, and, to a large extent in the organization as a whole, there are, of course, also other orientations. The newspaper provides space for political com-mentaries and debates, cultural news, etc. Very few organizations are based on a coherent and easily ranked set of values and ideas. What is expressed during the meeting does, however, say something important about some of the more signifi-cant understandings and orientations around the market and, by implication, the nature of the business, and the nature of the newsmakers themselves: the creation of the customers implies a particular self-construction. The shared meanings of the customers imply a certain view of the acts and the people that are to serve them with news and entertainment: offering the appropriate stuff calls for a parti-cular mentality: a particular organizational culture.

Through constructing 'newsmakers' and this newspaper as sales-oriented, gossip-providers, relaxed, playful, joking, a bit cynical and with some self-dis-tance, it becomes, at the end of the day, a bit easier to interpret events and act and operate in daily work. The shared understandings, and the confirmation of these during public events such as the news bill meetings, provide certainty and reduce feelings of isolation and personal responsibility. Even though the meeting in question appears to be highly irrational in terms of information processing, analysis and decision-making and problem-solving (see Kärreman and Alvesson, 2001), it facilitates coordination of work and confidence and focus in decision-making through the construction of a set of shared ideas and meanings about the cus-tomer, the product and, thus, the nature of the work and selves suitable in this kind of business situation.

Other subfields: networks, rationalizations and performance indicators

In this section I will briefly illustrate the relevance of a cultural approach also for a few additional areas of business, thereby further supporting and illustrating the claim that a focus on cultural meanings and organizational symbolism may benefit understandings and reflective practice in a variety of parts of management and organization.

The symbolic value of networks

That social networks and ties are of crucial importance in economic settings is widely recognized (Granovetter, 1985). The concept of network in itself does not imply a direct focus on cultural meanings, but in order to understand social ties the values, beliefs and ideas on how people and groups should relate to each other are important. Different cultures also influence how people, firms and other agents relate to each other, also in economic terms. Chinese firms for example often rely heavily on capital provided by networks and involve banks to a relatively low degree. Finance thus becomes partly a cultural issue. Successful investments are sometimes facilitated by similar cultural understandings amongst the parties, e.g. ideas on what is 'natural' and 'rational', what kind of social bonds and obligations that are seen as reasonable and that are sanctioned. Here is one illustration of the role of culture in the context of financial relationships. Taiwanese venture capital invested in non-Chinese-American high companies in the 1980s was, generally, unsuccessful due to language barriers and inefficient information flow. Investments in Chinese firms in USA were seen as more successful, partly due to better communication and the establishment of informal relationships between capitalist and entrepreneur (Tseng, 1997). Cultural patterns thus become vital for how the capital 'market' functions.

Another effect may follow from the symbolism of connections. The quality and characteristics of a company and its product is to a high degree defined through the networks. Relationships are seen as indicators of quality and a crucial element in corporate image. For companies claiming to be and offer something sophisticated it is very important to have (be broadly perceived as having) the right – advanced and demanding – customers, clients, joint partners and other organizations in the network. This is sometimes seen as important because it facilitates the development of new or better knowledge (Wikström, Normann *et al.*, 1993) and can lead to better access to substantial resources – such as loans or transfer of technology. My point is that the network is important also because it is typically read as confirming the claim of the quality of a particular company being able to associate itself with supposedly advanced other companies, e.g. in the form of technological sophistication. As Håkansson and Snehota (1989: 193) suggest, the invisible assets of companies 'consisting largely of knowledge and abilities, fame and reputation, are mainly created in external relationships. Furthermore they cannot be separated from these relationships'.

The symbolism of networks is salient in for example companies claiming to be knowledge-intensive, e.g. consultancy companies (Alvesson, 2001). One way of indicating that a knowledge-intensive company deserves this label is to point at prestigious customers or partners, with a reputation for *their* knowledge. A consultancy firm refers to having the 'right' client and the client refers to the use of the 'right' consultants. Through such mutual confirmations internal and external audiences 'know' that advanced knowledge is there.

The overall symbolic function of networks is thus significant in contexts difficult to evaluate. By being perceived as having close ties with (others) perceived as being knowledge-intensive one's own status is confirmed. The symbolism of for example joint ventures includes the value of being able to communicate that one's partner is (another) knowledgeable/technologically advanced actor. Of course, clients, customers, partners and associations also include substantive elements – such as expert advice or financial transactions – but the symbolism of one's network is important for internal and external meaning creation.

The symbolic value of rationalizations

Phenomena that may be seen as expressing a rather pure rationalistic, financial logic can often be understood in cultural and symbolic terms. Cost-cutting operations may for example be appreciated because of the cultural values they are symbolizing:

> ... reorganizations signal that change is for real, and as we know only too well, the stock prices of institutions in the course of reorganization thereby often rise, as though any change is better than continuing on as before. In the operation of modern markets, disruption of organizations has become profitable. While disruption may not be justifiable in terms of productivity, the short-term returns to stockholders provide a strong incentive to the powers of chaos disguised by the seemingly assuring word 'reengineering'. (Sennett, 1998: 51)

During the informal interaction following a seminar in which I had talked for a group of managing directors one of the group members presented the observation that he and others were generally rewarded for replacing people with technology, also in situations in which this was not profitable. He tried to get the others to respond, but they seemed to prefer to avoid the subject matter, treating it as slightly embarrassing, creating the impression that this subject was tabooed. It is not unlikely, however, that the replacing of people with technology broadly symbolizes rationality, progressiveness and efficiency, also in the absence of strong indicators on efficiency gains. The results, at the end of the day, may anyhow be difficult to establish.

Of course, rationalizations and cost-cutting sometimes are unavoidable and clearly improve results. Frequently, however, the short-term savings following from cutting costs are counteracted by long-term reduction of capacity due to the loss of competence following from downsizing. Some authors emphasize the significance of maintaining and developing competence as the key factor behind long-term success and view the emphasis on cost-cutting as shortsighted and adapted to the logic of the financial markets rather than enduring wealth creation (e.g. Pfeffer, 1994). This issue falls beyond a cultural approach to sort out. It is sufficient here to point at the uncertainties and ambiguities that are often involved and the significance of cultural assumptions and symbolism for what is happening. Frequently in organizations rationalization/cost minimization and competence-oriented logics co-exist, creating complex and confusing experiences for organizational members (Watson, 1994).

Various cultural ideas about people's ability in relationship
to performance

As discussed in Chapter 3, how results are interpreted must be related to cultural ideas and assumptions. Performance indicators are not simple and self-revealing, but call for sense-making and interpretation, relying on cultural background knowledge. Topics such as the time-span used in evaluations, values and meanings associated with performance measures, social rules for manipulation of results indicators, and assumptions about the relative significance of human efforts and coincidence for results can productively be understood from a cultural point of view. In some settings people believe that the relationship between effort and skill, on the one hand, and results on the other, is weak and accidental, due to the significance of factors largely beyond personal and sometimes also organizational control. A top executive interviewed by Jackall (1988: 70) expressed this opinion by saying that: 'I always say that there is no such thing as a marketing genius; there are only great markets'. In other companies there is limited belief in the role of coincidence and little worry that factors beyond the control of individuals determine the measurable results. Pepsi Cola, for example, according to Sculley's (1987) self-bibliographical account, was characterized by a strong belief in marketing geniuses and fierce internal competition based on the assumption that there are clear, simple and fair rules and that results were objectively measurable (which does not seem unreasonable regarding for example market shares and sales of soft drinks) and that the managers' skills and efforts were directly related to the performances of their units. The assumptions are the opposite of those held by the executive disbelieving in marketing geniuses.

Of course, one may say that in various circumstances and settings, results are more or less easy to determine (more or less ambiguous) and they may be more or less traceable to particular actors and efforts. In cultural terms, the assumptions, beliefs and values as well as the actions/arrangements and ways of reasoning based on these are of greatest interest. In some cultural settings, the 'effort and ability-determine-results' assumptions dominate, in others the 'ambiguity-chance' version is more frequently drawn upon.

Conclusion

In this chapter I have illustrated a cultural approach in some depth through two cases – of a business concept in a computer consultancy company and the construction of customers in a newspaper – and indicated its potential more briefly in a few other areas of management and organization.

An organizational culture approach has a great potential in illuminating a wide spectrum of business and management themes. This approach has also made some progress in transcending disciplinary borders and have now a presence in various subfields. However, with to some extent early work in strategic management as an exception, it is primarily the more superficial understanding of culture associated with functionalism and objectivism that is imported by the various subfields. In marketing, for example, there is little use of the interpretive and theoretical power of a cultural approach. Harris and Ogbonna (1999) and Desphande and Webster (1989) suggest that advances in the field of market orientation and organizational culture are dependent on marketing researchers taking theory and (qualitative) methodology in culture studies more seriously. They also propose a closer collaboration between marketing and organizational culture people. I agree, at least if that would include going beyond an interest in the comparatively superficial level of behaviour. One possible advantage of a greater interest from cultural research would be to illuminate significant areas of how companies function. Less concentration on 'pure' examples of symbolism – such as jokes, jargon, stories, rituals – and more on the cultural dimension of 'heavy' and influential management functions and activities, such as management control, marketing and the business concept, is to be recommended: at least if this can be accomplished without falling into the trap of a broad-brushed, superficial, functionalist approach. More about this in Chapter 7. The culture as a building block metaphor too easily becomes dominant when subfields with a strong normative bent, such as marketing, are involved. So I persist in raising the yellow warning flag: Go ahead, but do it carefully!

In general, spending less time on normative frameworks and being more empirically and conceptually open to what cultural interpretation can reveal about the richness and complexities of the meanings and symbolism in domains of business, appear to be fruitful. Such a closer understanding goes against the use of broad-brushed and non-informative abstract concepts such as those most popular in describing corporations (e.g. market orientation, high quality, value for money, growth) and inspire a more detailed and distinct approach where thick descriptions of individual cases are balanced with a consideration of themes that are common within an industry, a society, a type of organization and/or a *Zeitgeist*. In order to understand the meaning of e.g. 'market orientation', we need to investigate situations such as the news bills meeting, where views on the market and how one appeals to its 'needs' are expressed in a fairly unpolished manner.

5 Leadership and Organizational Culture

Leadership seems to frequently be used as a rather straightforward and uncomplicated concept. But, like culture, it too easily captures 'everything and nothing'. We need a more precise understanding of how the term leadership should be used. In this chapter a cultural approach to leadership is developed. It includes the organizational cultural framing of leadership as well as how the action of 'leaders' influences the meanings, values, ideas and feelings of others.

What is leadership?

There is a wide spectrum of definitions of leadership. Yukl (1989) says that 'the numerous definitions of leadership that have been proposed appear to have little else in common' than involving an influence process. This is then taking place within an asymmetrical relationship: the leader is exercising influence over the follower. Yukl himself defines leadership 'to include influencing task objectives and strategies, influencing commitment and compliance in task behavior to achieve these objectives, influencing group maintenance and identification, and influencing the culture of an organization' (p. 253). This definition is probably more thoughtful than many others in the literature. But one could very well let the words 'leadership' and 'culture' change place and then have a definition of culture. Or swap leadership and strategy. One could also replace leadership with organizational structure, job design, social identity or something else. As mentioned in Chapter 4, Weick (1985) has used this trick to show how some definitions of strategy and culture are roughly the same. Despite the shortcomings of definitions and the similarities of what a great deal of popular terms refer to, in practice they trigger different meanings and lead to different lines of thinking, related to the context in which the terms are used.

'Leadership' is typically defined in general terms. The ambition is to say something of relevance across quite diverse settings, and frequently to discover the success formula for effective leadership. The diversity of relations, situations and cultural contexts in which superior–subordinate interactions take place means that a coherent definition with universal aspirations may tell us relatively little in terms of the richness and complexity of the phenomena it supposedly refers to. It is then rather difficult to claim that 'leadership' as a general term and object of study stands in a clear relationship to a particular, distinct group of phenomena possible to conceptualize in a uniform manner. The efforts to capture variety through variables such as personnel orientation and initiating structure or democratic and autocratic are not very helpful. There are two interrelated problems: the social worlds of interest for leadership researchers do not easily lend themselves to neat categorization and ordering, and language use has its limitations in relation to the goal of fixing meaning through definitions.

Understanding leadership calls for careful consideration of the social context in which processes of leadership take place. Leadership is not just a leader acting and a group of followers responding in a mechanical way, but a complex social process in which the meanings and interpretations of what is said and done are crucial. Leadership then is closely related to culture – at the organizational and other levels. Understanding what a French plant manager, a female senior police officer in the USA, a Green Peace movement spokesperson in Russia try to do in relationship to people supposed to be following them, and why Brutus betrayed Ceasar, calls for a careful consideration of the specific cultural context of these relationships and interactions. This context then includes the societal, occupational and organizational – which all frame specific leader–follower interactions.

What is defined as 'leadership' calls for not just a theoretical definition but also close consideration of what a particular group mean by 'leadership' and how it relates to 'leaders' and 'leadership'. For different groups 'leadership' has different meanings and value. In the military and in professional groups, 'leadership' has very different connotations. Generally, and with the risk of overgeneralizing too much, it is a common impression that while North Americans seem to rate leadership favourably, many Europeans may be somewhat less enthusiastic. US society seems to favour an ideology of celebrating individualistic strong masculine characters that can lead (Lipman-Blumen, 1992; Prasad, 1997), although recent developments may have included a de-masculinization of management as teams, networks and knowledge are seen as increasingly salient features of contemporary organizations (Fondas, 1997).

US researchers dominate leadership research – in parts of Europe it is a less significant topic for academics to study. There are also variations between different sectors in societies regarding their attitude to leadership. Compared with business, researchers tend to ascribe less significance to leadership to explain performances and other outcomes in business. There is, in Sweden at least, a general trend to ascribe more and more significance to leadership as a way of solving organizational problems also in sectors that traditionally have downplayed the role of leadership, e.g. schools, hospitals and universities.

Of course, there is variation and debate also within academic camps about the meaning and relevance of leadership. One approach is to listen to various groups and organizations and find out when and why the 'natives' talk about leadership, what they mean by it, their beliefs, values and feelings around leadership and different versions and expressions of it. One can, for example, probably identify leadership-oriented organizational cultures of different and organizational cultures where the interest in, space for and/or emergence of leaders with a big L is less significant or even absent, e.g. as a consequence of a strong professional ideology or bureaucracy. The military and the university may exemplify this variation. Leadership may, by some groups, be seen as negative. An emphasis on leadership may for example, be seen as related to authoritarianism and non-professionalism ('qualified people need no boss to tell them how to think and behave'). Leaders and leadership can then be seen as organizational symbols, the orientations towards them are then not treated as 'facts' about leadership 'as such', but more as clues to understand organizational cultures. Does 'leadership' (or managerial work), in specific organizations, refer to the strong and decisive decision-maker, the superior technician or professional, the team-builder and coach, the educator and developer of people or the result-oriented number-cruncher carefully monitoring and putting pressure on people to perform? How people talk and in other ways express sentiments about leaders and leadership (managers and managerial work) is then indicating wider cultural patterns on human nature, social relations, hierarchies, power, etc. This approach would partly avoid the difficulties in defining leadership once and for all, valid over time and space.

Still, I refrain from restricting leadership studies to solely tracing the meanings and use of leadership vocabularies among people in organizations. Some theoretical ideas about what leadership as a theme may refer to is important to give some direction in the understanding. Given the tendency of many people talking about leadership – including many academics – to include almost everything, there is a risk that a study of language use may lead to the result that leadership talk may move in all directions, which can make it difficult to say much more than that there is this variation. Nevertheless, with this caveat, moving an interest in leadership from a standardized conception of the subject matter – expressed in for example questionnaire studies – to a greater sensitivity to cultural contexts and the meanings of leadership interaction, seems appropriate.

Bias towards abstract and thin studies of leadership

The leadership literature is enormous, but the academic work suffers from a heavily positivist bias and favours laboratory experiments or questionnaire studies that almost per definition neglect the organizational cultural context of leadership. It is revealing that in Yukl's (1989) and House and Aditay's (1997) extensive review articles of leadership research, the word culture is mentioned in passing only a few times, and then as something that is changed as an outcome of 'transformational leadership' (Yukl) respectively as national cultures possibly influencing leadership (House and Aditay).

Most studies of leadership focus on how a person identified as a leader is behaving or interacting with a group of subordinates and/or broadly is 'managing' the organization. In most systematic academic studies, the leaders lead small groups of people. As organizational culture typically refers to a larger context than a small group it is not something that the typical small-group leader has a significant impact on. (One may talk about small-group culture, but this misses the point with the culture idea referring to wider and historically related meaning patterns.) Senior managers lead, however, entire or large parts of organizations and then the situation with regard to organizational culture becomes different. There is some interest in top leader's influence on organizational culture in the literature. Frequently, the founder of the organization has been the target of attention (e.g. Pettigrew, 1979; Schein, 1985). A few studies have taken an interest in leadership in relationship to cultural change (Trice and Beyer, 1993). In these cases the leader is viewed as somebody that exercises a more or less far-reaching influence on culture.

There are not many good accounts of what leaders do and how followers/ subordinates react and act on the initiatives and efforts to exercise influence (Trice and Beyer, 1993). There are plenty of more popular writings of leadership, with a preference for hero portraits and anecdotes and that score higher in entertainment value than in terms of intellectual depth and insights. Self-biographies of famous executives in business are generally far from trustworthy, as well shown by Hansen (1996). Also in the academic literature rather thin descriptions prevail. Trice and Beyer (1993) provide an account of Lee Iacocca, who started as president of Chrysler during the late 1970s when the company was in deep trouble. Iacocca is frequently described as 'a designated leader whose leadership drastically turned around an organization's culture' (p. 271). At the time, most people thought that Chrysler, having huge debts and heavy losses, would not survive. But Iacocca generated 'a vision of a new Chrysler – one free of debt and actively competing in the national and international markets' (ibid. p. 271) which mobilized managers and other employees in the company. He also proposed and succeeded in getting the government to guarantee a very large bank loan, and thereby agreed to give the federal government a sizeable amount of control in monitoring the company. He succeeding in getting the president of the US auto workers appointed to the Board of Directors of Chrysler. He also prepared and delivered television commercials that phrased his vision in simple, convincing language to both the public and Chrysler's personnel. This was at the time seen as radical, but the response was positive. At one time, he cut his salary from $360,000 to $1 per year. By 1983, 'he had dramatically eliminated debts, produced deep cutbacks, manufactured a profitable new car, and paid back the government-guaranteed loans a year early' (ibid. p. 272).

Trice and Beyer believe that Iacocca 'turned around' Chrysler's organizational culture, but their account does not say that much if, and if so, how, this was done. According to at least some of his subordinates, Iacocca had the ability to 'switch on, to light up' so they 'wanted to go back to the office and work some more, to put in another couple of hours' (Lacey, quoted in ibid. p. 271). It is unclear to what extent this affected culture (patterns of meanings and ideas in the organization) – which is something else than people feeling (temporarily?) inspired to put in some extra work time. The 'vision' referred to above seems to be very general and lacks distinctiveness: being 'free of debt' and 'actively competing' are basic conditions in business. Getting loan guarantees from the government, appointing a union leader to the board and negotiating salary and benefit cuts with the union does not necessarily involve culture that much, although negotiating the meaning and appropriateness of these moves draw upon culture and the outcomes can be seen as involving a symbolic dimension through which broader shared meanings may be changed. The union leader on the board may symbolize a more consensual orientation in management–worker relations and a higher level of responsibility taking of unions, although it is uncertain whether this was understood in this way and even more if this led to significant cultural changes on a broader scale. Some of the other arrangements and outcomes can be seen as crisis management which do not necessarily imply cultural change at all, e.g. securing loans. Whether organizational culture did change or not is impossible to say based on the account, and Trice and Beyer's claim of the culture being 'turned around' seems to be speculative. Temporary reactions to threats of bankruptcy is not the same as cultural change. What is needed is a careful study of how organizational members broadly responded to the initiatives and arrangements of Iacocca and other senior managers. Also needed is research on any lasting consequences, e.g. in terms of new orientations to the company, to salaries, to union responsibility for the company, to competition, to how 'debt' is understood, etc. In the absence of any good indications on this, we can't really say anything about the possible effects of Iacocca's leadership on organizational culture. Getting people to temporarily adjust to difficult circumstances is not necessarily the same as cultural change. Most of his acts, such as negotiating loans and salaries, do not really concern leadership in any distinct sense, but refer to other aspects of management. While claiming to address leadership and organizational culture, in this case Trice and Beyer do not say that much about either.

Apart from the 'thinness' of most accounts of leadership in relationship to organizational culture, this example also illustrates a one-sidedness in the assumptions on how culture and leadership interact. In Trice and Beyer's narrative the 'leadership' is a product of Iacocca, his reading of the corporate situation and context and his charisma. Organizational culture, to the extent that these authors treat it, is portrayed just as an object which is reformed through acts of leadership. That organizational culture may frame leadership and that any possible effect of leadership is a consequence of how people interpret and develop meaning to various examples of leadership is hardly addressed. The salary cut of Iacocca to one dollar is of interest not in itself, but in terms of how it is read by various groups in the company. If it is seen as a publicity stunt, a signal of temporary sacrifices under extraordinary but shortsighted conditions or as a symbol of 'we-are-all-in-the-same-boat' and long-term corporate solidarity, the consequences are very different. It is here, on this interpretive level, that culture enters the picture, but this seems to be lost by Trice and Beyer – as well as by most other authors, not only pop-management writers but by many academics as well.

As with other examples of critique delivered in this book, this is not intended to be an exercise in faultfinding. The full realization of a cultural framework calls for an understanding of what may go wrong. An awareness of how aspirations of illuminating organizational culture may drift into focusing the behavioural level rather than the level of meaning, is important. The lesson here is that leadership as well as organizational culture calls for precision and depth to be understood, and much richer accounts than those typically produced are needed.

Two examples of rich studies of leadership

I will here briefly refer to two studies of leadership that take managers' intention and acts but also the subordinates' interpretations of these seriously. One is a study of Smircich (1983c) in which a CEO of an insurance company based on the merger between two companies tried to accomplish stronger cooperation. He devoted much time to teambuilding and encouraged the open sharing of viewpoints in the management group. He also launched the wheel as an organizational symbol intended to make people move together in a synchronized way. But all this never seemed to affect the 'real' differences in orientations and commitments among people in the organization. Despite the encouragement, at least on the espoused level, to present 'genuine' opinions and feelings, the tricky issues were never seriously aired in the meetings. The wheel metaphor did not work. It was re-interpreted in accordance with the understanding of the situation that people held, but was not aired in settings such as management team meetings. People said that the company is like a four-wheel van, but all the wheels move in different directions and with different speed. The symbol then created an opposite effect from the intended: rather than making people adapting the idea of cooperation and supporting a shared orientation, it reinforced their feelings of a diversity of orientations and objectives characterizing the different parts of the organization.

Another case is described by Hentze (1994). A young manager from the German corporate group was appointed as the production director of a French subsidiary in the printing industry. One intention was to strengthen the bonds between different parts of the group. The new director was well-educated and had modern ideas about participative management. He replaced a very experienced French manager that had worked himself up from the bottom and had superior knowledge about many aspects of the production technology of the company. The French predecessor had a direct, paternalistic style, dealt with his subordinates on an individual basis, had clear ideas about what should be accomplished and was fairly outspoken both on what he perceived as positive and negative results. The new production director was several times told about the personality and style of his predecessor and he was well aware that he represented something very different. He believed in participative management and management by objectives, explained the principles to his subordinates and started to implement this type of management. After some time he was convinced that it worked – production results did not indicate otherwise, a few managers left the company during his first months, but he carefully investigated their motives and concluded that they were not related to workplace issues.

But then the CEO of the company, the boss of the production director, received a letter from one of the production directors' immediate subordinates, an experienced manager that the production director had much respect for and whom he thought he worked well with. This manager, having been in the company for a very long time, expressed great worry about the state of affairs as well as of the future of the production department. He emphasized the good intentions and qualifications of the new production director, but compared him with the predecessor and this comparison was clearly in favour of the latter, whose direct, autocratic style and superior technical knowledge received great respect. People felt great uncertainty of the purpose of all the management meetings that the new director had initiated. This led to endless discussions without conclusions and decisions: during one month about a fourth of the working time of the managers were spent in the management team meetings, the manager had observed. People lacked decisions and directions and felt that they were asked to solve problems but without much support or clarification of what exactly they were supposed to do. Uncertainty led to anxiety – failure was at least under the previous director expected to lead to direct consequences such as people being informed about their bad performance in very clear terms.

The failure of the new production director can be ascribed to a lack of congruence between his management style and the expectations and assumptions of the people around him. They expected from a senior manager – at least in actual role – decisiveness, technical expertise and a strong mastery of the situation. They were also used to responding to relatively detailed instructions and to do this on an individual basis. Even though people broadly understood the principles of the new management style they only did so on a superficial level and did not value it. Meetings and discussions were seen as endless talk that seldom led to anywhere, as taking time and energy from 'real work' and as a bad 'surrogate' for the director telling people what to do. Group discussions also worked against a deeply engrained understanding of responsibility as an individual matter. As expressed in the letter to the CEO by the frustrated manager: 'at the end of the day we are only responsible for our own area of work'.

The deeper meanings of participative management and teamwork thus did seem to be lost in the managerial practices of this case: subordinates taking initiative and actively contributing with their expertise and ideas, people having some degree of shared responsibility – across levels, but also between people on the same level (management team) – and the group being an important unit in problem-solving and decision-making. To fully understand and work accordingly to these ideas calls for a deep understanding of them, involving also emotional adaptation.

Both cases illustrate that managers with good intentions and working according to what is today recognized to be good managerial practice may fail. The depth meanings associated with the cultural context they operated in were never touched upon in their acts of leadership – at least they did not connect positively to these meanings. Instead the cultural frameworks of the subordinates led to negative responses – the meanings intended by the managers and the meanings interpreted by their subordinates went in very different directions. The depth meanings leading to irony and distance in the first case, and worry, confusion and a feeling of waste of time and absence of direction in the second case, implied failures in leadership.

The selected cases powerfully illuminate that we need to take the meanings and interpretations of the subordinates seriously to understand leadership. Also the practical action of managers – at least when the 'voluntary' obedience of subordinates is called for (which is what leadership refers to) – calls for careful grounding in, and continuous interpretation of, what is on the minds of the subordinates and how they relate to the ideas and arrangements of the leader. The cases point to the need as well as difficulty in grasping 'in-depth-meanings'.

Varieties of leadership

Managers and leaders – instrumental and cultural?

Frequently, leadership is given a very broad meaning and includes almost everything that a manager or an informal leader does, as illustrated by Trice and Beyer's text just scrutinized. But managers clearly do much else than engage in leadership. As the great majority of all managers are subordinated to more senior executives or are accountable to various constituencies there are clearly elements of a manager's work time that can not meaningfully be defined in terms of leadership. Actually, with a precise and constrained view on leadership (see below) it may well be so that leadership only happens occasionally.

A note on the relationship between managers and leaders (management and leadership) might here be called for. Of course, not all leaders are managers, but may be political leaders or informal leaders. A distinction can be made between designated leaders, with a formally based position, including rights and obligations, and emerging leaders, which are entirely based on the support and legitimacy among the followers. During recent years many authors have proposed a distinction between managers, who are relying on their formal position and working with bureaucratic processes such as planning, budgeting, organizing and controlling, and leaders who rely on their personal abilities, work with visions, agendas and coalition building and mainly through non-coercive means affect people's feelings and thinking (e.g. Kotter, 1985; Zaleznik, 1977, etc.). Managers then can be 'only' managers or they can also be leaders. Zaleznik (1977) views the influence of leaders as 'altering moods, evoking images and expectations, and in establishing specific desires and objectives.... The net result of this influence is to change the way people think about what is desirable, possible and necessary' (p. 71). Leaders are then heavily involved in what Pfeffer (1981), reviewed in Chapter 3, refers to as symbolic management. In comparison, managers are much less omnipotent types.

According to Jackall (1988) it is common that top managers are described as 'leaders' by their subordinates and others, while managers on lower levels seldom are viewed as worthy of this label. This is not so much a matter of personal attributes as of social position. The formal social position makes people interpret and relate to the position-holder in a specific way. A story was widely told in IBM about how the founder Watson once, when accompanied with a group of executives, was stopped by a young female employee and asked to follow safety regulation, which he did, having stopped his escort of managers from giving the young employee a reprimand for telling the top person what to do (Martin *et al.*, 1983). The significance attached to one person obeying safety rules like everybody else illustrates that the formal position adds considerable 'mystique' to a him or her, and makes his or her act appear in a radically different light from that of the common people (Mumby, 1988). How cultural values and expectations determine and constrain the chances of people to emerge as 'leaders' is illustrated by the resistance of physicians in hospitals to re-label administrators managers. For administrators to appear as – be labelled as or seen as – 'leaders' would be highly difficult, given this culture, and of course, the political interests it is fused with (Parker, 2000).

I am not denying the possibility of leaders having the far-reaching influence proposed by advocates of the leader with a big L beyond the formal powers of the managerial position. It is, however, possible that most managers having a personal and non-coercive influence beyond pure 'management', are mixing elements of management and leadership and that the latter element is far from unconstrained by formal position and bureaucratic constraints, but typically intertwined with management. The following definition of the two concepts captures this.

> Management can get things done through others by the traditional activities of planning, organizing, monitoring and controlling – without worrying too much what goes on inside people's heads. Leadership, by contrast, is vitally concerned with what people are thinking and feeling and how they are to be linked to the environment to the entity and to the job/task. (Nicholls, 1987: 21)

In practice, managers frequently to some extent rely on plans, they coordinate and control and use burcaucratic means. But they also try to create commitment or at least acceptance for plans, rules, goals and instructions. Making people understand the purpose of, and create meaning around, what should specifically be done may transgress any clear distinction between management and leadership. At the same time, with the exception of talks in which the manager-leader tries to energize the masses, it is rare with acts of leadership addressing thinking and feeling and abstract connections between tasks and broader contexts on a very general level. Instead managers affect thinking and feeling in connection to managing specific tasks and goals, thus making 'leadership' and 'management' difficult to differentiate in practice. This view allows a combination of the two elements which I believe we can find in the activities of most (contemporary) managers and organizations.

Nevertheless, leadership is not productively used if it is supposed to cover everything that managers do. Everything that does not involve interaction with or indirect communication to subordinates falls outside leadership even if the activities could be seen as salient in management. In the case of Iacocca above, securing financial resources through getting a loan guarantee was a principle task for a president, but this did not mean an exercise of leadership, in any specific sense. And also in relationship to subordinates, parts of management have very little to do with leadership, e g when there is a strict behavioural and/or output measurement focus.[1] Leadership thus calls for a strong ingredient of management of meaning (Smircich and Morgan, 1982), in which the shaping of the ideas, values, perceptions and feelings of people is included.

This means that leadership is per definition seen as 'cultural', that is leadership must be understood as taking place in a cultural context and all leadership acts have their consequences through the (culturally guided) interpretation of those involved in the social processes in which leaders, followers and leadership acts are expressed. This, of course, does not imply that leadership means the significant impact on or capacity to shape and change culture at will. Leadership draws attention to the consequences within and through cultural meanings informing the thoughts, feelings and actions that leaders provoke.

Management – as different from leadership – is also cultural in the sense that interpretation and meaning are central also here – as in all social life. But management typically addresses 'simple' and taken-for-granted meanings, the level of thinking and feeling should be 'passed quickly' in control efforts, leading to predictable responses at a behavioural level. Management then is not primarily targeted at a cultural level as an 'end station' or as a significant site where a lot of things – thinking, sense-making – take place. Management as a mode of control is then thought to be able to bypass culture in its operations and minimize the involvement of values, unfocused thinking, and feeling.

Returning to the case of Iacocca, most of the activities mentioned did not seem to refer to a genuine concern with people's thinking and feeling in the organization, but more with PR work and instrumental issues. Getting people to accept cuts in salaries and benefits is mainly a managerial project, but it also includes an element of leadership. So is the case especially if the project does not stop with reducing costs and the workers grudgingly feel that they have no choice but to accept, but if the negotiations and communication around the issue lead to the workers developing an understanding and support for the outcome. The creation and maintenance of a 'cost-conscious' culture and the development of a particular sentiment towards sacrifice and responsibility is of interest to try to grasp here. Understandings within various communities around issues like this illustrate the fine distinctions between finance and culture, between management and leadership.

The ambiguity of leadership – a case of leadership or anti-leadership?

Leadership has traditionally been described as the traits of leaders or as a particular behavioural style. Occasionally, the need for a situation-dependent leadership style has been suggested. More fruitful is to see leadership as an act or set of acts within a social process. This de-coupling of leadership from a premature marriage with what a particular designated (or self-appointed) person does allows for a more open view. It also encourages paying attention to the meanings of all the people involved. It is then far from always clear if a particular act performed by a manager – or someone else – is productively described as leadership or not.

I will now present a glimpse of an event – a ritual – in a division of a Swedish industrial company (Alvesson and Björkman, 1992), with relevance for the interpretation of leadership. This organization is primarily populated by engineers or marketing people with an engineering background. Every third month there is an informational meeting for the 40 or so managers (here broadly defined, including also marketing personnel and supervisors) in the division. When Gustaf, the head of division, started with these information meetings not all the 40 or so people invited appeared and those who came sat rather widely distributed in a meeting room capable of hosting a larger group. Gustaf then emphasized that the meeting was obligatory ('please inform me if you can't attend', he wrote in the calls for the meeting) and asked people to take the front rows, thereby sitting close to each other.

At the time of our study no such encouragement is necessary. Most people attend and they take seats close to each other. Whether this reflects a new 'genuine' orientation or is a matter of behavioural compliance is difficult to say. All those present are men, with the exception of the female personnel manager and the secretary. Gustaf, the divisional manager, stands at the door and welcomes all the participants. During the introductory speech he gives a 'soft' impression, appears friendly and rather informal. The agenda is characterized by several speakers and Gustaf holds a relatively low profile. He could have done some of the presentations himself, and on the original agenda his name appeared as speaker on some themes but then he chose to let someone else take the centre stage. The atmosphere is informal and friendly. Sometimes Gustaf jokes with people and sometimes he is the object of their jokes. When the controller presents the results he uses Gustaf's picture aimed at showing changes in results on different markets in a pedagogical manner:

> 'Now we go over to Gustaf's own picture, the quantum physics diagramme'. (Everybody laughs)

After some comments, Gustaf asks the audience:

> 'Everybody laughs at me and this diagramme. Do you find it unclear? I think it is rather revealing'. Some people reply:
> 'At first glance it looks quite difficult (laughter), but when you have looked at it some time…' 'It is easier for me who is color blind'. (More laughter)

During the break, Gustaf serves coffee together with his secretary and the personnel manager. The overall impression from the meeting is one of community rather than formalism and hierarchy.

An interesting question is whether this is a case of leadership or not. It could be argued that this is the opposite of 'real leadership'. Gustaf is abdicating from a position as a leader, refraining from using the situation in order to exercise active influence on his subordinates. All the jokes about him and his pedagogical innovation can be seen as undermining his authority and weakening the asymmetry per definition characterizing the relationship between a leader and subordinates. The situation is mainly characterized by various people providing information about results and different problems that the company is working with. It has thus the character of information giving, rather than an opportunity for the leader to, through rhetorical skills and charismatic appearance, frame the minds, values and feelings of followers. In this sense one could say that Gustaf expresses 'anti-leadership' more than what is conventionally, and perhaps stereotypically seen as, leadership with a capital L.

But it is also possible to view the setup and Gustaf's behaviour as fully in line with leadership as defined by Yukl in the beginning of this chapter. Gustaf is downplaying hierarchy, he puts emphasis on community, an open climate and the free flow of communication. He also encourages other people through asking them to be responsible for presentation, which can be seen as strengthening their status, work identities and motivation. Through placing himself more as a host than an authority figure he sets the tone for others. Gustaf exercised cultural influence through delegation, emphasizing the value of everybody, underscoring social values, etc. The information meeting then expresses Gustaf's agenda of building an integrated organization through cultural means in which a traditional scepticism and antagonism between different functions – in particular marketing and production – can be overcome and a shared divisional identity and organizational community be developed.

An understanding of leadership then calls for considering not only the behaviour involved – through just observing what takes place at face value it may well be seen as the absence of leadership – but also the ideas and intentions. Through grasping the logic of the manifested social processes, we may see this as a case of leadership. But we also need to consider the reactions of those that Gustaf tries to influence. Neither intentions nor behaviour is sufficient or even the most vital components – the interpretation of and meanings of subordinates are really what matters, as these are basic for the responses to and effects of leadership acts.[2]

In the case of Gustaf actions like the information meeting and broadly in line with what it represents appeared to be positively responded to by his subordinates. People praised his social attitude and interest in trying to create shared orientations among the entire division. When Gustaf left after a restructuring of the company, which meant that his unit became part of a larger unit, people expressed some discontent with the more instrumental style of his successor. Within the subunit of the new division which partly overlapped the old unit that Gustaf was manager of, the senior person who took over some of Gustaf's tasks continued some of the events and practices he initiated. While most of the subordinates were positive to Gustaf, the depth and dispersion of his influence is difficult to evaluate. One worker viewed his behaviour as rather superficial and perhaps a reflection of a perceived inauthenticity of modern managerial practice. In many cases different orientations associated with functions and occupational cultures mattered more than the shared orientations and common organization-based identity that Gustaf's style and initiatives tried to bridge (Alvesson and Björkman, 1992).

One consequence of Gustaf's time as head of the unit was that people there developed more negative views on the practice of senior managers in the company, which was seen as much more technocratic, hierarchical and rational than communicative and sociocultural in intent and style. In that sense, Gustaf's leadership – or rather his way of being as a senior manager – seems to have had a cultural influence of some significance.

This case illustrates the need to take not only the actions of the leader, but also the ideas and intentions behind it, and in particular the interpretations and reactions of subordinates into account. Understanding leadership calls for the consideration of social process and cultural context, i.e. descriptions must be relatively rich or thick. The case also illustrates that what can be seen as leadership is an open issue. In informal, everyday settings it is even more uncertain what should productively be seen as leadership. In the case of Gustaf the manager-structured setup and his senior position make the leadership label appear appropriate, but it's well worth considering whether the use of the 'absence' of high-profiled leadership simultaneously can be understood as anti-leadership or as a particular version of leadership. The trick of sensitively grasping what goes on may sometimes be best accomplished through trans-gressing established vocabularies or at least through showing the uncertainties and tensions involved.

Leadership in the context of organizational culture

The relationship between leadership and culture is complex. Given the view on leadership expressed above – in which leadership deals with meanings, thinking and feelings more than it has a narrow behavioural focus – leadership may even be defined as agents working through culture as the medium and target of action. Leadership is culture-influencing activity, 'the management of meaning' as Smircich and Morgan (1982) expressed it. This does not necessarily mean that leadership creates or drastically changes culture, only that leadership is a cultural manifestation influencing other cultural manifestations, such as shared under-standings of objectives, technologies and environment.

In the interplay between leadership and organizational culture different kinds of relationships and emphasis are possible. In 'pro-leadership' management circles – such as most consultants, practitioners and some popular academics – leadership is seen as having a far-reaching impact on the cultural values and orientations of organizational members. We can then talk about assumptions about 'leader-driven organizational cultures', where a leader is influential in establishing or turning around certain core ideas, values and meanings.

The strongest case for leader-driven organizational creation or change is made by adherents of charismatic individuals in organizations. In order to be candidates for the label 'charisma' a top position seems to be required, at least for those writ-ing about it. Charismatic leadership emerges from the extra-ordinary influence exercised by a person, typically being able to get support for a radical vision, often in the light of a crisis, from a group of dedicated followers who are more or less spell-bound by the key person. They are willing to suspend critical thinking and disbelief and develop strong faith and emotional energy in the project of the charismatic leader. Charismatic leadership often involves the creation of some-thing new. The most well-known examples are from the political and religious spheres. Ghandi, Hitler and some leaders of religious sects are good examples. In the corporate sphere, the space for charismatic persons is probably much more restricted, partly due to the sobering impact of market mechanisms and competi-tion. Trice and Beyer (1993) do, however, refer to some examples of persons they think were or are 'genuine charismatics', including Iacocca and Steven Jobs, the founder of Apple. I will later in this chapter discuss a case of founders of a com-pany who were attributed charismatic characteristics by their followers.

Founders of organizations – whether seen as charismatic or not – are frequently viewed as also founders of cultures or at least significant sources of a set of values which the organizational members adapt and reproduce (e.g. Schein, 1985). Founders of organizations in a sense start from scratch, having a significant influence on the particular combination of people employed, choosing the direction of the company and thus frequently being able to put imprints on the shared ideas, beliefs and meanings that develop during the formative years of the company.

Although senior persons may be able to put relatively strong imprints on an organization (or parts of it) during special circumstances – crises, changes in circumstances calling for basic re-orientation, particularly favourable preconditions for strategic choice contingent upon market position and/or changes in the industry – it is debatable whether top executives normally can be seen as 'captains of culture'. Arguably, culture forms leadership rather than the other way around. So is at least the case for the large majority of all people designated as or emerging as leaders. As Biggart and Hamilton (1987: 435) put it: 'All actors, but perhaps leaders especially, must embody the norms of their positions and persuade others in ways consistent with their normative obligations'.

In a sense societal and business cultures set limits for the kind of managerial behaviour and arrangements that have a chance to be approved of. There are subgroups in society, such as religious sects, criminal groups and others, that deviate from broadly shared orientations and here there is space for leadership that would lead to sanctions in more 'open' contexts. Most organizations are, however, exposed to societal cultural values. This is accomplished through mass media attention, through the inflow of people carrying cultural orientations picked up in education and at other workplaces and through organizational members being citizens affected by the ideas and values expressed in various extra-workplace situations. Cultures in organizations are also affected by the interaction with suppliers, customers, authorities and others. All this counteracts deviation from the shared cultural understandings within a society or an organizational field that makes cooperation possible. When Iacocca reduced his income to $1 per year for some time and appeared on television with messages about the company, this was innovative, but of course it appealed to broadly shared values rather than challenged or changed these. What a senior manager or other kind of leader does must in a fundamental sense be perceived as in line with some broadly shared values. As a lot of what executives do is at odds with some social values (e.g. honesty, coherence, rationality, democracy, ecology-friendliness), and there is balance between drawing attention to what tends to be seen as good and natural and away from those values that one's actions are not in accord with.

Culture can be seen as a repertoire of positively and negatively loaded meanings. Leadership to be perceived as successful involves trying to attach positive meanings to one's intentions, acts, arrangements and outcomes and steer away from people – within and outside the organization – ascribing negative meanings and beliefs to what one is up to. In the case of Gustaf above, drawing upon and invoking values such as making people grow, participation, building organizational community and identity make his acts appear in a favourable light. On the other hand, if Gustaf should be evaluated in terms of ideals such as establishing authority, being in control, giving direction, the leader as a great communicator, etc. the verdict would be less positive.

Culture does not only limit, frame and prescribe leadership on a general, societal level, but also *within* organizations. Any particular organization represents a mix of general societal and industrial expectations and ideas, and of local, more or less organization-specific ones. Organization-specific cultural ideas and meanings in various ways direct and constrain managerial behaviour and leadership. Senior managers pass on (or modify) organizational culture through being role models, using selective recruitment to managerial positions and through sanctioning or discouraging deviations. Also subordinates have a strong impact on how leadership is shaped. If we disregard the use of 'pure' power – breaking the wills of people through the use of the whip (threats of being fired, etc.) – leadership means having some kind of appeal to people, to their hearts and minds. Visions, instructions, suggestions, goals, constructions of corporate reality must be perceived as legitimate and meaningful. The actions of the leader must then be fine-tuned to the frameworks and norms of those that are to be influenced. In this sense the subordinates as a collective – sharing certain cultural ideas – 'decides' what works in terms of leadership. This of course does not mean that the leader is totally subordinated to a given set of orientations or is forced to adapt to a specific style and just reproduce a given set of meanings and ideas. The leader can change these, but gradually and must in order to do so proceed from an appreciation of people holding certain ideas, values and preferences. The leader is involved in the negotiation rather than the imposing of new or revised orientations on people. Cultural change then tends to be gradual, partial and an outcome of social processes in which a group of subordinates have as much if not more to say than the leader.

It is not uncommon that managers are located in between values and norms held by senior managers and those promoted by their subordinates. 'Top management' culture – sometimes seen as corporate culture – and 'functional cultures' (associated with production, R & D, personnel or marketing) frequently differ and may conflict, and here leadership may partly be a matter of negotiation between different kinds of normative frameworks and views on corporate reality.

This can be illustrated by the case of a US coastguard officer who found his men – mainly college graduates whose expectations, interests and motives were at odds with the routines and lack of discretion of military life – bored and negative. Instead of trying to impose military discipline in a traditional way, he made a deal with his men about more discretion and certain liberties in exchange for more positive behaviour (Wilkins, referred to in Trice and Beyer, 1993). The case illustrates, among other things, how the values and orientations of a group of subordinates trigger a change in 'leadership' (if this is the right label in the case) so that it resonates better with their values and meanings.

I assume that most people expected to exercise leadership in their jobs are much more strongly influenced by organizational culture than they are involved in actively producing it. Apart from structural conditions (job task, resources, position, formal rights, etc.), which to some extent are cultural manifestations and have consequences through the cultural meaning attached to them, the cultural context guides the manager to how leadership should be carried out. So is done for example through prescribing that 'leadership' goes beyond relying solely on formal authority, and involves influencing the ideas, values and orientations of subordinates on how they should interact with managers, e.g. in terms of the appropriate degree of subordination.

The 'culture-driven' nature of leadership is neglected in most of the literature and in talk by management gurus and practitioners. This is to some extent because the cultural dimension has traditionally been neglected in leadership research. More significant, however, are the ideological overtones of a lot of talk on leadership. There is a broad tendency, in leadership research and among practitioners, to stress the manager as a superior, unidirectionally interacting with subordinates, and neglect that almost all managers also are subordinates and thus have a hierarchy above themselves (Dervin, 1990; Laurent, 1978). There is a wish among many people to ascribe strong impact to leaders, reflecting a want to see somebody as responsible for different outcomes, good or bad (Pfeffer, 1978). This fits the self-image of many managers and reinforces their status and claims for high wages, prestige and authority in companies and society. Management writers, teachers and consultants will probably find that their market would be smaller and less sympathetic if they should argue for the significance of other factors than management and leaders, as well as the complexity and ambiguity of how to account for performances. Generally, the strong faith in leadership, the attribution of causal powers to it and the heroization of leaders may be seen as interesting cultural manifestations – reflecting socially invented 'truths' and worthy of investigation.

Sometimes external dependencies and structural restrictions for leadership are noticed but the phenomenon of 'cultural subordinancy' has not been treated seriously in leadership research. Leadership as the adaption, mechanical reproduction, reinforcement, creative variation and/or of rejuvenation of dominating cultural orientations in organizations is a potentially fruitful line of thinking.

To sum up, culture is often seen as affected by the leadership of in particular the founders, but to some extent, and certain conditions, also of senior managers, at least if they are 'charismatic' persons. Leaders are said to work *on* culture rather than to work *within* culture. In the present book leadership is rather understood as taking place within and as an outcome of the cultural context, although under extraordinary circumstances leaders may transcend parts of existing cultural patterns or even contribute to the creation of culture. Also in such cases cultural context and cultural constraints must be considered. A precondition for changing culture is to connect to it. The next section will treat different kinds of leadership as creating versus created by organizational culture.

A case of initiator-leadership and follower-leadership

I will here return to the case of the computer consultancy company that I addressed in Chapters 3 and 4 and first treat leadership during the formative years of the company and then also address the notion of charisma. I will then provide an account for leadership in a post-formative phase. (For details of the study, see Alvesson, 1995.)

Leadership during the foundation and expansion of the company

The three founders of the computer consultancy company Enator headed it during the first seven to eight years of its, at the time of my study, ten year long history, and exercised a very strong influence of the ideas, beliefs and values subsequently characterizing the organization. The persons that participated in the first five years of the history of the company express almost lyrical tales about the functioning of the top management, i.e. the three founders. Despite the fact that a large part of the work was carried out at the clients' workplaces there was a strong feeling of closeness and involvement within the company.

According to the subordinates the founders exhibited energy, enthusiasm, high availability and an engaging and supporting attitude to the employees.

> One had a management that was very engaged. You had direct contact with the management. The management always was ready, always were available and always listened. You always got a motive.

The founders expressed a strong interest in the employees. Good performances were noted, acknowledged and communicated within the organization. The spotlights were put on the person that had done the right thing. He or she encountered positive feedback from all directions. Not only the praiseworthy person was told about how good he or she had been, but also other persons, who contributed to the positive reinforcement. Often a bottle of champagne was opened to celebrate the achievement.

The founders succeeded in tying together the everyday life of the personnel with the company's activities on a larger scale. The personnel felt that they were a part of the centre of the company, not only in different consultancy projects, but also in ideas and business developments, including contracts on new projects, joint ventures and acquisitions of companies.

> When we had morning meetings one of the owners was always there. We got a lot of inside information. On the present development, etc. We felt very much a part of what was happening.

The founders broadened the sphere for social influence that leadership in corporations is normally about. Through 'dramatization' of passing on information employees felt close to the running of the company and a part of an inner, trusted circle. Through frequent participation in social activities, also outside normal working time, the leisure time became to some extent a part of corporate life, to the benefit of experiences of community and knowledge sharing.

As we will see below, the orientations that the founders powerfully promoted were shared broadly in the organization and guided also the work of subsequent managers. The founders may well be seen as initiators of an organizational culture. For their subordinates this was partly a consequence of the charismatic qualities of the founders. It may be tempting to emphasize the heroic qualities and the leader-driven nature of cultural patterns in the company, but as said it is important to consider the social and cultural context in order to avoid a one-sided understanding. The computer consultancy business was, at the time, young and expanding. Of course not all companies were successful, but the expansion possibilities facilitated the distribution of positive interesting information and a dynamic atmosphere. In Enator, as in the rest of the industry, mainly relatively young and well-educated people were employed, providing a good ground for feelings of organization-wide community, an interest in social activities after work and so on. Swedish societal patterns are comparatively informal and non-hierarchical providing a value-basis for interaction between hierarchical levels. Enator was not entirely unique in the cultural orientations that developed but shows some resemblance with other companies in the industry. This is not to minimize the significance of the founders or to suggest that they just reproduced societal and industrial templates for cultural management. Given appreciation of the context and social factors which they were guided, constrained and formed by, they still were, compared to most other managements, highly influential in creating and shaping a particular version of organization culture with significant impact on corporate development as well as on the work life experiences of the personnel.

Charisma at Enator

Most of the literature and common talk on charisma in management contexts devolve on a limited number of public figures, such as Jan Carlzon, Lee Iacocca and Steven Jobs (Bryman, 1993; Trice and Beyer, 1993). Fame and mass media attention may contribute heavily to their aura and make their cases very special and perhaps of limited relevance for the understanding of less atypical managerial situations.

The founders of Enator were not media celebrities. Nevertheless, for the people in the company they scored highly in terms of charisma.

They are looked upon as gods. They are never criticized. People look up to them.

Christer (one of the founders) radiates entusiasm. He can turn some damnable setback into something positive. He has exceptional charisma. Everyone wants to talk to him.

The employees then developed strong faith and loyalty for the founders and to make efforts exceeding what is common in working life.

You could go through fire and water for the founders.

You felt for being part of it. To make an extra effort.

Enator's founders meet at least two of the characteristics of being charismatic leaders, they were deemed to be exceptional by the followers and enjoyed great personal loyalty. A third characteristic, having a mission or vision, is somewhat more ambiguous in this case. For Weber, who developed the idea, 'the bearer of charisma enjoys loyalty and authority by virtue of a mission believed to be embodied in him' (quoted by Bryman, 1993: 292). This is a bit difficult in business life, as the 'mission' (ultimately to make profit) may be less capable of making the pulse beat quicker for most persons in an organization. Iacocca's 'vision', discussed above, is for example, rather pale. Nevertheless, for some of the people of Enator, the business concept of Enator and the way the founders run the company had considerable attractiveness (Chapter 4). A fourth criterion for charisma to appear, according to some authors (e.g. Trice and Beyer, 1993), is that the leader faces and solves a crisis of some kind. In a 'cool' situation, followers are less inclined to see the leader as so exceptional, to grant him or her so much authority and/or to be so devoted. In the case of Enator, there were, of course, occasionally significant problems, but no major crises. On the contrary, things went well: the company grew quickly and was successful in all respects.[3]

Charisma is often understood as a personal trait of a person, although certain circumstances may be called for in order to make the followers inclined to see the person as truly exceptional and be strongly devoted and loyal. Crises and anxiety help. When leaders in business must attend to a lot of administrative duties as part of normal management practice or when results are no longer good, the perception of the leader as charismatic may vanish. It is important to consider not only the leader's qualities and his or her behaviour but also the context and the characteristics of the followers to understand charisma. It is perhaps better to see charisma as a quality in the relationship between a person and a group following him or her or even as a perception or attribution of the group. A person seen as charismatic may well have certain qualities – self-confidence, rhetorical skills, knowledge, personal courage, an original idea – but this in itself does not lead to people responding with deep devotion. Whether a Ghandi, M. L. King, Iacocca, Jim Jones (leader of a religious sect that committed collective suicide) or Hitler are seen as charismatic or not, is mainly a matter of social situation, cultural context and characteristics of the followers.

In the case of the founders of Enator one may, in addition to personal qualities and a thought through and systematically applied leadership style with a strong appeal, also point at charisma-facilitating conditions. One can ask how did they manage to be perceived as charismatic, which is per definition the same as being successful as leaders in the sense of having far-reaching influence and being able to get a high level of loyalty and work motivation.[4]

One important element here is to (choose to) be in a business on an expanding market. Being successful increases the chances of being perceived as charismatic. For a person wanting to be perceived as charismatic this is an alternative to following the more conventional path of facing and solving a difficult situation and thereby appearing as a saviour for a group ('the crises route'). Another important aspect concerns recruitment. It is more difficult to appear as charismatic for a diverse audience, with different values and inclinations to interpret and react on talk and other forms of action. The recruitment policy of Enator strongly facilitated a good spirit within the organization. Many of the employees were a part of the contact network of the three founders – who knew a lot of people – and were consequently personally known by the founders from earlier workplaces or in other ways. The average age of the personnel was low.

There is a general tendency for new organizations to start with recruiting a homogeneous group of people in order to shape a good base for confidence and mutual understanding (Kanter, 1977). In relationship to leadership, a homogeneous group of followers makes it much easier to adapt a style and tailor a message that all respond to in a similar way.

The people recruited may have been inclined to respond to the ideas, practices and personal style of the founders in a highly positive way and perhaps positively disposed to ascribe charisma-like qualities to the founders.

In order to understand charisma – the chief criterion being what subordinates see as exceptional qualities in leaders and a willingness to turn themselves into devoted followers – then several aspects need to be considered: not just the personal characteristics of the leaders and their leadership style, but also the socioeconomic situation and the orientations of the followers. The relations being formed in the Enator case then is not simply charismatic persons triggering certain reactions, but a more complex interplay between the characteristics of those involved (including the youth of the personnel), favourable context (the rapid growth on the market) and processes involving an effective leadership style and high-intensive interaction (including attention, feedback and publicly visible praise to the personnel, frequent social events outside work, etc.).

Post-founder leadership

This history of leadership at Enator provides the background for the common features of the exercise of leadership within the company at the time of my study of the company, i.e. ten years after it was founded and two to three years after the founders withdrew from the operational management of the company. (One had left entirely, the two others were still major shareholders, one of them the chairman of the company, the other involved in more informal ways.) The patterns initiated by the founders continued to be distinct to the company. Group cohesion, friendship, have fun at the workplace, openness and generosity with information to the employees, etc. are important values.

From the view of Enator's management an important task is to create a totality, to get the parts of the company together. What may be referred to as social integrative leadership is a matter of inducing a common orientation and direction to the operative units (the subsidiaries, the project groups and the individual consultants), to contribute to the identification with the company and a feeling of loyalty with this, to achieve social cohesion both on the micro level, within work groups and subsidiaries, and on the overall level, within the company as an entity. Social integrative leadership does not primarily addresses technical and operative issues. It is a matter of transferring ideas, meanings and orientations that counteract the disintegrative tendencies inherent in consultancy work. It facilitates convergence in thinking, feeling and acting which increases the chances of people staying in the company, getting along, being able to cooperate efficiently within and between units.

Social integrative leadership is partly a matter of boundary keeping. The key group in the company here is the subsidiary managers – heading units of 30–50 people (when a subsidiary grows and employs more than 50 persons, it is divided up into two units). The company prides itself for decentralization and a very flat organization. In consultancy companies, as in some other service companies, the boundaries between company and customer are often unclear. The projects are carried out on behalf of the client, in cooperation with the client's personnel and often at the client's workplace. This may trigger loyalty conflicts and identity problems might follow from this.

You are out there with the customer and keep your face. But you easily get into problems with loyalty. And if you will be on the right side of the border you have to go home occasionally and discuss the situation …

For subsidiary managers it is then important to create and maintain strong social bonds between the company and the consultants.

If you are working for a customer all by your own you have a tremendous need to have contact with your manager. To feel that you are not only earning money, but that you also are a person and important as such.

The subsidiary manager is important here as a representative of, and symbol for, the company as well as having a personal relation with the consultants. It is important that he or she is both respected and well liked. A related important aspect concerns the internal social cohesiveness and atmosphere within the company. The subsidiary managers should be socially active and express a positive and engaged spirit. The expectations are high in this regard in the company.

I will now give two brief illustrations to how what may be viewed as leadership in Enator is exercised, in ways aiming to ensure that the right values and orientations are accomplished. Both illustrations are from the recruitment and selection process, which reproduce and reinforce culture through selectivity in who is employed and also what the process signals to the newcomers. One example came from observations of a manager, responding to calls on a recruitment advertisement. Having described the company and the jobs and answered questions, he asked the persons calling if they were interested in applying, to write to the company and say something about themselves and their qualifications, what they wanted, and what they were like as persons. He asked them not to send academic grades, etc. He was not interested in formal documents. This signals an informal approach, in which trust is indicated. It also communicates that it is personal characteristics and orientations, rather than technical skills or the job as best carried out in a depersonalized way, that is valued in this company.

Another example, also from the recruitment process, came from another manager. He asks personal questions like 'are you religious?' 'jealous?', 'is it important for you to speak the truth?', etc. He also talks with the potential employee's spouse about the job, what it might mean in terms of travelling, being away from home, etc. before agreement of employment is made.

In the second case there is also an emphasis on the informal as well as a broader view of the personnel in the workplace. The manager goes far outside what is traditionally conceived of as being part of the work role. Thereby it is indicated that his and the company's interest in the personnel goes much further than their way of solving computer problems between 8 and 5. Openness and informality as well as the importance of the personal life and the link and overlap between work and home life are stressed. The new employee and his/her spouse are also expected to commit themselves to the demands of the company in terms of overtime, travelling, etc.

Dominant values in, and to some extent distinct for, the company means that there are certain local institutionalized expectations on managers. These are related to the style and values of the founders that have put strong imprints on the organization as a whole:

> There is an opinion, a certain education that you get on how to be a manager in this com-
> pany and that comes from the old leaders, the founders of the company. The leaders are
> seen as very important, to be a sort of cultural carrier and to be an ideal for the per-
> sonnel. As a leader you must participate in all social arrangements. You should preferably
> be the funniest of all, you should be visible all the time and give a direction to the com-
> pany and the personnel in the way you wish that the company will function, type nice
> parties and stories and things like that. (Subsidiary manager)

One manager expressed this as 'in Enator you only employ managers that can become buddies with their consultants' and that 'the employees have the expectations to have a beer with the CEO'. The personnel had more or less the right to veto candidates for subsidiary manager positions. One person failed to live up to expectations about providing information. He tried to put out smokescreens around a bad financial result during his first year in relationship to the subordinates. They found out, and this contributed to them demanding his removal and the person had to leave the company.

In the case of this company there is a rather strong and explicit cultural framing of leadership at the organizational level. Top management, but perhaps even more so the personnel, have certain values and expectations on management and leadership to which the managers must respond in order to be credible, legitimate and effective: to be active in social arrangements, to downplay status and prestige and emphasize close and informal social relationships, put personnel and team building into focus. All this breaks with traditional hierarchies. For managers, this is a constraint but also a guiding framework in their leadership.

Enator is, of course, as all companies, in many ways unique. It is a young and, in terms of cultural orientations, very explicit and high-profiled organization. Many other companies incorporate perhaps less distinct, less espoused and more taken-for-granted ideas, beliefs and expectations. Still, there are cultural institutionalized orientations carried by superiors, colleagues and subordinates which means a selectivity in terms of who is recruited to and allowed to stay in managerial positions, and cultural rules for what kind of leadership that is seen as acceptable and that people respond positively to. The case of Enator then illustrates how organizational culture shapes leadership.

Summary and conclusions

In this chapter I have tried to make six interrelated points on leadership. A cultural understanding of leadership calls for appreciating local meaning. Leadership can be defined as about influencing the construction of reality – the ideas, beliefs and interpretations of what and how things can and should be done, in the light of how the world looks like. An understanding of leadership calls for the nuanced interpretation of the relation and context of interaction between superior and subordination. But not all aspects of this interaction are best understood as leadership. Many researchers suggest a distinction between manager and leader. The leader then supposedly relies on formal means and addresses 'substantial' concerns, but exercises an influence through the heads, hearts and values of people. This calls for paying attention to specific instances of leadership – acts in which this kind of influence is exercised. Such acts may be relatively rare and call for careful interpretation to be grasped. However, managers always, in some way or another, 'manage' culture. Even strongly bureaucratic and number-counting managers reinforce rules-and measurement-focused cultures and thus affect thinking, feeling and values. Also non-managerial organizational members contribute to cultural formation/reproduction, but typically from weaker positions.

A second point concerns the balance between academic a priori definitions of leadership and openness to the meanings of the people being studied. It is important to be somewhat careful in imposing a particular definition on leadership and instead be open to the meanings ascribed to 'leadership' by the natives. Interesting themes then become when, how and why do the people in an organization talk about 'leadership'? What meanings – coherent, varying or contradictory – are expressed around 'leadership' and what particular acts and arrangements are seen as 'leadership'? What hopes, fears and expectations are there? How do people react to various styles and acts seen as expressing leadership? What is perceived as leadership? Who is seen as a 'leader'? Which metaphors for leadership seem to inform understanding of this phenomenon? Commander, coach, visionary? Interpreting the local meaning of leadership offers a route to an understanding of organizational culture. And vice versa.

Even if the emphasis in leadership theory should not go so far as to 'delegate' the meaning of leadership altogether to the people in various organizations, but to retain some theoretical idea of what leadership refers to, it is a good idea to put less emphasis on the leader and what he or she does and more to how people relate and respond to acts of managers. The effect-triggering element in leadership is less what the leader does *per se* than how subordinates perceive, interpret and react on the leaders' acts. One and the same behaviour may for example be read as 'authoritative' and 'capable of making a decision' or 'authoritarian' and 'out-dated', with very different implications for legitimacy, trust and motivation on behalf of the subordinates.

A third point concerns method – how we go ahead in studying leadership. This would imply an approach in which leadership is studied through thick descriptions. This is something completely different from the majority of anorectic leadership studies and talk preferring abstract variables – such as personnel orientation or task orientation – or promoting a recipe for what is claimed to be a superior leadership. Thick descriptions devote attention to details and rely on the powerful example to develop insights. One may for example follow a manager during a work day or a few events in which s/he is interacting with others and then pay attention to specific acts of leadership – the case of Gustaf in this chapter partly illustrates this approach. A thick understanding of leadership is not of exclusive academic interest, but also offers a basis for organizational change intervention. The objective is not so much to develop very broad generalizations, but to say something of more relevance for a particular sector of organization or a kind of situation (as illustrated by the example of leadership in the computer consultancy company referred to above).[5]

A fourth point concerns the influence of culture on leadership. As leadership is normally not carried out from a sociocultural point zero, but always takes place in a context of already developed meaning patterns – those of the leader and those of others – there is always a strong element of cultural determination of leadership. Promotion is often dependent on being perceived as well as adapted to dominant orientations of senior managers, which means that managers typically fit into corporate culture and tend to carry rather than deviate from dominant patterns. Most leadership is culture-driven in the sense that shared beliefs and norms inform the manager how to act. Culture here may refer to the organizational level, but also societal, industrial and occupational cultures may be central. Leadership is then better seen as 'within' rather than 'outside' culture. Within culture-driven leadership the skilful manager may exercise considerable influence. Cultural constraints are seldom very strict, but may give rather broad parameters. Sometimes the acts of managers and informal leaders also more independently shape elements of culture. More significant examples of culture-shaping leadership (leadership-driven cultures) are rare, but in certain situations, particularly when organizations are founded and during major crises, where a significant portion of key personnel are replaced the situation is more open for the re-framing of ideas, beliefs and meanings.

A fifth point, also related to the earlier ones, concerns the role of leadership in organizational change. This is frequently viewed as an outcome of leadership, and without new forms of leadership organizational change is difficult if not impossible to accomplish. Organizational change is not, however, only or mainly about letting a superior 'leader' loose in order to transform organizational culture. In the culture literature there is a peculiar emphasis on the highly extraordinary situations of planned cultural change in which top leaders are treated as if they were 'standing above' corporate culture. The normal leadership situation with regards to culture is far less spectacular and grandiose. As leadership is a cultural phenomenon – and any act that is not interpreted as meaningful will lead to negative responses (confusion, resistance, loss of legitimacy, reluctant obedience) – cultural change rather means the cultural re-definition of leadership. Cultural change, to the extent it is related to leadership at all, includes and brings about new forms of leadership. The relationship between leadership and other cultural manifestations is then not 'external' or causal, but intertwined. I will treat this issue further in Chapter 8.

This brings us to charisma and a sixth point. In those examples where powerful leadership appears to have a strong impact on the radical transformation of culture, it is often viewed as charismatic leadership being in operation. When a person is ascribed charisma it means per definition a far-reaching preparation to let oneself be influenced by a person. The question is under what circumstances followers can be moulded so strongly that they radically transform their frameworks and beliefs through the impact of a big leader. In business and public administration this is probably rare, and claims of the charismatic president turning round an organizational culture sometimes seem rather spectacular, as I tried to demonstrate in the case of Iacocca. To understand charisma, not only the charismatic superhero, but also the context and the orientations of the subordinates need to be considered. I illustrated this with a case of founders of a Swedish computer consultancy company. Among other things, recruitment practices and selectivity in employment and promotion provided fertile soil for 'hot' responses to the personal qualities of the founders.

To sum up this chapter, I am arguing that the leadership of managers (and even more so of informal leaders) is typically strongly constrained by, and draws upon, the cultural and ideological context(s) of the organization. New ideas and initiatives are more likely to succeed if they are broadly in line with the dominant values and understandings. Recognizing that there are exceptions, leaders are normally better understood as 'transmitters' than as 'masters' of culture. Managers may more or less intentionally, more or less skilfuly act as 'cultural engineers'. They are typically significantly more influential in the ongoing reproduction and revisions of cultural meanings than other organizational members.

Notes

1   Some authors do, however, include a broad spectrum of highly diverse orientations, tasks and behaviours in leadership (e.g. House and Aditay, 1997).
2   One could argue that the most significant aspect of leadership is its effect on corporate or unit performance. As so much influences the latter and it typically is difficult to determine performances, it is seldom easy to identify any direct links between leadership and results. Even when reliable indicators on leadership behaviour and performance can be discovered, this does not tell us how leadership actually works.
3   This of course does not mean that the situation was idyllic. A high stress level at work was not uncommon. Some of the employees felt, in retrospect, that what they got from work did not really correspond to their efforts and contributions during that time. When the company expanded and the founders had earned a lot of money they moved on, while the co-workers continued more or less as before, feeling slightly betrayed, because what may be at the time felt to be a genuine social relationship in retrospect may appear as an instrumental, exploitative one.
4   As Trice and Beyer (1993) point out, charisma also has some considerable drawbacks. The strong emotions and the bracketing of critical thinking in relationship to the leader may lead to irrationality. There is also a strong risk of disillusion when the high expectations on the leader are no longer met. Even though charisma means highly influential leadership, companies do not necessarily benefit from charismatic leaders
5   This point about method is not solely of relevance for academics. Everybody in organizations that are engaged in evaluating and developing leadership, need to do more or less systematic observations and develop understandings of leadership. Superior managers need to have an empirical basis to provide feedback on junior managers or evaluating their potential for promotion, as do HRM professionals and consultants working with aiding specific managers in leadership and developing training programmes. Ideas on method are relevant here.

6 Culture as Constraint: An Emancipatory Approach

As pointed out before, culture facilitates, indeed is a necessary condition for coordinated human life, and thus organization. Organizational, occupational and other forms of culture thus fulfil vital positive functions: they provide group members with a shared understanding, feelings of clarity, direction, meaning and purpose. But there is also a dark side of culture. When leaders influence culture or act based on a set of understandings and meanings that all involved take for granted, a subtle and frequently penetrating form of power is being exercised. Cultural meanings that are engineered by powerful and skilled actors counteract questioning and independent thinking. The power aspect of socially dominating ideas about what is true, natural, good and possible must be taken seriously. That a work group or an organization seems to share certain ideas, beliefs and values do not necessarily mean that this should be viewed as an expression of consensus or harmony. Before drawing this conclusion one should seriously consider the possibility of powerful actors or ideologies being central for the development and reproduction of these orientations. It is also important to investigate whether a commitment to ideas and values are 'genuine' or a matter of conformism and compliance. Asymmetrical relations of power and dominant ideologies representing sectional interest may lead to people adapting certain orientations without carefully thinking through these.

But culture does not work as a source of domination solely through the more or less deliberate acts of managers and organizational arrangements – such as symbols of hierarchy or carefully orchestrated rituals. Culture can also be seen as carrying ideas and values that everybody – social elites as well as regular employees – takes for granted and subordinates themselves to. Cultural assumptions, e.g. about gender, careerism, affluent consumption and technocracy, may fix also the minds of senior organizational members. As with all cultural meanings, they are a mix of societal, industrial, organizational and group-level phenomena.

Cultural meanings can then be seen as the freezing of social reality. People subordinate themselves to existing forms, values and social patterns. They take certain interests as given and/or good and refrain from considering alternative ways of creating social reality. In Chapter 2 I mentioned the compass as a common metaphor for organizational culture. It indicates that cultural ideas and values show people the 'right' way. In comparison the blinder and world closure metaphors – also introduced in Chapter 2 – point at how culture prevents people from critically exploring the reasons for embarking on and sticking to a particular path and from seriously considering alternative ways of how to live one's organizational and personal life.

The idea of pointing at the negative, constraining aspects of culture, proceeds from an emancipatory view on knowledge. The task is then to provide inspiration to liberation from some of the constraints that culture exercises. Less ambitiously, this task can be seen as encouraging questioning and resistance. This does not necessarily aim at full-scale liberation from prison-like elements of culture, but may be a more modest project and include some kicking back against being too strongly sucked into the templates for thinking and being that powerful agents design for others in their efforts to engineer culture.

Of course, the critical investigation of cultural meanings may be useful not only for the emancipatory efforts of people, but also for getting input to organizational change aiming to improve corporate performances. Repressive ideas on gender or the pressure to conform to managerial fashion may be critically explored to the potentially valuable advantages of both facilitating liberation from ideational and normative constraints and improve management through a better use of female talent and a more careful and selective adaptation of new management ideas. Frequently, however, critical scrutiny and the ideal of emancipation are less in harmony with goals of improving corporate performance.

Culture as a counterforce to variation and autonomy

As argued, the basic idea of a cultural understanding of organizations gives considerable weight to more or less integrated patterns of ideas and meanings that provide some stability and point of departure for coordination. These ideas and meanings – which include hierarchic and other relationships and the acceptance of objectives, rules and various frameworks for operations – often lead to the absence of questioning, or at any rate of serious questioning, of existing social conditions. In this case, basic conditions tend to be taken for granted and the social world will be regarded as natural, neutral and legitimate (Alvesson and Deetz, 2000; Deetz and Kersten, 1983; Frost, 1987). There is little room for any conscious awareness that social reality can be experienced and understood in radically different ways, and that an infinite number of approaches are, in principle, possible. This acceptance calls for selectivity in the view of experienced social conditions, and 'complementary' selectivity in interpreting and assessing what is heard and seen. There are limits to the openness and rich variety with which this social reality could be appreciated, and to the ways in which what is real, unreal, good, bad, sensible, problematic are defined. This is, of course, to a large extent unavoidable. If a given social system is to function and to be reproduced, the ideas and meanings involved must thus be limited and a great many alternative interpretations – alternative in relation to the dominant interpretations, typically treated as truths, must be excluded from, or at least marginalized, in human consciousness and public life. This is partly what culture is about, and these selectivity mechanisms are characteristic of socialization processes in society at large and in organizations.

This does not, of course, imply a highly conservative social reality. In important ways contemporary society and corporations are dynamic and drive or respond to market and technological changes. Such changes also include the re-definition of meanings. But such changes do not necessarily concern 'core meanings and values'. A gradual re-definition of gender towards less pronounced sex roles and some opening up of new paths for men and women, do co-exist with deeply rooted tendencies for men and women to locate themselves and sanction each other so that traditional notions of masculinity and femininity still bear their imprints on men and women in terms of education, job type, wages, domestic duties and sexuality. More about this later in this chapter. There is a strong interest in fashion in Western management and working life, but this orientation often reflects more a dominant cultural valuing of novelty, a naive belief in progress and strong conformism, than a genuine openness in terms of how relate to organizational issues. It frequently represents the opposite of autonomous thinking. I will come back to this issue in Chapter 8.

There are practical-organizational as well as psychological-existential reasons for culture as constraint and a denial of the openness of human life and the arbitrariness of contemporary social forms and dominating values. That is, arbitrariness in the sense that we, given our biological inheritance, could develop other cultural forms to guide social life than those of the present historical period. This limiting and freezing of ideas about reality is contingent upon existential reasons as well as practical constraints: we want a coherent picture of the world and it is far too time-consuming and distracting to be constantly wondering about different ways of interpreting the world. An extreme pluralism in ideas on how to manage, work and give priority in life lead to endless doubt, anxiety, indecisiveness, debate and conflict. Arguably, some cultural closure is necessary for cooperative social activities and for individual well-being. It is impossible to question everything. But a certain amount of unpacking of dominant meaning and counteracting forms of cultural closure that are evaluated to be socially unnecessary and repressive may encourage more autonomous personal choices and the development of social meanings based on careful considerations.

Culture and power

There are 'spontaneous' or organic restrictions associated with cultural 'belongingness' – constraints associated with language, tradition, taken-for-granted assumptions and ideas specific to a particular group or society. As we are born into or enter a particular cultural context – a society or a workplace – certain shared orientations and some degree of subordination to these are internalized, without any agent being of particular significance. However, frequently powerful agents make a difference for how meaning is developed and a group relates to the social world. Power relationships thus matter for the shaping of culture, perhaps particularly so at the local level, e.g. the organization or the work group. A view of reality is then to a significant degree the result of negotiations between actors involved in asymmetrical power relationships. The actors in these relationships have access to different resources – material and symbolic – and have different possibilities when it comes to deciding how reality is to be defined. This is a crucial aspect of power, at least in modern society (Frost, 1987; Lukes, 1978).

Connecting culture to power, politics and conflict refutes a common orientation within organizational culture studies in which culture is viewed as implicating mainly consensus and harmony, culture is seen as shared values (e.g. Hofstede *et al.*, 1990; Schein, 1985). Sometimes culture is treated positively – as something worth striving for – because the concept is seen as standing for harmony and consensus (Schein, 1985), sometimes culture is rejected as an explanation for the same reason (Wilkinson, 1996). A more sophisticated understanding is reluctant to see culture as grounded in 'genuine', organic consensus. Culture is thus not seen as standing for the consensual, collective, coherent and integrated, but may also be interpreted in terms of contradiction and (hidden) conflict, dominant ideologies, class and gender bias, and so on.

A great many different theories and definitions of power exist, but I will refrain from surveying them here.[1] Briefly, most of them can be located on a scale ranging from theories which try to define power as something delimited and behavioural, such as the classic definition of power whereby A makes B act in a certain way despite resistance on B's part, to theories which look at more complex phenomena and emphasize structural relations and the influence of ideas, preferences, self-images, etc. The classical theories focus on individual and behavioural factors and disregard the less obvious, but perhaps today's most significant elements of power. Another weakness of traditional conceptions is the connection of power with competition and conflict. Power is seen as a matter of defeating and preventing opposition. This is sometimes referred to as instrumental power (Pfeffer, 1981b). Critics have argued that power is also and particularly significant when not brought to the surface:

> If we define power as the capacity for a personal or impersonal instance (Instanz) to bring someone to do (or to abstain from doing) that which left to himself he would not necessarily have done (or would possibly have done), it is immediately obvious that the greatest conceivable power lies in the possibility to preform somebody in such a way that, of his own accord, he does what one wants him to do, without any need for domination (*Herrschaft*) or for *explicit* power (*Macht/Gewalt*) bringing him to do or abstain from doing. It is equally obvious that a being subject to such shaping will present at the same time the appearances of the fullest possible spontaneity and the reality of a total heteronomy. Compared to this absolute power, any explicit power and any form of domination are deficient and exhibit an irreparable failure. (Castoriadis, 1992: 275)

The following empirical observation endorses this view:

> The most important kinds of power were already constituted as being those occasions when A's didn't have to get B's to do things because B's would do those sorts of things anyway. Simple empiricism would not be sufficient to reveal this. (Clegg, 1987: 65)

Power is highly relevant also in explaining the absence of conflict. Power does not only produce visible effects, but it is also vital to an understanding of inaction: why grievances do not exist, why demands are not made, why conflict does not arise and why certain actors appear as authorities whom people voluntarily obey (Lukes, 1978). Here it makes sense to talk about symbolic or ideological power. Another critique concerns assumptions about the deliberate nature of power. Rather than assuming power to be intentional, an instrument held by the powerful over the powerless, it is the structural and systemic character of power that is emphasized. Ideologies and mechanisms may exercise power beyond the intentions or control of the elites, who benefit from dominating forms of power but who are also subjected to them. Managers, for example, may be subordinated to cultural ideas and values that they take for granted. Intentions are not neces-sarily central. Power may thus be in force even if particular agents such as managers have limited control over it, and some of its functioning and effects are unintentional.

There thus seems to be a strong trend away from 'episodic, agency, causal, mechanical conceptions of power as if they were the whole of power' (Clegg, 1989: 186). Yet a great deal of power research continues to use what critics view as a mechanical approach, presumably partly because it is most convenient for empirical studies, but also because there are many phenomena that seem to fit this understanding. There are a variety of forms and manifestations – and as said also 'non-manifestations' – of power, and there is little point in saying that power is only or solely of a particular kind. In this book, it is the cultural-symbolic forms of power that are focused upon. Here, 'power is implicated in meaning through its role in upholding one version of significance as true, fruitful, or beautiful, against other possibilities that may threaten truth, fruitfulness or beauty' (Wolf, 1994: 226).

One of the drawbacks of the modern comprehensive theories is that power becomes difficult if not impossible to delimit or define. Foucault (1980) contends that this lies in the nature of the phenomenon. There is little point in trying to pro-duce a precise definition in such a case. Instead we must, like Bachrach and Lawler (cited in Hardy, 1994: 220) 'ask not what is power but to what does the notion of power sensitize us'. More important than formal definitions is thus a line of thinking which provides a focus and a sharp edge in reasoning and inter-pretation. The idea of using the concept of power should be to draw attention to some kind of agency – perhaps people or formal institutions, but as Foucault (1980) has emphasized also forms of knowledge may involve the exercise of power through the capacity to define what is real, true and normal and thus regu-late and constrain people, e.g. specify how a good manager should be. Power also signals subordination and repression.[2] Even if power is not solely negative, the concept draws attention to how someone is being subordinated and shaped in accordance with a particular regular force, giving priority to certain interests and neglecting others.

Culture theory, managerialism and consensus

Sometimes culture theory, especially in the context of management and organi-zation studies, is accused of being consensus-oriented and of avoiding or trivial-izing issues of power and politics. This, of course, is not an inherent characteristic of culture theory but is a result of the way many researchers have chosen to work with the concept of organizational culture. As mentioned in Chapter 3, this liter-ature has a pro-managerial orientation, based on the assumption that management acts in the common interest. It is argued that by managing culture, e.g. creating ceremonies, rites, slogans, specific expressions, etc. it is possible to facilitate a range of positive outcomes, beneficial for employees as well as shareholders. There is a strong belief in the superiority of management and the legitimacy of asymmetrical power relations, in which subordinates become the material to be worked upon by managers. Trice and Beyer (1985), for example, appear to assume that top management is the legitimate interpreter of the appropriate ideologies and values in an organization, and various means for controlling the ideas of subordinates are suggested. Non-managerial organizational members enter into this text only as objects of managed rites or as a conservative force that might, according to management, jeopardize the needed cultural change. Except for recognizing that management might also resist genuine change, the major problem, according to Trice and Beyer, concerns the risk that management's efforts are not successful enough.

The risk that management might have the 'wrong' values and ideology or that resistance to cultural change may make good sense for a specific group, is hardly recognized by (pro-)management authors. They assume that the cultural significance of managers in organizations is great, and that this group supports the common good and has the moral right to decide upon 'desirable' values and ideals.

Many of these studies are in a sense dealing with issues of power, without explicitly addressing this topic and without taking seriously the potential negative consequences for subordinates of being the objects of cultural control. Nor is there a serious consideration of the possible drawbacks for companies when subordinates are not recognized as having a say in which ideas, meanings and values should govern organizations. A reluctance to recognize and address how certain actions and arrangements sustain and reinforce asymmetrical relations of power, makes functionalist studies political naive. There is a smokescreening of issues of power behind a technical and misleadingly neutral vocabulary. However, as will be seen below, there is also a rich collection of ideas and insights within the field of organizational culture that encourages a critical and reflective approach to the power-aspects of the management of culture.

Cultural control and management of meaning

As pointed out in the previous chapter, the creation and utilization of existing as well as novel ideologies and symbolic means of control are crucial features of management and leadership (Kunda, 1992; Rosen, 1985; Willmott, 1993). In modern companies symbolic power is particularly salient, compared to technical and bureaucratic means of control, although all kinds of control typically co-exist. Also the use of modes of control not primarily targeted at consciousness but on output, rules and other constraining measures also involve cultural control. Bureaucracy, for example, calls for managerial efforts to develop and maintain respect for and the valuing of rules and standards.

Addressing these issues in terms of power rather than, or in addition to, management and leadership means that issues such as repression, constraints and (potential) conflict of interest are considered. While the language of leadership typically indicates the channelling of thinking and effort into a direction upon which there is (or becomes) a consensus and from which everybody involved benefits, the vocabulary of power frames the issue in somewhat darker or more sceptical light. Power indicates that certain interests and voices are either not respected or never raised and some options and degrees of freedom become blocked. While the term leadership typically is used in a ways that trigger association in a 'positive' direction, many people talking about power (conflict, interests, domination) raise doubts over the legitimacy of arrangements and acts in which power is expressed.

Corporate culture as expression of power may be seen as taking the form of systematic efforts to establish a certain world view, a particular set of values and/or emotions among corporate employees. Ray (1986) refers to corporate culture as 'the last frontier of control'. Critics have called this management strategy 'cultural engineering' (Alvesson and Berg, 1992; Kunda, 1992). Ideas about what exists, what is good and what should be accomplished are being communicated by management. The purpose is to attain a monopoly of the definition of appropriate values and ideals.

> Through the careful design and dissemination of corporate values, employees are exhorted and enabled to acquire 'a love of product' or the equivalent, as their sense of purpose. (Willmott, 1993: 522)

Such systematic efforts to make people think and feel in a particular way sometimes are realized, but frequently only partially so. A lot of the nice-sounding and glamorous ideals typically communicated in programmes for the installing of new values and mindsets are at odds with corporate practice. Anthony (1994: 72) claims that there is 'a disparity between managers' experience of cultural reality and the presentations of corporate culture which they are required to believe'. This disparity is difficult to grasp because the attempts of cultural control are accompanied by self-censorship and norms and practices suppressing the espousal of critique. Of course, this would make it difficult to back up generalizing statements such as Anthony's with empirical evidence. However, there is some support. Jackall (1988), for example, attended a seminar in a company where the senior manager in charge startled a room of juniors by saying:

> Fellows, why aren't any of you asking about the total lack of correspondence between what we're preaching here and the way we run our company?

Even though such outspokenness is rare, it may well reflect what many managers privately think. This would indicate some problems in exercising cultural control, at least over some organizational employees and managers. There is, however, frequently expressed worry that corporate culture succeeds in partially taking over the minds of those exposed to it, despite the lack of full correspondence to practices and despite some conscious distancing of employees to the messages and the symbolism (Kunda, 1992; Willmott, 1993).

A slightly different approach involves the management of meaning, which was briefly addressed in Chapter 3 and to some extent in Chapter 5. This is not necessarily tied to large-scale efforts to manage corporate cultures, but is part of the everyday leadership. This is regarded as symbolic action and means that powerful agents draw attention to certain things, and away from others. Language is carefully used in ongoing communication. Objects and issues are framed in a particular light, encouraging certain understandings and sentiments, typically reflecting managerial interests and objectives – which sometimes overlap with what may be seen as the interests of broader groups, and sometimes not. This control is centred around the ideas and meanings that management or individual managers want employees to embrace (Barley and Kunda, 1992; Pfeffer, 1981a; Smircich and Morgan, 1982). Consequently, it implies the counteracting of a multiplicity of ideas and meanings which could hamper cooperation and the reproduction of the organization (Willmott, 1993). Thus the managerially biased presentation and creation of social reality reduces the number of available variations in the way things can be perceived, when the possibilities of describing understanding and evaluating workplace conditions and objectives are being negotiated. The crucial issue of power does not thus consist of large-scale, visible moves, whereby resourceful actors decide for oppositional, or weaker actors; rather it is the creation or shaping of particular ideas and understandings whereby the ground rules of the organization are accepted.

> Generally, dominance is manifested not in significant political acts but rather in the day-to-day, taken for granted nature of organizational life. As such, the exercise of power and domination exists at a routine level, further protecting certain interests and allowing the order of organizational life to go largely unquestioned by its members. (Deetz and Mumby, 1986: 376)

One illustration of this is the communicated meaning of age in many contemporary organizations. There is often a negative view to middle age and a denial of the worth of a person's experience (Sennett, 1998). Age is seen as associated with risk-aversiveness, inflexibility and lack of energy. This meaning of being middle-aged, although probably often ill-founded and prejudiced, then is being used in order to get rid of senior employees. The laying off of organizational 'deadwood' in a turbulent time calling for capacity to and willingness for change appear highly reasonable and an example of efficient management. Of course, there are variations between organizations and competing meanings whether seniority primarily means 'valuable experience' or 'rigidity'. A particular motive behind the latter meaning is the preference for many managers of relatively young subordinates; these are often seen as more malleable and submissive. Older employees are more loyal with their institutions than with their managers and they are more inclined to speak up against what they see as bad decision-making – while younger employees, due to less organizational loyalty, may quit instead, Sennett argues.

Another, but more specific, illustration of how operations of power form meaning is the CEO of a large US company who, when starting this job, found no one at work when he arrived at his usual time of 6.30. He quickly changed this situation through leaving notes on the desks of his executives saying 'call me when you get in'. As he also had the habit of staying at the office until very late, he effectively prolonged the working day of the managers. A part of the 60–70 hours long work week was spent by reading newspapers of more or less business relevance, social mixing with other managers (Jackall, 1988: 51). Nevertheless, signalling that executive work means a very long work week and that it is normal for a senior manager to arrive very early reduces the autonomy of individuals and effectively obstructs the possibility to take responsibility for family matters.

The example can be used to illustrate the difference between behavioural and cultural control. The signal about and monitoring the time of arrival at work may be seen as behaviourally focused and people may react through responding only to explicit monitoring – so when the CEO is away the other executives may arrive later. But it may also be seen as symbolic management leading to consequences on the level of meaning. People may internalize the idea that senior managers do work very long hours and a 'natural' commitment to work means an early arrival as well as a long stay at the workplace. This may be motivated for several good reasons, but as the case illustrates can also be seen as an effect of the exercise of power, in which there is an element of arbitrariness. If people then, which is common, rationalize their behaviour through pointing at or inventing reasons for it rather than acknowledging it to be solely an effect of the pressure of the CEO, this should not lead us to neglect the power aspect. Of course, the meanings and values attached to time spent at work are not developed in a societal vacuum but are closely connected to various societal ideologies. Turner (1971) says that the general emphasis on punctuality in working life is not so much motivated by functional reasons as by the symbolic aspect: it is part of the disciplination of the workforce to adapt a specific work regime and the hierarchical differences are also played out through different emphasis on punctuality in different social classes.

Dominance is exercised chiefly by ensuring that specific meanings supporting the current social reality is regarded as natural, rational, self-evident, problem free, sensible, etc. and the leading actors as good and legitimate representatives of this reality (in our case the organization). A senior subordinate (e.g. a middle-level manager) may be constructed as 'experienced but not change-oriented', which paves the way for dismissal, subtle discrimination and/or the persons targeted themselves lowering their ambition and/or retiring. People not arriving very early and staying very late may be seen as 'lacking commitment' or 'being too soft' and therefore not being seen as candidates for promotion. Managers may be seen therefore as agents of power creating or reproducing shared meanings, ideas and values through acts of communication which freeze social reality or, at least, counteract an open, questioning approach to how it should be negotiated.

Culture as a source of taken-for-granted assumptions

Culture limits opportunity

As said, that powerful organizational actors use cultural and symbolic means in their exercise of management control and thus define the reality and the ideals for others is not the only rationale for a critical approach to organizational culture. Of equal, if not larger, importance is to look at more broadly shared, taken-for-granted cultural assumptions that tend to lock people in constrained, unimaginative patterns of thinking and relating to the world. What appears to be expressions of variation and individuality may sometimes be seen as clearly grounded in a common set of ideals, and thus contingent upon cultural constraints and social conformism. The idea of being an 'individual' and showing one's individuality is often surface-phenomena and barely hides the background of shared norms and rules. To appear as a 'real' individual calls for sophisticated adaptation to social norms – otherwise the person appears as 'odd', having bad taste or being socially incompetent. To express one's individuality through following fashion and choosing between prefabricated life-styles indicates the cultural-conformist basis of 'individualism'.

Arguably, cultural meanings and symbolism are not only tools for management control. Similar to culture 'leading' leaders through guiding, constraining and conforming them, culture subordinates also members of social elites to psychic prison-like patterns of relating to the world. As said, executives may use the cultural idea of passing 50 implying reduction of entrepreneurial capacity in order to get rid of middle-aged employees but at the same time suffer from the consequences of losing and marginalizing experienced people. They may sooner or later be caught by this negative view of age themselves, e.g. experience distrust and self-doubt when they approach 60, even if they should be intellectually and physically in good shape. Of course, at the most senior levels it is easier to avoid the rules and meanings that are deemed to be valid for others do not apply to themselves. But the celebration of youth penetrating the entire Western culture making ageing basically negative put strains broadly on the population.

Another example of how a group that in many respects benefits from a certain set of cultural ideas also may suffer from them is the meanings of gender. Cultural ideas on gender often mean that men are seen and see themselves as more instrumental and committed to work and career than women, which give them some benefits in terms of career options and wages, but the cultural meanings of men being masculine may bring about constraints, doubts, anxiety and impoverished social relations. Broadly shared cultural meanings associating women with domesticity and sexuality are often intentionally exploited by managers and husbands *vis-à-vis* female subordinates, competitors and spouses. Cultural meanings of gender mainly work behind the back of and severely constrain also men being privileged in terms of social position, income and exercise of formal authority. Masculine meanings of a 'man' then, despite being a source of benefits, also regulate and constrain men to define self-worth and identity in relationship to career and income.

Culture as a constraint through tradition and broad societal or international trends bringing about certain assumptions and ideals calls for critical exploration also in the absence of group oppression or exercise of power. Apart from age and gender, possible themes for such exploration include affluent consumption and hedonism fostering an orientation towards immediate gratification and a 'shallow' orientation to what matters in life (Fromm, 1976); a strong interest and cultivation of the level of the image, appearance and surface over issues of 'substance', materialized in public consumption activities and the emphasis on the brand (rather than product qualities) (Boorstin, 1960; Alvesson, 1990); the celebration of novelty, change and fashion (Ramsay, 1996); the institutionalization of an increasing number of forms of expertise, knowledge and practices of questionable usefulness (Meyer and Rowan, 1977) but which tend to create uncertainty and dependence as individuals and organizations lose faith in their own capacity (Lasch, 1978); and various forms of managerial ideologies defining what is rational and effective and through which people measure themselves and their superiors and subordinates (du Gay, 1996). These are, of course, only examples. A couple of these themes have been touched upon earlier and/or will be further addressed later in this chapter.

Western managerial culture is often taken for granted

The narrow view of organizational culture described in the previous chapter has come about partly because of the close association between researchers and management culture that is more or less universal at the higher levels of business in the Western world and, to a considerable extent, in industrialized countries in general. Basic elements of Western culture – progress, efficiency, rationalization, productivity, masculinity, exploitation of nature, control, hierarchy, and affluent consumption, among others – are shared by management researchers writing about organizational culture. Perhaps because of this, these values generally go unexamined. Organization theorists, especially in the United States, tend to share their views on subject matters with managers. One may even criticize organization researchers for frequently subordinating their intellectual understanding to the interests of the dominant elites (Alvesson, 1987). This is probably sometimes a conscious choice but often to some extent an effect of the confusion of the managerial interest with 'neutrality' and the general interest:

> Most organizational research implicitly adopts this managerial bias, not simply because it is more interested in the managerial perspective, but largely because the so-called value-neutrality of scientific research is easily co-opted by dominant managerial interests. Research questions thus get framed from a managerial perspective, and findings are couched in managerial language. (Mumby, 1988: 2)

There is a peculiar assumption behind much thought that neutrality and objectivity is the same as taking dominant social order – including its language use – as given and unproblematic. The tendency to view culture primarily through metaphors such as that of a resource or an instrument means that attention is concentrated on the manageable dimensions while the 'deeper' layers of culture and the cultural context of organizations and managerial action are taken for granted. By 'deeper' here I mean aspects of a collective consciousness of which people are not fully aware but which they experience as the natural order or as pure rationality. Bourdieu (1979) addresses this basic level in terms of 'schemas' and 'habitus' acquired through socialization, and, as we have seen, Schein (1985) speaks of basic assumptions on a pre-conscious level. Researchers tend to view the cultural phenomena they encounter as natural, part of the world order, rather than as specific to national or late-capitalist/post-industrial society and business culture.

The parochialism in management and organization research and practice in the USA in particular is shown by Boyacigiller and Adler (1991) and Prasad (1997).

A more genuine interest in cross-cultural comparisons and a refusal to take results produced in the USA as necessarily valid or relevant for other cultures are important, but there are also shared cultural orientations of a more global nature that call for scrutiny in order to be opened up and made the object of reflection and redefinition. If for example discrimination against women is a feature across several nations or if US management ideas colonize business world-wide then there is perhaps a need to look at the broad pattern and not only focus on the cross-societal variations encouraged by comparative studies. Global culture and its manifestations in specific organizational settings are not best understood through cross-cultural comparisons.

That organizational culture research does, on the whole, perform badly in this respect is ironic, since the proponents of a cultural approach sometimes claim that 'the essence of culture lies in the unstated premises or ethos that are taken for granted and so are largely implicit' (Trice and Beyer, 1984: 664). Gregory (1983: 359), an anthropologist, has observed that the literature concerned with organizational culture often says 'more about the culture of the researchers than the researched'. This kind of research problem is in fact more generally recognized by anthropologists (Marcus and Fischer, 1986); some even warn against the study of one's own society. Leach (1982: 124), for example, writes that:

> fieldwork in a cultural context of which you already have intimate first-hand experience seems to be much more difficult than fieldwork which is approached from the naive viewpoint of a total stranger. When anthropologists study facets of their own society their vision seems to become distorted by prejudices which derive from private rather than public experience.

An interesting illustration of this cultural blindness is the fact that few organizational culture researchers have observed that the preoccupation with 'managing', 'organizing', and making as 'efficient' as possible is a key feature of Western culture and of business organizations in particular. Smircich (1985: 56), however, has speculated on the way in which anthropologists a thousand years from now may characterize our societal and organizational culture:

> These people were crazy for organization. They valued discipline, order, regulation, and obedience much more than independence, expressiveness, and creativity. They were always looking for efficiency. They wanted to control everything. They had a fetish for 'managing'. They managed stress, time, relationships, emotions, but mostly they managed their careers.

The reduction of the culture concept to fit instrumental concerns and the tendency to take Western managerial culture for granted may be viewed as quite independent of each other. Normative research aiming to improve business does not necessarily exclude creative efforts in which cultural phenomena previously taken for granted are investigated in a novel light (despite certain weaknesses, the work of Peters and Waterman [1982], for example, did manage to shed new light on conventional wisdom); and a broader approach that addresses not only minor, company-related cultural variations but also the common assumptions and ideas in Western business and working life is of course no guarantee of the achievement of new insights. However, the two problems do overlap to some extent. The instrumentally guided conceptualization of culture which typically focuses on values deemed to be relevant for profits is a reduction of the potential richness of culture. From another angle, the inability to recognize and interpret the basic cultural patterns of organizations leads to a focus on what is specific to a certain company, for example, its particular strategy or management style, and from this focus may spring an emphasis on the instrumental elements of corporate culture specific to that company. Our ability to think culturally in an open and opening up-oriented manner is thus threatened from two directions.

The two problems are also related in a specific and significant way. Because the ideal of instrumental rationality is (though often imperfectly realized) a key feature of Western society and, in particular, of business life (Alvesson and Willmott, 1996; Deetz, 1992; Horkheimer and Adorno, 1947; Marcuse, 1964; von Wright, 1986), equating instrumentally relevant aspects with culture uncritically reproduces rather than explores a dominant feature of culture. Thus not only what is focused upon – instrumental values and norms – but also the very framework guiding research reproduces and reinforces a kind of thinking in which instrumental rationality is taken for granted. These two deficiencies of current organizational culture research – the focus on instrumentality and the tendency to take Western managerial and organizational culture as given – then clearly merge on this vital point. If this tendency can be avoided, then perhaps the narrow focus on instrumental aspects of corporate culture could be prevented: the preoccupation with such aspects would be recognized as a cultural phenomenon, and thus not accepted as a natural and self-evident guideline for research.

The somewhat obsessive preoccupation with profit, economic growth, higher wages, and increased consumption in the world's richest countries, for example, might well appear surprising and calling for careful investigation, in particular as they do not seem to lead to increased satisfaction and well-being (Fromm, 1976; Hirsch, 1976; Leiss, 1978). In many organizations, there is strong competition and high pressure from financial markets, but also people in companies having more of an option, e.g. partnership companies, frequently give a one-sided emphasis to goals such as profits and growth, sacrificing autonomy and quality at work (Covaleski *et al.*, 1998).

One major rationale for addressing the cultural aspects of organizations is the prospect of achieving a better understanding of 'self-evident' organizational and managerial patterns. Researchers should then distance themselves from the phenomena under study and ask why (cf. Alvesson and Deetz, 2000). This could also be done within a functionalist perspective and in instrumentally oriented studies. Schein (1985), for example, suggests that a methodology for cultural studies could include looking for 'surprises' in the culture – things that are different from what the outsider expects. International business oriented cultural studies may perform better here than studies that work solely within a particular country. The things that surprise a researcher with a managerial orientation are not necessarily the same things that an anthropologically oriented researcher would regard as 'surprising'. The latter may be inclined to view the modern business and organizational world as rather odd and strange in its very nature. Distancing does not of course mean that the researcher should employ 'objective' methods such as questionnaires – these are more likely to reproduce cultural taken for granted ideas as they mainly capture superficial attitudes and also reflect the researcher's assumptions of what is relevant to 'measure'. Instead the basic approach should be 'interpretive' and should combine closeness and distance in relation to the subjects (Smircich, 1983b) but simply accounting for subjective meanings is only half the research job. Many interpretively oriented scholars stop here rather than going on to place meanings and symbols in a broader cultural perspective. But:

> To understand organizational reality, then, is to ascertain why a particular meaning system exists by examining the conditions that necessitate its social construction and the advantages afforded certain interests. (Deetz and Kersten, 1983: 160)

Here we have history, language, ideology, and material practice as possible conditions worthy of investigation. These patterns of meaning are better understood if they are approached from a wide spectrum of reference points by a researcher who is both emphatically and observationally close to and, at periods, intellectually distant from the subjects of the study. Being able to view cultural manifestations as exotic, strange, arbitrary and constraining is important here. Such distancing can be achieved by way of broad theoretical knowledge and reflection and at the same time a kind of naivete. A good question to ask is 'What in earth are these people thinking?' Those aspects of an organization's life that its members take for granted, not only as a result of socialization and everyday experience in the particular organization but also because they are members of society, should be the targets of research interest. For ideas on a critical methodology involving de-familiarization of organizational phenomena see Alvesson and Deetz (2000).

Eye-opening studies: cultural limits to rationality

There are a few studies that put culturally dominant ideas and meanings into a perspective, exploring the shortcomings of dominant ideas on Western management rationality. The examples that I will review here are not particularly radical in the sense of questioning these ideas and meanings from a critical theorist's point of view, nor signalling any explicit emancipatory interest; they may, however, be mobilized in this direction. Feldman and March (1981: 178) address the meaning of information in organizations. They suggest that preoccupation with information is widespread not for any instrumental-rational reason but because of the cultural value attributed to information. Information symbolizes reason, reliability, security, even intelligence and is thus a matter of legitimation:

> Using information, asking for information, and justifying decisions in terms of information have all come to be significant ways in which we symbolize that the process is legitimate, that we are good decision makers, and that our organizations are well managed.

Paradoxically, it is the cultural value placed on instrumental rationality – on reason, 'facts', and the other things that information symbolizes – that accounts for deviations from the ideal. In other words, people emphasize information, viewed as a cornerstone in instrumental rationality, far more than is required or can be used from an 'objective', instrumental-rational point of view. Too much focusing on information prevents the practical use of it, and takes attention, energy and time away from intuition, creativity, interpretation and critical reasoning.

Still another such study is Ouchi's (1981) comparison of US with Japanese organizations, which offers a new perspective on Western cultural understandings of hierarchy, control, career paths, and specialization. It inspires the rethinking basic characteristics of US and many other Western companies. It indicates alternatives to the fast-track and short-memory orientations common in these companies, and the encouragement of short-term result-optimizing behaviour (milking) and other forms of opportunism that was treated in Chapter 3, referring to Jackall's (1988) work. Ouchi's book, however, has a number of drawbacks from a critical and questioning perspective. Its many prescriptions for success tend to 'freeze' thinking and inspire instrumental behaviour based upon it. Thus the eye-opening elements are limited to the initial phase in a process of re-orienting managerial understandings (cf. Alvesson and Willmott, 1996). The element of questioning is limited and a new and better solution is suggested, whereby the reader is encouraged to adapt a new position without much reflection about its constraining powers.

Although the two texts are very different in objectives, style and themes addressed, both illuminate broadly shared values, symbolism, and assumptions in Western organizations and indicate the limitations of apparent rationality. Ouchi illuminates how managerial principles, far from representing rationality, are located in a particular cultural context and possibly self-defeating. March and Feldman can be read as indicating that symbolism steers thinking and feeling away from what is functional, reflective, and psychologically mature – how mastery of information serves as a surrogate for reason and judgement and includes a denial of the ambiguity of the contemporary organizational world. A prolongation of this line of reasoning may include a critique of the arrogance of technocracy and management as conventionally understood, encouraging a stronger element of doubt in relationship to current organizational arrangements and practices.

Anthropological studies of organizations which have the objective of investigating basic assumptions and values can in fact be seen as dealing with rationality in a critical way: showing what is behind this notion, illuminating its relative and often ethnocentric character. The two texts of Feldman/March and Ouchi are referred to here because they illustrate how comparatively 'moderate' texts can contribute to eye-opening cultural studies of organizations. I will in the following sections address a few topics that invite even more ambitious enterprises.

Gender and organizational culture[3]

One of the most salient areas of organizational culture in which critical thinking has tried to challenge conventional assumptions and meanings is gender. As with all areas of interest from a cultural approach what is seen as given, natural and reasonable and to which people must adapt, the socially constructed nature of ideas about men and women is examined. The focus of relevance here is on how cultural ideas frame and restrain what men and what women should think, feel and do.

Some views on masculinity and femininity

Conventionally, at least as manifested in mainstream management and organizational literature, organizations are presented as neutral in terms of gender. Such a claim is, however, difficult to sustain. Many authors argue that sex discrimination 'is embedded in cultural values that permeate both organizations and the concept of organization itself' (Mills, 1988: 352). Discrimination exists in 'a number of overt (low pay and low authority status) and covert (images of domesticity and sexuality) forms that serve to constrain female opportunity, not only within, but in access and recruitment to, organizations' (p. 361). A cultural system which associates women with 'domestic life' and men with 'public life' restricts entry to jobs or channels women into a narrow range of occupations, normally of a caring or domestic type, serving (superior) men. Organizational culture is (normally) male dominated, involving notions of gender and sexuality in language, stereotypes, values, beliefs, and assumptions (Alvesson and Billing, 1997).

Organizational and occupational structures, processes and practices may be viewed as culturally masculine, as feminine or as neutral in terms of gender. Masculinity and femininity are not essential, natural categories but should be seen as cultural meanings which groups ascribe to various phenomena. 'Gendering organizations' means making explicit how cultural meanings are informed by ideas of gender. It usually means paying attention to how organizational structures and processes are dominated by culturally defined masculine meanings. Feminine meanings do less seldom dominate although they may be central in some organizations. Masculinity is a vague concept, but can be defined as values, experiences and meanings that are culturally interpreted as masculine and typically feel 'natural' to or are ascribed to men more than women in the particular cultural context. The same reasoning is valid for femininity. There are variations between different classes, nations, occupations, ages, organizations, and ethnic groups in terms of what they perceive as respectively masculine or feminine. Some forms of working-class masculinity may, for example, be quite antagonistic to management and white-collar work, which is perceived as non-masculine, e.g. the safe, physically undemanding and polished job of an executive (Collinson, 1988). For middle-class people, being an executive may instead be seen as masculine: it may be constructed as calling for toughness, instrumentality and a capacity to lead, not suitable for women.

The concept of masculinity overlaps with what Marshall (1993: 124) views as male values or the male principle: self-assertion, separation, independence, control, competition, focused perception, rationality, analysis, etc. This view on masculinity is perhaps more pronounced among the upper and middle classes, among managers and professionals, than by the traditional, now diminishing working class, engaged in body work. Femininity is defined in complementing and corresponding terms: interdependence, cooperation, receptivity, merging, acceptance, awareness of patterns, wholes and contexts, emotional tone, personalistic perception, being, intuition, and synthesizing (Marshall, 1993: 124). What is defined as masculine typically is valued higher than femininity in contemporary society and organizations, although some changes in business and working life – towards more of network and team organization – may involve some de-masculinization and a less clear-cut valuing of culturally masculine ideas (Fondas, 1997).

The concepts of masculinities and femininities can be used to describe cultural beliefs without connecting these very closely to men and women. Masculine meaning may therefore be traced also in language, acts and artefacts loosely coupled to sex/human bodies, e.g. strategy and sports talk, whisky drinking and cigars. To explore how people think, feel and make sense in relationship to these categories is vital for understanding gender relations and gender identities. Ideas about what is masculine/feminine and what is natural/normal for men and women in relationship to these qualities guide, constrain and trap people in all respects from occupational choice to acceptance/rejection of tasks in everyday working life, although people may be more or less independent in relationship to these guidelines and constraints. Facilitating such independence may be viewed as one purpose of gender-conscious cultural thinking (Alvesson and Billing, 1997).

Division of labour, sex typing and gender symbolism

In society and in different organizations there exist more or less profound ideas that certain types of education, career choices, work and certain positions are connected with a certain gender. Labour markets as well as work organizations are divided according to gender. Most jobs are sex-typed. They are defined as feminine or masculine and thus seen as natural for women or men, respectively, to occupy. One could also say that a job has a certain gender symbolism (Billing and Alvesson, 1994; Gherardi, 1995). Symbolism refers to objects – words, physical things and acts – which are seen as carrying a broader meaning than they 'objectively' do. A symbol is rich in meaning and evokes a subjective response, shared by people who are part of the same culture. The concept of gender symbolism goes a bit deeper than sex-typing, meaning not only that a particular job is openly viewed as women's or men's work, but that it refers also to non-explicit meanings, unconscious fantasies and associations. While sex-typing only means that some jobs are defined as suitable (only) for men, or women respectively, gender symbolism refers to the cultural logic behind such typing. Most work does not appear to be gender neutral but is attributed some form of masculinity or femininity, either vaguely or in the shape of more specific ideas about what the work involves and the kind of qualities typically possessed by a 'man' or a 'woman'. Examples of occupations with a strong masculine gender symbolism are fireman, postmortem examiner and army officer, while secretary, seamstress, fashion creator, hairdresser and nurse are as a rule connected with different versions of femininity.[4] (So appears to be the case at least in the part of the world where I live or more indirectly am familiar with). Jobs perceived as including affirming, beautifying, enhancing and celebrating the well-being and status of others, are typically seen as feminine, while jobs seen as calling for the jobholder to be stern, impassive or cool – as in policing or bank management – are more seen as masculine (Cockburn, 1991). Many technical jobs are constructed as masculine, and thereby as antithetical to women (Burris, 1996).

As Leidner (1991) shows, almost any job may be socially constructed as either male or female, through emphasizing some dimensions and labelling them in a particular way. (The exception is mainly jobs calling for physical strength, which 'naturally' may be seen as suitable for some men and only exceptionally physically strong women.) Leidner has studied insurance salesmen in the USA. These people had the task of visiting potential customers at their homes, establishing contact ('warming up the prospects'), going through the basic sales presentation to counter any objections raised by the prospects and to persuade them to buy as much life insurance as possible. Most people they contacted were motivated to prevent this sequence from being fully materialized, making the work not easy. Despite that this kind of job is interactive and may equally well be said to call for 'feminine' qualities, e.g. service-mindedness, almost all the salesmen in the company were men. The male persons Leidner interviewed felt strongly that women would be unlikely to succeed in the job. The manager said that he 'would never hire a woman' for the job. Leidner notes that this kind of job is done primarily by women in Japan and, also in a US context, requires skills that are not generally viewed as 'manly'. Salesmen must swallow insults, treat people with deference and keep smiling. Of interest therefore is how the salesmen construct their job through re-interpreting some features and de-emphasizing others. According to Leidner the company's trainers and agents 'assigned a heroic character to the job, framing interactions with customers as contests of will. To succeed, they emphasized, required determination, aggressiveness, persistence, and stoicism' (p. 166). Through stressing toughness as a key quality the job was constructed as manly. Women were felt to be too sensitive, too unassertive and not able to withstand repeated rejection in sales calls, according to some salesmen. In other sales organizations employing mainly women, qualities such as nurturance, helpfulness and service were viewed as crucial. These qualities were not absent in accounts of work in the insurance company, but they were clearly less pronounced. The conceptualization of work as an arena for enacting masculinity has several consequences. The salesmen become more inclined to accept conditions that otherwise may have been seen as unacceptably frustrating and demeaning. The definition of the work make the men employed unprepared to accept women jobholders.

Gender symbolism is not restricted to the work or occupation but also to the social field and organization in question as well as to specific activities. Also social positions are sometimes loaded with gender symbolism. Generally, masculinity is associated with higher positions, while assisting work is not just subordinate but also regarded as feminine.

A cultural approach to gender goes clearly beyond an interest in measuring differences between men and women in terms of differences and inequalities. Men and women are not seen as fixed objects to be counted in organizations. Instead it is conceptions and meanings about men and women, the masculine and the feminine, and the constraining consequences of these that are focused upon. As important social phenomena, gender relations thus influence the fundamental functioning of organizations and our general way of thinking about aim, rationality, values, leadership and so on (Calás and Smircich, 1992a,b). The cultural appeal of masculinity may for example bring about exaggerated ideas of the strong person acting as a leader providing visions and definitions of reality for the (less masculine) followers. This valuing of masculinity may also favour a strong interest in commander-oriented models of strategic management. The military origin of the strategy concept may have contributed to its popularity (Knights and Morgan, 1991).

A cultural approach to the theme of gender and organization means a gendered-organizations perspective – in which the gender over- and undertones of a wide spectrum of cultural manifestations are taken seriously. This then differs from a gender-in-organizations approach, in which representatives of gender – men and women – are focused on, in the light of the organizational environment they are in (Hall, 1993). This means that 'gender is not simply imported into the work-place: Gender itself is constructed in part through work' (Leidner, 1991: 170). Gender is thus partly seen as an organizational accomplishment, as culturally created at the local level, although of course ideas associated with the societal-level are central. Workplace culture thus is seen as constructing beliefs about and self-understandings of men and women, what is masculine and feminine, thus shaping gender identities.

Ethical closure in organizations[5]

An important field that has attained considerable interest during recent years is ethics. Within a cultural perspective it is not the development of ethical principles for solving moral conflicts in various business situations that are of interest, but how moral consciousness is being shaped in social contexts.

Jackall's book *Moral Mazes* shows that managerial occupational ethics, at least in the USA, is primarily shaped by the oppositional forces of the, on one hand, need to conform to internal pressures towards instrumental achievement and adapt to organizational politics, and, on the other hand, external pressures to 'look good' and comply to broadly espoused moral ideas in the face of the public. In particular, he points at and explores the enigmatic and highly ambiguous moral terrain managers face, and their habitual and routine ways of coping with it. Contrary to common belief, Jackall claims, are bureaucratic contexts not morally objective, neutral or indifferent:

> Bureaucratic work shapes people's consciousness in decisive ways. Among other things, it regularizes people's experience of time and indeed routinizes their lives by engaging them on a daily basis in rational, socially approved, purposive action; it brings them into daily proximity with and subordination to authority, creating in process upward-looking stances that have decisive social and psychological consequences; it places a premium on the functionally rational, pragmatic habit of mind that seeks specific goals; and it creates subtle measures of prestige and an elaborate status hierarchy that, in addition to fostering an intense competition for status, also makes the rules, procedures, social contexts, and protocol of an organization paramount psychological and behavioral guides. (Jackall, 1988: 5–6)

Jackall shows the problems in acting in accordance with high or consistent moral principles in the US corporate world. Dealing with morally sensitive issues – typically having negative consequences such as increased costs, bad publicity or counteracting the personal interests of senior managers in the company – is like walking on a mine field. Being explicitly moral is viewed as an indication of reduced reliability in a corporate world in which ambiguity and politics call for flexibility, teamwork, pragmatism and a willingness to support one's superiors and other people in the organizational network. A person insisting on high-profile moral standards is less likely to be described as courageous and with high integrity than as having a rigid mind, being religious about the issue or a troublemaker. Most companies do respect personal convictions such as unwillingness to work with products for the nuclear industry, but this is still seen as a source of doubt. When people want to raise moral issues, one rule for getting acceptance is to couch them in business language, Jackall says. One may argue against the use of bribery by saying that it is unfair business and point at avoiding negative publicity as a reason for reducing pollution, for example. Jackall argues that corporate values typically minimize moral issues as a legitimate concern. Moral problems still regularly turn up and must be faced, thereby creating all kinds of pitfalls for the people involved.

A study of moral issues and reasoning in Swedish mass media companies, in particular a newspaper, also indicates a highly constrained view on ethical issues (Kärreman and Alvesson, 2000). Moral dilemma is often framed – reduced – into the question whether one should provide material that identifies the people in a story, or not. (Swedish mass media is much more inclined to respect private life than e.g. the UK counterpart.) This seems to be *the* ethical question for journalists we studied. However, as some informants made clear, journalistic ethics covers more than name publishing:

> There exist a well documented and elaborated ethical responsibility, codified in the rules of the games. They are the ethical foundation for the trade.... They are developed in a collaboration with several stakeholders; the union, the owner's organization and the publisher's club [a professional organization]. It is part of the freedom of press-articles in the constitution, that the press is self-regulated, rather than government-regulated. And it regulates issues of name publishing. It regulates the separation between editorial content and advertising. And it concerns the journalist's integrity, how involved one can be – which means that one cannot. (Morning paper senior columnist)

Name publishing, editorial purity and integrity (in the sense of not having a personal interest in a subject matter). Put bluntly, it is around these issues that Swedish newsmakers are expected to develop a professional conscience, guided by agreed-upon 'rules of the game'. These are the issues that are generally perceived as relevant for the occupation, ethically speaking. Ethical issues are seen as regulated by a set of written rules. Ethics is thus viewed as compartmentalized to certain issues and taken care of in a bureaucracy-like form.

Journalists do not generally claim that these issues exhaust the realm of ethics. However, it is quite clear that other issues, at least those the outsider would expect to have ethical relevance for journalists, have a difficult time to make it as issues that are relevant for the profession. Such potentially relevant issues include respect for private life rather than intruding and exploiting it, telling the truth (as far as possible) rather than producing half-truths, misleading or questionable information or even lies, illuminate important phenomena (thus serving society and democracy or informing the public of global problems) rather than focusing on nonsense (such as celebrity gossip or fairly trivial mistakes or immoral behaviour by politicians). Journalists do not necessarily deny that these issues are ethical issues. But they are not considered to be particularly relevant for the profession – at least not on the workplace level – in the sense that they are issues that regularly are intraprofessionally considered from an ethical point of view. Issues that concern violations of the integrity of individuals, such as lies and rule- or norm-breaking behaviours by famous people, are rather considered as useful ingredients in newsworthy stories. They allow journalist's to cast the story from a moral point of view, but this point of view is not typically used to inform and evaluate professional conduct. They are, in that sense, 'dead' as ethical issues.

We can conceptualize this minimization of the area of recognized ethical issues and a disinclination to raise ethical problems or to engage in reflection and dialogue about these as *ethical closure*. Ethics is then viewed as belonging to private life, only exceptionally to be considered in the business world. The process of ethical closure relies heavily on reifying practices. This is beautifully illustrated in the newsmaker context by the way ethical judgments are converted into rules of the game. As such, they are looked upon as bureaucratic protocol, to be followed or bent, rather than a particular perspective on the human existence.

> The journalistic ethics in use in Sweden is, more or less, a following of rules. So it is not, apart from a historical point of view, based on moral judgment. Everything is put together in a pamphlet: this is what you are allowed to do. The limits and boundaries are expressed there, everything is regulated in there. Everything, from Freedom of Press-bills to the ethical, moral rules of the game, as they are called, and which really is nothing but recommendations. (Evening newspaper editor-in-chief)

The codified, and almost formal, nature of 'the rules of the game' makes them impersonal and lends them a pretence of objective existence. The reference to extra-personal institutions (unions, employer organizations, professional organizations, and legislative bodies) as key guardians of the book of rules further detaches them from their origins as outflows of concrete human judgement, thus making them appear more 'objective' and less part of subjective human experience. Morality is here based on the seemingly superior rationality of certain institutions. As a consequence, moral judgement becomes an exercise in converting rules into practice; into yet another area regulated by bureaucratic protocol.

Usually, this makes it easier for newsmakers to instrumentalize themselves in their professional role: they view themselves as instruments of the trade. This view substitutes the notion of being a human agent, guided by conscience and practical reason, with the notion of being a functional utility regulated by external constraints. They are 'the messengers, not the message', and they are 'only printing stuff people want to read'. They are no longer full humans in the sense of bearers of moral consciousness: they are conduits of information and mere expressions of supply and demand. As a medium linking more powerful forces one's moral agency become minimized. This means the projection of moral responsibility to others and a retreat from any exercise of moral judgement in an organizational context.

This mechanism, once again in no way restricted to Swedish journalists, is also strong in Jackall's case studies and is nicely illustrated by the following statement of a UK manager, who in the interview first speaks in favour of environmental issues, and then adds:

> But it is not for me to bring personal prejudice or my own opinions into the marketplace. What's important from my point of view is to reflect my customer's requirements. So whatever I happen to think is irrelevant. I must give the customers what they require. (Fineman, 1998: 243)

Here, the marketplace and customers' requirements are constructed as standing above prejudices or opinions. Customers' requirements are presumably partly based on their 'prejudices' and 'opinions'. The moral is that one should not let one's own prejudices and opinions interfere, but obey what may equally well be referred to as the 'prejudices' and 'opinions' of others. This is not, however, typically viewed as a moral standpoint. It involves a claim of the moral superiority of being amoral to positions in which a certain conception of what is right and good is acted upon. The customer as king motto could be seen as cultural value that includes a distinct ethical position, legitimating retreat from active ethical reflection on specific issues, and as a personal prejudice and opinion actually brought into the marketplace. That this opinion about the moral superiority of letting the market decide is broadly shared does not, of course, change this.

The empirical work in this field indicates the predominance of cultural values embracing a primarily amoral view on organizational life in many organizations. People in organizations, in particular managers, tend to avoid moral reasoning or the use of explicit moral vocabulary. The meanings ascribed to organizational arrangements and acts are thus only exceptionally based on ethical considerations and the language of ethics saved for more ceremonial circumstances (such as official corporate statements on ethical rules). Cultural values and meanings creating ethical closure or ethical minimalism involves self-discipline and a highly constrained way of relating to social issues, counteracting autonomy and responsible stances in business and working life, and are thus important to critically scrutinize. Even if an organizational culture characterized by ethical closure facilitates the smooth and profitable operation of business and organizational life, the negative consequences of ethically dubious practices and arrangements for various stakeholders can be significant.

Corporate culture and closure at Pepsi Cola

I will now go somewhat more into depth with a particular case illustrating domination in a cultural form. The case illustrates how performance-orientation and reduced autonomy – culture as powerful guideline for how to think, feel and act as well as a prison-like web of meaning – can co-exist.

The case is Pepsi Cola, as described by the former vice president John Sculley (1987). In a chapter with the headline 'bootcamp' he provides a dramatic account of the tight atmosphere and intensively communicated ideals, norms and symbolism of the company. A ritual among the top marketing people in Pepsi Cola described illustrates how a ritual may work.

Like other meetings, this one was a ceremonial event. We marked it on our calendars many weeks in advance. Everyone wore the unofficial corporate uniform: a blue pin-striped suit, white shirt, and a sincere red tie. None of us would ever remove the jacket. We dressed and acted as if we were at a meeting of the board of directors. (p. 2)

People entered the room in hierarchical order. First came people from the marketing investigation consultancy company, then junior executives entered the room and subsequently senior managers arrived in order corresponding to their ranks. Corporate formality dictated where people sat. The company's top officers gravitated to the front of the table, the junior executives toward the back. The core of the meetings was the monitoring of results. These monitoring sessions were often harsh:

These sessions weren't always euphoric. Often the tension in the room was suffocating. Eyes would fix on Kendall (the chairman) to capture his response at every gain or drop in every tenth of a market share.... An executive whose share was down had to stand and explain – fully – what he was going to do to fix it fast. Clearly in the dock, he knew that the next time he returned to that room, it had better be fixed.... Always, there was another executive in the room, ready to take your place. (p. 4–5)

Pepsi is described as a place characterized by heavy, but fair and open internal competition. Frequent, short-term, precise measurement of results – in particular market shares were focused – meant that the contributions of executives were perceived as easy to determine. This was a workplace for the best and the brightest and also the toughest. War metaphors were frequent. Managers describe themselves as the Marine Corps of the business world. They are physically and mentally very fit. In the 'Cola wars' – the intensive competition between Coca and Pepsi about market leadership – there were many 'victims', but people did not complain. All this according to Sculley's book.

Can we trust his book? It is hard to tell. It is clearly Sculley's account, but Pepsi and Apple – the company he went to after the years at Pepsi – and specific people and events there are mentioned and the author has strong reasons not to say something that a large group of people could protest against or witness that this is simply wrong. Sculley also refers to and discusses a number of mistakes he made. In accounts like this, we must consider a number of biases. One is the author and his apparent interest in appearing in a particular light and also to produce a favourable picture of the company he or she currently works for.

Sculley emphasizes the importance of loyalty and gives a lot of space to account for his problems and pains in resigning from Pepsi Cola and not to any more work for the chairman of the company to whom the ties are described as very close. Even more detailed and personal is the account of how he was forced, as he puts it, to get rid of Apple's founder Steven Jobs. One can read the book as a confession where he tries to convince the world about his moral qualities in the light of suspicion for lack of loyalty and trustworthiness. But these qualities seem mainly to characterize relations to very senior people. He mentions, in passing, that he fired four assistants, apparently without any hesitation or need to motivate why in detail. This is used as an indication of his result-orientation and impatience with substandard performance. A certain 'misfit' between how relations to senior, powerful people are characterized by a lot of loyalty and great care on the one hand, and a somewhat more cavalier attitude to at least some subordinates can thus be detected.

Another issue worth paying attention to when evaluating the book concerns the limited outlook of the author. He talks about the corporate culture of Pepsi Cola, but he mainly describes a version of how it may have appeared for successful senior managers. The organizational life of less senior people may have appeared quite different from the one at the executive suite of the 'elite' he refers to.

A third aspect concerns the American character of the book. It clearly reflects US business ideas and societal values, one may even say mythologies about success and masculinity, and about how brightness and a strong will – rather than politics, chance and luck – determines glory and results. To fully understand the meaning of Sculley's metaphors I guess that good knowledge about US society is called for. For a Swede, at least, the idea of viewing salesmen of sweetened water as the Marine Corps appears slightly ridiculous, but it may make more sense for Americans.

A fourth aspect concerns the business motive of the author and how this may have led to a particular framing of Pepsi. Sculley presents this company as the old business world before he moves to Apple, which he was CEO of at the time of the production of the book. Pepsi can be seen as used in order to frame Apple. It is then the Other, invoked and described in a way that makes what is to be understood and appreciated appear in a particular light. Against the efficient-oriented, but rather stuffy Pepsi we discover the nature of the highly innovative, progressive company of today and the future – Apple.

All these aspects are, of course, highly relevant from a cultural point of view, but one must then bear in mind that they do not target the corporate culture of Pepsi Cola, but give clues to understanding aspects of the contemporary business world more broadly and how this is presented in public.

Leaving the possibility that the text is best viewed as fiction, entertainment, a confessional tale or the marketing of Apple, and instead addressing it as a witness to some aspects of executive corporate life at Pepsi Cola in the late 1970s, let me offer a few interpretations of the case.

From a technical-instrumental point of view, the case gives us some clues to the success of Pepsi at that time. The values, norms and symbolism apparently had effects on motivation, emotions and identity. People felt pushed to do their outmost – to focus strongly on results, work very hard and give relatively little consideration to other values of work and extra-work life. Friendship relations and social support behind what strictly instrumental considerations called for did not seem to matter that much. Also family life appeared to be fairly marginalized. Emphasis on competition – between and within the company – supported by rich vocabulary and rituals giving this a strong presence appealing not only to the abstracted calculator, but the energized, feeling person strongly identifying with a masculine character oriented to prove his worth, appears to do the trick.

We can, of course, also raise some hesitations to these arrangements, values, norms and understandings. Fierce competition obstructs cooperation, people may combat each other, experience an impoverished work situation, work too hard, being too heavily focused on short-term results, etc. The corporate culture may appear as outdated and have less appeal to younger generations. The exaggerated masculinity is hardly in line with equal opportunity ideals and female talent may easily be lost.

From an emancipatory point of view, the comments just made – in particular its gender bias – is of relevance, but other aspects are more important to bring forward. Here it is interesting to note how embraced the executives of Pepsi seem to be. There is little of reflection or doubt about the meaning or purpose or any of all the rigid rules around the game. People seem to be caught in an almost totalitarian ideology in which any sacrifice for the cause – increasing market shares and being promoted – appear to be self-evident. The executives participate in rigid rituals as if programmed in detail. The verbal metaphors – taken from the military and sport fields – the strict clues for physical appearance and the hierarchy-reinforcing meetings all interact in creating and colonizing a closed mind of the masculine, docile, performance- and career-fixated subject. I may be exaggerating, but Sculley's description points in this direction.

It is worth confronting the engagement and energy of Sculley and his co-executives with what the company accomplishes. One could not imagine a scientist being about to finding a cure for cancer or a person in an aid organization trying to rescue a number of people from disaster being more committed or experiencing greater meaning or value than the 'heroes' of the case. And for what? At the end of the day Pepsi's 'substantive' contribution to human kind is partly about negative effects on health, teeth and self-esteem. The effect on self-esteem needs perhaps to be explained: the massive promotion directed to teenagers in which young, beautiful, happy youngsters in fantastic scenarios are portrayed is powerful and trigger responses through the discrepancy behind this ideal picture and the self-understanding of most young people. This discrepancy increases the vulnerability of the self and a fluctuating self-esteem (Lasch, 1978).

I feel almost inclined to do as Braverman (1974), having the capitalist worried about productivity increases 200 years after the industrial revolution in mind, quoting King Ahab from the Bible: 'my means are wise, my goals are insane'.

Conclusion: Methodology for critical inquiry

A major motive for a cultural approach to management and organization is its emancipatory potential. Culture bears the imprint of power. Actors, more or less intentionally, use culture in the exercise of power. At the same time all people are to various degrees subordinated to the constraining effects of taken-for-granted assumptions and meaning patterns. Culture can be seen as world closure, reducing reflection, questioning and dialogue. There are thus strong reasons for the critical illumination of various cultural ideas and manifestations in business and organizations. This approach to culture may be seen as more relevant or useful for a person in an academic or academic-like context – a research or a student project or an ambitious consultancy investigation – than for a member of a work organization. Space for deep reflection but also for the thinking and possibly speaking out of non-conformist talk certainly encourages critical thinking and its application in the form of communication of critical insights. But also for reflexive practitioners critical cultural thinking is an option. If the organizational situation is too negative to any airing of the concerns following critique of ethical concerns, such as overt or covert sex, age or race discrimination, environmental pollution or waste, manipulative commercial practices, etc. then it may be wise to exit the organization.

Arguably, research and education should not only contribute to increased effectiveness, but improving corporations may also include the ethical qualities of organizations – capacity for, attention to and space for reflections, clearsight and dialogue within the workplace.

Much thinking, writing and efforts to use ideas on organizational culture draw upon a compass metaphor for culture. Through visions, ideals, values and norms the employees are united and guided in the right direction, it is assumed. Of course, there may be a misfit between culture and strategy, or environmental changes may call for cultural change, so occasionally the culture compass needs to be repaired – the task of a competent top management possibly supported by consultants. But the route that the compass shows may be inherently problematic. It may be so in relationship to performance and profit objectives, but also in relationship to other legitimate concerns. The value set of hedonism, consumption, exploitation of nature is frequently coherent with financial performance ideals, but they may well contradict ideals such as autonomy, environmental protection and non-materialistic values. The culture compass may guide people into life projects that are not necessarily satisfying and developing in the long run. Perhaps more frequently than culture framing thinking and objectives in a 'bad' direction, the culture compass indicates arbitrarily a particular route and provides a false security. It closes the world for unprejudiced inspection. We should not be dismissive about this need for security and stability in life. We certainly need some sense of order and direction and as this needs to be shared by others there are limits to the openness with which we can approach social reality. Sometimes managerial action to reduce such openness and variation at the organizational level is needed for practical and existential-psychological reasons. But this is not the sole relevant 'need' and the opposite may favour informed choices. Also, cultural studies may inspire the disclosure of the world through directing critical attention to ideas, beliefs, values and meanings that are evaluated to be (a) taken-for-granted and frozen, and (b) repressive and unnecessarily constraining.

From an emancipatory point of view then, less of cultural closure and more eye-opening ambitions and insights should govern research, education and cultural thinking in organizations. The conceptualization of culture as a psychic prison, a set of blinders or source of domination is then accompanied by a cultural research project of de-familiarization, disclosure and eye-opening. Realism and modesty about these ambitions should not prevent us from acknowledging that this is a powerful rationale for thinking culturally.

Notes

1   For discussions and criticisms of the various concepts of power, see e.g. Clegg (1989), Clegg and Hardy (1996), Hardy (1994) and Lukes (1978).

2 There are, of course, authors that treat power in a more liberal way, trying to be neutral about power and its effect, expressing a kind of 'some win-some lose' mentality, reflecting a misleading view of social science as neutral, impassionate in relationship to different social actors, ideologies and interests (for a critique, see Alvesson and Willmott, 1996). I – and a great many authors – prefer a sharper concept of power connecting this with constraints and domination. Power is not necessarily bad and it can't be avoided, but an interest in emancipation calls for a questioning-sceptical rather than a 'neutral' approach.

3 This section is based on Alvesson and Billing (1997).

4 These jobs are, of course, also sex-typed. That the jobs are sex-typed according to a male/female dichotomy co-exist with a much more varied gender symbolism. The masculinities, typically ascribed to the work of a fireman and a postmortem examiner, respectively, have little in common.

5 This section draws upon Kärreman and Alvesson (2000).

7 Multiple-level Shaping and Ambiguity of Culture

Frequently the term organizational culture is used to indicate a view of organizations as typically unitary and unique, characterized by a stable set of meanings. Most organizations are then viewed as mini-societies with a distinct set of meanings, values and symbols shared by, and unique for, the majority of the people working in the organization. This view is in several ways problematic. It can be challenged with arguments from below as well as from above. The challenge from below emphasizes the pluralism of organizations: different groups develop different outlooks on the world. This is often referred to as organizational subcultures. The challenge from above point at the powerfulness of ideas, values and symbolism shared by broader groups of people, associated with civilizations, nations, regions, industries and occupations. Taken together this means that the local as well as more macro contexts need to be considered to understand cultural manifestations at the organizational level.[1]

In this chapter the question of focus in cultural research will be pursued further and micro and macro 'forces' will be investigated. Related to this fundamental issue of the level of culture are aspects such as what are the key elements in the production and reproduction of cultural manifestations in organizations? What are the 'major driving forces' behind the shared understandings, beliefs, values, and norms in an organization or a part of it? Are these shared orientations locally produced by work groups, engineered by management or imported from macro level 'units' such as society or occupation?

Partly concomitant to the issue of how cultural manifestations can be related to a variety of levels or sources of culture shaping organizational life is the need to unpack culture as a stable set of meanings and values. Arguably cultural manifestations are far from always neatly organized, values not easily ranked and cultural ideas may be unsystematic and incoherent. The complexity and dynamics of organizational life and the multitude of culture-shaping forces affecting organizations call for the appreciation of variation, fragmentation and incoherence. Ambiguity and contradiction thus become vital aspects of organizational culture.

The appeal of 'pure' symbolism uncoupled from material practice

A lot of the interest in, and hopes attached to, the idea of organizational culture as a vital element in management control is related to the attraction of (a) the possibility of moving the entire organization in a similar direction and (b) to do so through idealistic means (ideas, values). This has led to great efforts in managing specific, often strongly visible and explicit forms of symbolism and a lot of talk about visions and corporate values. The significance of such 'substantive' activities as productive work, the structuring of tasks, the formalization of procedures, the technical and bureaucratic control of work, cost management and the reproduction of power relationships is often neglected. It seems to be widely assumed that symbols and meaning in work organizations and vision talk can be understood without paying much attention to the specific work context, i.e. what people actually do. Instead corporate culture is viewed as effective throughout the organization despite – or because – of very general and vague messages. Paradoxically, the emphasis on instrumental values that we have noted goes hand in hand with a neglect of 'core' or concrete instrumental activities associated with work and labour processes.

Within management and organization theory there is a strong interest in vision and values talk and less of interest in what this talk actually leads to, if anything. Researchers

> focus heavily on the rhetoric of spokesperson and its interpretation and seem to ignore the actual settings within which normative control is formulated and applied and its meaning for those for whom it is formulated. There is scant contextual evidence concerning the use of ideology, its meaning in the context in which it is used, the practices associated with it, the nature of life supposedly resorting to normative control, and the consequences for individuals. (Kunda, 1992: 16)

This rhetoric is frequently targeted at the entire organization and consequently very general and vague. A typical example is the 'vision' of Iacocca, addressed in Chapter 5. Whether this kind of message has an impact on broader groups of people in the everyday work situations cannot be assumed.

Using the culture concept and borrowing from anthropology – at least in terms of jargon – organization theorists have discovered new aspects of organizational life to study: jokes, coffee breaks, the way people dress, the functions or consequences of the corporation's Christmas party, seating arrangements at meetings, the 'rite' of firing people, the stories told about present and former figures of authority, and so on (e.g. Boje, 1991; Dandridge, 1986; Martin *et al.*, 1983; Trice and Beyer, 1984). The content and form of these activities and behaviour often seem to be considered of some importance in themselves, that is, viewed as contributing to the forming of organizational life (through their sense-making, meaning-creating, norm-setting, and spirit-enhancing capacities). Sometimes, in contrast, they appear to be viewed as an important source for the illumination of culture but not necessarily of any significance in themselves.

The relationship between a particular cultural manifestation and broader cultural patterns may be weak and uncertain. This possibility is neglected in the literature focusing on a single symbolic element. Martin *et al.* (1983: 439), for example, report that 'stories were selected because they generate, as well as reflect, changes in organizations', but this one-to-one relationship between organizations and stories cannot be assumed. The degree to which a story mirrors an organizational culture must be an open question. An organizational story may give us a limited and misleading impression of the larger setting in which it is told, especially if this setting is equated with the entire organization. It may not represent that much beyond 'itself'. Martin's later writings clearly support this view; we have already examined her view of culture as non-ordered and contradictory (Martin, 1992; Martin and Meyerson, 1988). Another possibility is that stories provide an ideologically biased view 'by mediating "realistically" between organizational members and their perception of the organization, constructing a reality that serves the interest of only a handful of organizational members' (Mumby, 1988: 114).

From this we can conclude that in order to get at the significant aspects of organizational culture – the meanings, understandings, and symbols that are most vital for members of the organization in developing orientations within their communities and work settings – great care must be taken to include those expressive and symbolic forms that are related to everyday life thinking and feeling, i.e. the cultural reality in which people live.[2] Such a focus may, as will be elaborated below, be more connected to a group within an organization and not necessarily be equated with the organization as a legal entity. One may, as also will be considered later in this chapter, advocate a more fragmented, postmodernist picture of the cultural aspects of organizations (see, e.g. Calas and Smircich, 1987; Linstead, 1993; Linstead and Grafton-Small, 1990), in which the assumption that a cultural manifestation will reflect a broader totality becomes even more dubious. More about this in the final part of this chapter.

Some of these problems follow from the seductiveness of anthropological concepts (Helmers, 1991), but perhaps mostly from the, for managers, very appealing idea of accomplishing wanted outcomes through such inexpensive means as visionary talk and engineered symbolically loaded events. Rather than limiting the scope of the cultural approach, it is more reasonable to shift its focus from what may be fairly peripheral aspects of organizational life to the activities central to the work of the organization or a specific group of people within it. Organizational culture research should benefit from less attention to 'pure' symbols loosely linked to everyday social and material conditions and more attention to the latter, where the culture approach can illuminate the more important aspects of organizational life.

A greater interest in labour process and the interaction settings of everyday work life may then make a cultural approach better equipped to understand what employees, beyond senior managerial groups, feel to be important in organizations.

Taking work and social interaction into account

A redirection and extension of a cultural approach would cover potentially more important aspects of organizational life than are focused in the idealistic streams of culture thinking:

> In anthropology, where the concept is most fully developed, culture concerns all aspects of a group's social behaviour.... Applying this anthropological approach in corporations leads one to study participants' views about all aspects of corporate experience.

These would include the work itself, the technology, the formal organization structure, and everyday language, not only myths, stories, or special jargon. (Gregory, 1983: 359)

It is of course impossible to consider all aspects of organizational life simultanously, but it is important to avoid a systematic selectivity that neglects common experiences of organizational life. Cultural manifestations are 'not generated in a socioeconomic vacuum, but are both produced by and reproduce the material conditions generated by the political and economic structure of a social system' (Mumby, 1988: 108). In particular, the type of work people are engaged in and the conditions under which it is carried out interplay with culture, i.e. there is 'interaction' between behaviour, material conditions and cultural meaning. Job content, work organization, level of skills, hierarchical position, differential opportunities, and the demands and patterns of interaction in different groups and strata should all be carefully considered.

Work conditions and culture

Focusing on the cultural aspects of people's work situations may lead to reduced interest in phenomena such as stories or jokes communicated by managers as a means to influence people. The point is whether these are 'picked up' in everyday work settings.

Everyday work activities and material circumstances of the majority of employees are frequently 'protected' from the powerful impact of at least senior managers and centralized efforts to engineer corporate culture. The specific work context affects values, beliefs, cognitive styles, opinions about work and the company, etc. According to organizational and work psychology, the content of work, including its skill level, variety, scope, degree of freedom, and perceived significance, is important for job satisfaction, motivation, mental health, and off-the-job behaviour (Gardell, 1976; Hackman *et al.*, 1975). The intellectual complexity of work content seems, for example, to affect values on authoritarianism and belief in the possibility of influencing one's life situation (Kohn, 1980). There is also some evidence that the degree of discretion in the job has an impact on the general level of activity/passivity in and outside the workplace (Karasek, 1981; Westlander, 1976). These influences mainly address the level of individual reactions, but may indirectly affect the cultural characteristics of the workplace.

Whereas culture can be seen as the medium through which people experience their environment and organize everyday life, it is related to the material basis for existence and social interactions connected to these – work activities and concrete social relationships (cf. Foley, 1989; Löfgren, 1982). Cultural elements are embedded in both the material situation and the social structures of organizations. To be clear and to repeat one of my key points in this book, this view does *not* suggest that the culture concept in itself covers behaviour patterns, material things, etc. As I have said, culture refers to the ideational level of ideas, understandings, meanings and symbolism. The point is that these cultural manifestations are frequently affected by, anchored in and closely related to sociomaterial reality – they are not freely floating around. On a higher level, the task of an organization appears to affect cultural patterns. This is sometimes self-evident and almost trivial to point at. One example of this is Schein's (1985) in Chapter 3 reviewed example of the chain of stores in which cleanliness was an important value. Hofstede *et al.* (1990) report that four of the six dimensions of the 'perceived practices' which they see as part of organizational culture are related to the organization's task. Given that most organizations do a variety of different tasks – in a hospital, for example, some do cleaning, others drive ambulances and others sit in meetings and talk about plans and budgets – a more specific appreciation of task may be connected even more tightly to cultural manifestations.

There is of course no mechanistic or one-to-one relationship between material and cultural levels. The former affects cultural manifestations, but do not simply mirror material and social conditions. Of course, the meaning given to work tasks, material conditions, etc. is also central and intermesh with how the materiality of work content and labour process contribute to the shaping of consciousness and interpretations of the social world. Materialistic reductionism and mechanical reasoning must be rejected. An example of such reasoning can be found in an article by Jones (1983), which argues that culture is determined by production conditions and that the ways of regulating exchange between employer and employee are contingent on these. He imagines three types of cultures – production, bureaucratic, and professional – that is implied to follow directly from structural features.

The interplay between the material and cultural aspects of the work situation is shown by Burawoy (1979). He studied a factory on the shopfloor level and found, among other things, a work culture built around 'making out' – managing to produce enough to keep the piece rate. This was not only or even primarily a matter of pay; instead, it was an act, a gamble, which reduced boredom and provided a basis for discussion, jokes, and integration among workers:

> Even social interaction not occasioned by the structure of work is dominated by and couched in the idiom of making out. When someone comes over to talk, his first question is, 'Are you making out?' followed by 'What is the rate?' If you are not making out, your conversation is likely to consist of explanations of why you are not: 'The rate's impossible', 'I had to wait an hour for the inspector to check the first piece' ... (p. 62)

The connection between work content, labour process and cultural phenomena may of course be a bit looser and less direct than in Burawoy's study, where the cultural manifestation is a rather direct response to a boring work situation. In other cases, more complex psychological processes account for the creation and maintenance of particular cultural patterns. Anxiety-producing and stressful work such as that in hospitals (Menzies, 1960), psychiatric institutions (Kernberg, 1980), or social agencies (Sunesson, 1981) may trigger emotional reactions leading to or at least reinforcing, for example, social defence-oriented work practices and organizational structures, rigid attitudes to rules, formal procedures, and the reification of patients/clients. The cultural elements are significant in affecting psychological reactions to the task and mediating the implementation of rules, procedures, and other structural arrangements. Of course, forms of anxiety other than those directly related to work tasks and labour processes can also affect culture; being in a risky business can e.g. trigger collective, paranoically coloured reactions which influence understandings, beliefs, etc. (see, e.g. Brown and Starkey, 2000; Kets de Vries and Miller, 1984, 1986).

Also cultural orientations of white-collar workers and professionals, where specific sources of anxiety such as the work with social and emotional problems associated with suffering, pain and death, may be less pronounced, can be understood in the context of the work they do. Lawyers and people in government tax offices seem to develop critical attitudes in relationship to for example managerial ideas and initiatives. Lawyers are used to arguing and taking the opposite position in much of their work – in court and in negotiations – and this seem to characterize their attitudes and orientations more generally in law firms, making management and more ambitious, large-scale cooperation difficult (Winroth, 1999). In a study of tax authorities that I conducted interviewees reported that people regularly working with the critical monitoring of tax sheets were inclined to look for errors and weaknesses also in areas of work other than their 'core tasks'. This sceptical attitude then coloured broader orientations at the workplace and was a significant element in organizational culture. Managers complained that subordinates were difficult to 'flirt with' and to get approval from in for example change initiatives. Something similar can be said about academics. Also among this group, a critical, fault-finding attitude viewed as a vital part of the job put its imprint on the organizational level.

As indicated by these examples, different types of interaction exist between the type of work undertaken and the cultural characteristics of the workplace. My purpose here is not to explain in detail the different types of relationship between work (in the sense of job content and other central dimensions of the total work situation) and culture; I only want to stress the importance of investigating these relationships in organizational culture studies.

The variety of work practices often tend to lead to a variety in cultural orientations within organizations. It seems likely that the marketing research department and the blue-collar workers in the same company will develop at least partly different work cultures, sometimes referred to as subcultures. This is not so much because of the different efforts of the organization's executives to communicate the same appropriate virtues to all concerned as because of differences in tasks, labour process and general working conditions. This may seem trivial, but in the more managerially oriented organizational culture literature it is often not self-evident. But also in academic writings, the work aspect is often neglected. In the collection of papers of Frost *et al.* (1985), based on a conference called 'Organizational culture and meaning of life in the workplace', there is scarcely any mention of labour processes, work content, sociomaterial work conditions, or anything else clearly related to social practice. When, for example, such physical aspects of organizations as architecture are considered, they are often viewed not as sociomaterial situations – the materialization of former activities, functioning at present to restrict or provide opportunity for action (Österberg 1971, 1985) or to influence ideas and meanings – but as clues to values and assumptions (Deal and Kennedy, 1982; Schein, 1985). The impacts of organizational material structures upon ideas and meanings have not been sufficiently considered (Gagliardi, 1990).

An example illustrating my point is the following event in an industrial company. A young worker was asked to report to the marketing manager who tried to persuade him to say 'business' instead of 'product' when referring to the rock drills produced by the company (from Alvesson and Björkman, 1992). It was part of a corporate effort to make the firm more 'market oriented', to make people in production recognize that there are customers buying the 'business'/product, and to create a common orientation across the different areas of the company. This attempt to adopt the term 'business' instead of 'product' encountered sustained resistance from some employees. According to the shopfloor worker:

> Roland (the factory manager) has also been brainwashed with that term. I am convinced that the expression originates from the marketing manager. I have nothing whatever to do with the 'business' rock drill. It is the marketing side which has to do with the business. *There* it is a matter of business, but not *here*. I am not interested in getting closer to the market. I have enough to do as it is. [The marketing manager] tried to impress upon me that it is a matter of businesses, not of the product. He tried to find out what kind of person I am. I thought it was a damned thing to do. His job is to deal with the market. He should not come down here and mess with me, that's the task of my own boss. Roland also thought it was a bit unpleasant. (He was also there). One wonders what kind of people they have up there. (Alvesson and Björkman, 1992: 147)

The worker's strong negative reaction can partly be accounted for by reference to his work situation – it is the physical product that he operates on, not a financial transaction. The term 'business' simply does not appear meaningful and relevant. The effort to impose this kind of meaning on his work experience backfires heavily and the result is the opposite of what the marketing manager wants to accomplish – instead of a common understanding and more appreciation of customers and market considerations, the outcomes are the underscoring of differences in world view, negative perceptions and distance between marketing and production people.

This kind of outcome is presumably not uncommon in efforts to manage meaning and engineer culture in organizations. Managers base their interventions on what make sense for themselves and not for their subordinates, which often backfires.

Work situation and social interaction shaping meaning

One reason why what people do is important for cultural orientations is that it affects interaction patterns. Physical closeness and need for cooperation between workers involved in a labour process is central here. Shared work experiences means frequently the development of shared meanings around work. Work content and labour processes are frequently closely related to specific social interaction processes, which is central in the development and expression of meaning. As Young (1989: 201) puts it:

> It is precisely at this level of everyday, at the level of the detailed social processes informing relationships between organizational interests, that the content of organizational culture is continuously formed and reaffirmed. What appears as prosaic detail is actually the development of norms and values whereby events and relationships in the

organization are given meaning. The mundanity of the everyday is an illusion, for it is within these details that the dynamics of organizational culture come into being and use.

Van Maanen and Barley (1985: 35) suggest that cultural patterns 'cease to exist unless they are repeatedly enacted as people respond to occurrences in their daily lives'.

Studies of shopfloor cultures such as the reviewed one by Burawoy (1979), but also many others, e.g. Collinson (1988) and Linstead (1985), support this position. These studies often deviate from mainstream organizational culture studies both in terms of depth of method (often long periods of participant observation) and in the picture of organizational culture that emerges. Of course, 'organizational culture' here is shopfloor culture, something many writers would call a subculture. However, from a cultural point of view, boundaries are not defined in legal or formal terms, but are based on identifications, interaction and the development of shared meanings and ideas. And frequently a 'unit' such as the shopfloor may then be treated as a 'cultural whole', even though this 'whole' is seldom contradiction-free as other divisions may also be important (as I will elaborate upon later in this chapter).

This then is something quite different from the communication of visions and values to broad and diverse groups from executives. Often executives may be quite remote from what is expressed within work groups and departments at lower levels within the overall organization. Sometimes executives do, however, have an impact across specific social settings and in spite of the lack of everyday or more elaborated interaction patterns with subordinates. Skills in communication and 'charismatic qualities', corporate practices broadly in line with rhetoric and an 'extra-ordinary' corporate situation which captures the attention of employees (crises, success) may contribute to such influence. Systematic and ambitious efforts to control cultural orientations may, as said, also work in this direction. Here corporate ideology may have a far-reaching impact and 'flatten out' variation in meanings and values associated with specific work group experiences associated with material work situation. Such a strong impact from a distance can not, however, be assumed. Typically, groups and occupations engaged in 'natural communication' have a significant say in the development and modification of guiding ideas, beliefs and values and they may marginalize any impact from top managers communicating values.

A modest proposal for a redirection of cultural understanding

It is difficult to capture the 'essence' (if there is one) of an organizational culture only or primarily through its 'idealistic' aspects – the realm of 'pure' symbols. A shift of focus in organizational culture research might draw upon a view of culture such as the following:

> The cultural cannot be separated from the social as an independent system. Ideas and beliefs are parts of material existence and of people's everyday life on the labour market and in 'politics'. Culture is a driving force behind social change; people's consciousness is developed in intimate interaction with social pre-conditions. Material is dead and without impact without its cultural meaning. Material is a base for ideas, but without ideas, material does not exist. (Dahlström, 1982: 143)

The main thrust of research might then be shifted along the following lines:

1   From a purely idealistic orientation to a broader emphasis upon the material aspects of organizational life (including the cultural aspects of technology and work, equipment, architecture, etc.).
2   From off-the-job activities such as Christmas parties and other fairly atypical events to *work-related activities* as the focus for examinations of expressions of culture.
3   From the organization (or a particular part of it such as a division or department) to the various communities within it (based on social class, profession, age, gender, etc.) as the point of departure for cultural studies. (Of course, sometimes formal entities and communities may coexist and overlap.)
4   From excessive concern with beliefs and values of a rather abstract nature to an emphasis on social practices as the basis for the reproduction of the cultural attributes typical of a particular natural cultural category. Social practices offer the basis from which beliefs and values can be abstracted, as well as the key theme for anchoring these abstractions.

Needless to say, the shift of focus proposed here is not the same as abandoning studies of 'peripheral' aspects of organizational life. Phenomena 'outside' everyday work activities may be of considerable importance and interest. Management rhetoric and organizational rites may be of significance for the development of broadly shared orientations on issues of common concern, such as 'rules' about social interaction, the general sense of corporate direction, etc. I am more concerned with the lack of balance and, in particular, with the neglect of the link between peripheral cultural phenomena and social practices. The challenge is to relate the study of ceremonies, stories, and other expressive phenomena to what I suspect to be the 'core' aspects of organizational cultures associated with work. This means paying attention to everyday life and the meaning-shaping processes taking place in social interaction. Of course, sometimes leadership involves such interaction and frequently engineering efforts and managerial communication from above are important input to such local, face-to-face interaction; but what takes place at this level means a translation and re-interpretation of 'cultural management', being important for its effects.

Organizational cultural research, in the midst of addressing organizational men/women as storytellers, humorists, rite performers, and myth believers, in short, symbol lovers (cf. Ray, 1986), should not forget that they are also producers and workers. The latter terms are not normally understood as metaphors, but in the sometimes strange world of organizational culture studies they seem to belong to a foreign frame of reference. 'Worker' or 'producer' might (provocatively) be used as a metaphor to throw light on organizational culture.

Conceptualizations of culture in terms of social level

The previous sections led to an interest in what is often referred to as subcultures and this will to some extent be considered below, but I will also move in the opposite direction and address macro aspects of organizational culture. In other words, I will also discuss various ways of conceptualizing culture in terms of the social level concerned. There are different concepts of 'size' involved in talking about culture – for example does the entire organization or a part of it correspond to (what is treated as) a culture or is organizational culture a reflection of society? We can talk about macro and micro/local orientations to organizational culture. The issue of size or level of analysis, I will argue, is related to the way we see the 'engine' behind cultural manifestations.

Level-related metaphors for culture

Let us now return to the question of metaphors for organizational culture. These metaphors are relevant not only to conceptualizing the content of culture, i.e. those aspects of organizational culture that are illuminated by the metaphor, but also to the way cultural manifestation on the organizational level can be understood in terms of the different social entities involved. An overview of different formulations of culture makes this point clear. Some authors see organizations as micro entities embedded in a larger societal culture; others regard the work group as an entire culture with certain idiosyncrasies and strong boundary lines between itself and other groups. Most authors fall between these two extremes. Berg (1982) talks about organizations as 'cultural products', Wilkins and Ouchi (1983) speak of 'local cultures', and Martin *et al.* (1985: 101) of 'umbrellas for (or even arbitrary boundary lines around) collections of subcultures'.

The expressions used for culture frame our understanding of phenomena. Cultural studies are very much a matter of discovering subtle patterns, and our conceptualizations must encourage sensitivity for these. The choice of phrase expresses a particular metaphor of culture and should not be taken lightly. Van Maanen and Barley (1985), for example, explicitly reject the label 'organizational culture' because it suggests that organizations bear unity and unique cultures, something that they find difficult to justify empirically. I agree with their hesitation about the phrase 'organizational culture', if it triggers off associations with 'unitary and unique' cultures. However, 'organizational culture' can be used to signal an interest in cultural manifestations in organizations without any assumption about unitariness or uniqueness, but it must then be supported by clear signals against any such connotations. Parker (2000) is uncomfortable with the term organizational subcultures, as it assumes that organizational culture is the 'natural' starting point for culture talk, which may be quite misleading.

Approaches to organizational culture, in the respects here addressed, can be described in terms of four major dimensions: (1) the degree to which an organization is considered unique and as producing idiosyncratic cultural patterns; (2) the degree to which an organization is seen as a coherent cultural whole; (3) the degree to which it is seen as independent of culture-producing forces external to the organization (societal culture, professional and class cultures); and (4) what is considered the appropriate 'level' for illuminating cultural phenomena (individual, group, organization, society, etc.). The organizational culture literature earlier commonly assumed the existence of a local culture covering the entire organization that is unique, coherent, and independent and strongly influenced by the founder's ideas, but this has become disputed (Martin *et al.*, 1985). One could argue, however, that an organizational culture can be unique without being coherent or independent – the combination of different subcultures rooted outside the organization leading to unique patterns and dynamics with a strong 'local touch'. This presupposes that the subcultures interact rather than exist independently and isolated within the organization, for example, in different departments or on various levels in the hierarchy.

Whereas the phrase 'organizational culture' or 'corporate culture' in itself – when used as an empirical concept (intended to 'mirror' a certain reality) rather than as a signal of an interest in cultural manifestations in organizations – may lead to assumptions of uniqueness and unity, other expressions suggest other views. Conceptualizing an organization as a 'culture-bearing milieu' (Louis, 1981) is more open-minded and cautious. This is fairly neutral in terms of level and the significance of various 'forces' for culture creation and reproduction. Most studies do give priority to macro or micro issues.

Macro understandings of organizational culture: reflections of societies

A strong case can be made that societies – nations or groups of nations with similar characteristics – put strong imprints on organizational cultures.[3] The idea of an 'industrial subculture' draws attention to the fact that culture most fully corresponds to a society and that the sphere of industry includes 'a distinctive set of meanings shared by a group of people whose forms of behaviour differ to some extent from those of the wider society' (Turner, 1971: 1). Turner's point of departure is his experience that when 'moving from one industrial organisation to another, it is possible to observe certain similarities' which differ from behaviour elsewhere in society. Here the entire industry is conceptualized as a subculture. Individual organizations then may appear as sub-sub-cultures. By drawing attention to the cultural context of the focal object, it encourages a broader view of it.

The so-called institutional theory school emphasize isomorphism, a trend implying that organizations become more and more alike. Meanings patterns are imported from various instances outside individual organizations. For reasons of legitimacy as well as for reason of adapting a cognitive view of the social world as ordered and comprehensible, people in organizations are sensitive to the meanings, ideas and definitions of what is natural, rational and good developed by various institutions, such as professions, state agencies, science, management consultants and so on (DiMaggio and Powell, 1983; Meyer and Rowan, 1977; Scott, 1995). Local meaning creation is thus seen as less relevant, as it is assumed to exhibit fairly little variation. Instead the overall level driving organizations to conformity is viewed as more crucial in order to understand organizational reality. From a cultural point of view – at least as it is used in the present book – institutional theory tends to embrace a rather crude idea of meaning. Institutional theory illuminates structural arrangements (organizational forms, techniques, policies) associated with fairly standardized meanings and constructions rather than the more nuanced and specific meaning-creating processes and symbolism. Institutional theory is not emphasizing interpretive and cultural depth and, as a consequence, may over-emphasize homogeneity and conflate meaning. Nevertheless, it draws attention to valuable macro aspects of meaning creation and the large amount of studies clearly shows the need to go outside the individual organizational level and consider the macro aspects in operation.

Associated with a macro approach is also the long-term history of a cultural tradition putting its imprints on the organizational level. Prasad (1997) shows this nicely in a study of how cultural orientations developed by the first immigrants from Europe, connected to a particular version of Protestantism and a Frontier mentality, still are important in shaping the beliefs, values and norms governing US business, typically favouring white men, and making access to managerial jobs more difficult for women and people from other ethnic groups.

A macro view on organizations does not necessarily mean a neglect of variation within organizations. Quite the contrary, appreciating the role of ethnic groups, classes, gender, age, occupations and other sources of social differentiation that in no way are restricted to be characterizing the individual organization, mean that variation at the organizational level can be taken seriously. Conceptualizing the organization as a 'melting pot for work cultures' (Alvesson and Sandkull, 1988) for example points to the importance of phenomena outside its formal boundaries and how they contribute to create local dynamics, with more or less of unique processes and effects.

Local understandings of organizational culture: subcultures

In contrast to the macro view, a micro or *local* perspective typically views the organization as the macro context and cultures within it as the more important phenomena.[4] Such a local perspective may use the term subculture, but frequently its proponents refrain from explicitly or implicitly giving priority to the organizational level, i.e. defining 'sub' in relationship to it. A local view is closely associated with an emphasis on work context and social interaction, but authors also point at other origins or vital mechanisms for the development of cultural orientations within a specific group of people.

In an influential local approach to culture, Van Maanen and Barley (1984, 1985) call attention to the existence within organizations of groups that have different backgrounds and professional affiliations and high degrees of internal interaction and consequently share rather little. Van Maanen and Barley (1985) argue that 'unitary organizational cultures evolve when all members of an organization face roughly the same problems, when everyone communicates with almost everyone else, and when each member adopts a common set of understandings for enacting proper and consensually approved behavior' (p. 37). These conditions are, of course, rare. These researchers emphasize subcultures created through organizational segmentation (division of labour hierarchically and vertically), importation (through mergers, acquisitions, and the hiring of specific occupational groups), technological innovation (which creates new group formations), ideological differentiation (e.g. when some people adopt a new ideology of work), counter-cultural (oppositional) movements, and career filters (the tendency for people moving to the top to have or develop certain common cultural attributes) (pp. 39–47). Parker (2000) found three major sources of differentiation in his case study organizations: spatial/functional (associated with geographical location and work function), generational (connected to age and length of time in the organization) and occupational/professional.

Van Maanen and Barley (1985) consider their model both structural and interactionist in content, implying that it is not strictly micro: 'theories that treat meaning as pure social construction jump into the centre of the culture-building process and fail to appreciate the fact that people's actions and interactions are shaped by matters often beyond their control and outside their immediate present' (p. 35). They write that 'only when the ratio of intragroup ties to extragroup ties is high will a common frame of reference regarding ecologically based problems be likely to develop among the members of a collective' (p. 34). As a counter-point to the view of organizational culture as unitary, this remark is important and the approach of focusing ties and interactions productive. There is a risk, how-ever, that it directs attention to highly local (group) cultural manifestations and away from the larger cultural context. There is, after all, also communication across different settings and tight interaction is not the only means through which meanings and values are developed, shaped and maintained.

Generally, the idea of a single, organizational level corporate culture, frequently accompanied by the assumption of management being able to shape it, was very popular earlier (e.g. Davis, 1985; Martin *et al.*, 1985). Today most scholars empha-size the presence of subcultures in organizations. Sometimes they are viewed as co-existing with organization-wide umbrella cultures.

Linking subcultures and society

In-depth cultural studies of organizations typically offer a careful investigation of a limited empirical terrain and frequently lead to a strong focus on cultural orien-tations shared by a group within an organization. Only rarely do they not relate cultural elements to what is shared by larger collectives. Exceptions are typically critically oriented studies which relate organizational manifestations to the capi-talist economy or class relations (e.g. Rosen, 1985) or studies involving groups of professionals which clearly are informed by frameworks and ideas originating from broad occupational communities. These are connected or associated with professional schools, associations and informal networks. Cross-cultural studies and institutional studies of course also note the impact of national and/or societal culture on the organizational level, but here there is often limited depth in the understanding of local manifestations as national cultural difference and broadly shared homogeneous patterns are frequently emphasized.

More subtle connections between the local level and the broader context are difficult to detect. The idea of, for example, an industrial subculture and the pos-sibility of there actually being shared understandings, meanings, and assumptions among broader groups is neglected. An example of this may be found in Wilkins and Dyer's (1987) study of a company called Modtek. Founded in 1965, Modtek had developed strong commitment among its employees, who were very productive and rebuffed efforts by the local union to organize them. Around 1980 this situation changed; productivity dropped, and many employees voted to support a union. Wilkins and Dyer argue that the change was partly a result of the founders having built a new luxury corporate headquarters building and withdrawn to some extent from daily contact with the workers and partly a consequence of a decline in profits and the ensuing discontinuation of profit-sharing bonuses:

> The lack of interaction with top management made it difficult for the workers to continue to support the view that they were all 'one happy family'. Thus they sought for an alternative 'frame' to understand the new situation. This alternative frame came from previous experience, from union organizers, and from stories employees had heard from friends who worked in other companies. The new frame that emerged was one that emphasized the adversarial nature of employee–management relations as opposed to the more harmonious feelings of family which characterized the previous frame. (Wilkins and Dyer, 1987)

Wilkins and Dyer talk about 'frames' or definitions of situations and view a change in 'frame' as a cultural change. This approach diverts attention from the broader meanings and understandings best understood on a macro level that inform change in 'frames'. One and the same 'macro culture' can help us make sense of quite different situations. I suggest that a general cultural understanding of employee–employer relations informed these employees' responses to their close relationships with the founders, explaining the notion of 'one happy family' not as a simple reflection of those relationships but as contingent upon the belief that such relationships are usually not 'family-like'. The high degree of commitment and productivity were based, then, on the broader cultural understanding that this situation was exceptional. When these relations were perceived to have changed, a new understanding ('frame') was indeed created, but this cannot be understood on the group level alone. If the employees had not proceeded from certain general cultural assumptions about normality, they might have defined the situation in many ways – for example, judging their employers frauds (finally showing their true character) or crazy, showing erratic and unpredictable behaviour. But after some time of confusion they defined it in a way that was perfectly in line with the general cultural understanding of normal employee–employer relations and called for a union rather than a psychiatrist. The new 'frame' is best understood from the point of view of 'macro culture'; I doubt that the people of Modtek had to hear stories from other workplaces to discover it.

As researchers conducting ethnographic work on organizations get close to the culture and attempt to understand patterns of local meaning and symbolism, what is directly in front of them in the form of interview statements, observed cultural expressive events, and other empirical material often obscures the more distant sources of cultural influence. Informants may not be aware of them. Hannerz (1988: 9) points out the significance of indirect cultural influence: 'There are people in the world who engage habitually only with a rather limited range of ideas, drawn from a handful of nearby sources. But there are also those others whose ideas involve them with much more of the world; those ideas maybe of more kinds, coming directly or indirectly from more sources.' That people can develop similar ideas and understandings without having actually met is clear from the relative ease of interaction of professionals sharing the same scientific paradigm on international scientific conferences. The common work situation and the shared understandings following from similar experiences, the exchange of ideas, and the development of shared frameworks through international publications produce cultural similarities across geographical boundaries in the absence of direct interaction. To understand culture, we cannot limit ourselves to the local level – the ways in which people make sense of the problems they are facing and influence each other through direct interaction. This is, in particular, important from an emancipatory cognitive interest. Broader, historically anchored cultural ideas tend to create unquestioned understandings that restrict our autonomy. Variations on the group and organizational levels may obscure these underlying understandings.

Organization as a site of local culture and reflections of macro cultures

The idea of a unique and unitary organizational culture is contested, then, from two different viewpoints: first, that organizations are basically products of macro-level phenomena (society, class, industrial sector)[5] and, secondly, are normally similar and that variations within organizations are much more profound than unitary patterns because of the diversity of the groups involved. These viewpoints are not contradictory: for example, some of the social and cultural variations within organizations can often be related to similar variations on the societal level. There are several reasons why it is important to consider the relations between organizations and 'macro culture' (national, regional, Latin, Western, late-capitalist, etc.). There is an obvious interplay between these 'entities' in the production of cultural manifestations (Hofstede, 1985). The interesting cultural aspects of organizations are, as we have seen, not what is unique for a single organization, but deeper and broader patterns that to some extent are a part of a more general business, industrial, or societal culture. Understandings of cultural manifestations in organizations should not take the organization as a self-evident starting point. Organizational (i.e. formal) and cultural boundaries cannot be equated. A further reason for understanding the subcultural nature of *all* the cultural manifestations in organizations, even those that are dominant and broadly shared on the local level, is that it makes us realize that management's influence is, after all, restricted. National culture, class culture, and the cultures of professional and occupational communities put strong imprints on organizations.

As many researchers have noted, the view of organizations having unique and unitary cultures is widespread, and it encourages the treatment of their cultural dimensions as closed systems. That people sometimes emphasize the impact of the 'environment' (e.g. crises caused by a changed market situation) on culture does not mean that they advocate an open view of culture in organizations; the 'environment' is viewed here as non-cultural and as affecting organizational culture only through reactions to circumstances and conditions that have consequences for operations. (As briefly mentioned in Chapter 4, in the strategic-management literature there are, however, a few examples that take the cultural nature of the business environment seriously (e.g. Smircich and Stubbart, 1985).) The production of culture in the public sphere, particularly through mass communication (including ideas on management and organization), is of obvious significance. But in organization theory the relationship between 'environment' and culture is normally treated as weak and indirect. Direct and open cultural flows are seldom seriously considered. Research often seems to be guided by an understanding of organizations as 'cultural islands' or 'mini-societies', inherent in the view of organizational cultures as unitary and unique. These are not very good metaphors because they divert attention from the organization's cultural embeddedness and its open relationship to the cultural aspects of its environment.[6] The literature does contain valuable counters to the 'cultural island' metaphor. Meyerson and Martin (1987), for example, consider it 'more informative to define organizational culture as a nexus where broader, societal "feeder cultures" come together', and Beck and Moore (1985) use the phrase 'host culture' to represent the societal context of organizations.

In addition to noting the complicated embeddedness of organizational cultures, it is important to realize that there is seldom a simple way of determining how 'feeder' or 'host' cultures should be conceptualized and demarcated. As Helmers (1991: 65) has put it:

> Recognizing the contours or drawing boundaries of a culture is not only problematic in modern organizational settings – there are international, multicultural organizations, networks of intermarket relations, transorganizational stock-holdings, branches, acquisitions, etc. – it is a problem in the traditional areas of anthropological studies as well. Some people see themselves as belonging to a uniform, dissociate society or tribe, as the Tolai of New Britain or the African Wodaabe would; others assign themselves to certain totems, languages, villages, communities or modes of production (Elwert, 1989). The problem of perception is the same in both cases.

One way of handling the dynamics between organizations and their cultural environments might be to talk about *cultural traffic*. Such traffic includes, but is not restricted to matters of organizational demography such as recruitment, selection, and socialization of newcomers and people leaving the organization. It is a matter of members being citizens and as such influenced by societal culture. Changes regarding environmental protection, gender and ethnic relations, age, attitudes to work, new ideas on business and management, and so on, affect people not only outside but also inside their workplaces. Cultural traffic is a key feature of modern organizations, counteracting any unity and unique character and limiting the influence of management.[7] This theme will be developed in the next chapter.

Ambiguity and contradiction: a plurality of values and commitments

There is an increasing awareness about the multiplicity of cultural orientations in organizations. Not only the idea that a single, overall organizational culture creates unity among people in organizations, but also the counter-idea that organizations typically are characterized by stable and well-demarcated subcultures are increasingly being disputed.

Emphasis on ambiguity as a central feature of organizational culture is a response to the dominance of the idea that a culture (or a subculture) is a clear and known entity that creates unity and harmony within an organization (or a group within it) and solves problems. Also many authors moving beyond functionalism and embracing an interpretive approach somewhat one-sidedly focus what is shared and how common problems can be handled: 'Through the development of shared meanings for events, objects, words, and people, organization members achieve a sense of commonality of experience that facilitates their co-ordinated action' (Smircich, 1985: 55). 'In crude relief, culture can be understood as a set of solutions devised by a group of people to meet specific problems posed by situations they face in common' (Van Maanen and Barley, 1985: 33). Schein's (1985: 149) assertion that 'all definitions of culture involve the concept of shared solutions, shared understandings, and consensus' represents the old mainstream view, but is incorrect in so far that many authors and definitions do *not* emphasize broadly shared consensus. In several writings, Martin (1987, 1992, Martin and Meyerson, 1988) has emphasized an ambiguity perspective on culture. (In later writings she talks about fragmentation instead.) She points to the 'black hole' in our definitions of culture produced by the exclusion of ambiguity – uncertainty, contradiction, and confusion. Instead of culture creating order, it is rather seen as disorder.

This interest in ambiguity can perhaps be seen as a reflection of the *Zeitgeist*. So-called postmodernism – which stresses uncertainty, paradox, problems of representation, etc. and can be described as 'an assault on unity' (Power, 1990) – is very popular both in social science in general (Featherstone, 1988) and in organization theory (e.g. Cooper and Burrell, 1988; Hassard and Parker, 1993).

Martin (1987: 5) suggests that 'descriptions of cultures that excludes ambiguities would be incomplete, misleading, and of very limited utility'. I agree that cultural studies should not equate culture with solutions, clarity, and consensus. Careful cultural research must take contradictions and uncertainties seriously, even within a cultural category, whether it is the organization, the management, the division, the occupational community, the shop floor, or the society. I am, however, somewhat hesitant to give cultural ambiguity the prominence Martin accords it.

Ambiguity as construction

In a sense, issues of uncertainty, contradiction, and confusion could perhaps be studied just by asking people whether they are uncertain or confused. The problem is that on many (non-trivial) issues, most people are neither absolutely certain nor extremely confused. In investigating cultural ambiguity, the criteria are themselves very ambiguous. It is hardly possible to say that if x per cent of the group feels rather or very uncertain about the meaning of y per cent of a set of cultural manifestations (themselves difficult to isolate), then ambiguity is present.

Martin and Meyerson's concept of culture corresponds to a very large number of phenomena: thoughts, feelings, meanings, understandings, official policy, social structure, informal practices, rules. In fact, most of their illustrations of ambiguity are not self-evidently cultural but concern rules and procedures, limited knowledge about what is going on outside one's own level of the hierarchy and the division, criteria for promotion, etc. A more value-oriented example concerns egalitarianism in the company:

> Employees are confused about [the organization's] commitment to egalitarianism. They hear relatively egalitarian rhetoric about the distribution of resources and nonfinancial rewards, open office spaces, consensual decision-making, and lateral promotions. However, their own experiences, and those of other employees, leave them confused about what the purposes of these policies are, whether these policies are desirable, how these policies are implemented, and why. (Martin and Meyerson, 1988: 115)

Egalitarianism is a topic that frequently is characterized by confusion and contradiction. In organizations managers frequently emphasize the family-like, informal and communitarian spirit, but everyday practices and relations often deviate from this ideal (Alvesson, 1995). It can sometimes be debated whether a discrepancy between policy and practice is an example of cultural ambiguity. Ambiguity is a figure (or anti-figure) that emerges against a ground of clarity, and culture emerges against a background of non-culture. The more confusion, contradiction, and uncertainty that we relate to the sphere of non-culture – contingent upon earthquakes, ignorance, structural arrangements, rapid changes in sociomaterial conditions – the less ambiguous culture appears and the less need there is for an ambiguity perspective on culture.

Martin's (1987) empirical material, partly drawing on the writings of others, is somewhat more clearly cultural in nature. One case, originally studied by Feldman (partly published in Feldman, 1991), concerns the US Department of Energy, 'a culture engulfed in ambiguity'. This organization had brought under one roof rather diverse (and partly conflicting) tasks, and changes in the political environment had created much uncertainty. The confusion was reflected in metaphors such as 'a lot of people trying to do a little bit of good – bumping into each other – all on a different wave length – with the same echo system, going crazy' and 'a combination of the Three Stooges Comedy Act, Ringling Barnum and Bailey, a three-ring circus, and five-year-olds playing in a nitroglycerine factory' (Feldman, quoted by Martin, 1987). This view seems to have been widely shared in the department, and Martin concludes that 'ambiguity is a central component of employees' experiences at this agency. Not surprisingly, then, ambiguity is central in the symbolic systems of this culture' (p. 8).

One hardly doubts that the organization can be described in terms of ambiguity, but the symbolic system itself appears to be quite the opposite of ambiguous – the metaphors mentioned indicating a clear and rather consistent understanding of the organization. One gets the impression that the organization's members developed a common understandings about the character of their workplace, e.g. it being circus-like. These understandings were *about* ambiguous situations and conditions, but the cultural level in itself does not seem to have been characterized by confusion and uncertainty – as might have been the case if some people had referred to the department as a well-oiled machine or even as impossible to describe while others had used the metaphors just mentioned.

Again, it is not self-evident how the degree of ambiguity in an organization's culture can be assessed. (Another doubt concerns whether the concept of organizational culture is appropriate in this case – whether the department 'had' an organizational culture.) One could perhaps say that even though structural arrangements and environmental changes had created confusion, the cultural manifestations in the organization reduced the degree of uncertainty, confusion, and contradiction experienced by members – that metaphors and other symbols articulated a shared understanding and helped people anticipate and cope with ambiguity. My point is that ambiguity in structural arrangements and organizational processes does not necessarily call for (or correspond to) a perspective that focuses on ambiguity as an aspect of organizational culture. As was emphasized in Chapter 1, culture and social structure is not the same (Geertz, 1973). Ambiguous social structures may be accompanied by cultural meaning patterns that reflect them in a way that creates shared understandings. Thus a conventional view of culture can deal rather well with many cases of organizational ambiguity.

Uncertainty, confusion, and contradiction, are, moreover, partly a matter of how closely one looks. Cultural manifestations such as myths, rites, stories, etc. are, according to most definitions, ambiguous in themselves (e.g. Cohen, 1974). Even if people are, for example, familiar with a story and share attitudes to it, their interpretations of it may differ. This is to some degree inherent in cultural phenomena and not something about which most researchers are concerned on the level of the collective. On a certain level, however, ambiguity is the very stuff of cultural analysis.

The ambiguity paradigm views organizational culture in itself as ambiguous, and the more closely organizational reality is studied, the more material supporting an ambiguity view appears. Let us continue with Martin and Meyerson's example of an organization's claim to egalitarianism:

> Resources and non financial rewards are supposed to be distributed at OZCO in a relatively egalitarian fashion. However, how one actually obtains a better office space, a nicer desk, or a newer computer (or any other physical object that can have status connotations) is not clear to some employees. Need, status, power and tenure all come into play, but there certainly does not seem to be a formula, even within the divisions. (1988: 113)

On a general level, the ideal of egalitarianism gives some understanding of the organization. On a more detailed level, the situation is, of course, more complicated. That certain things are not clear to 'some employees' or that egalitarianism is not the only source of particular outcomes emerges partly from a closer look at what is going on. From this example it seems that, in order *not* to be ambiguous, egalitarianism would have to be in almost perfect harmony with social practice and the distribution of resources would have to be transparent to nearly all employees. The criteria for avoiding the label of ambiguity are thus rather tough. And a closer look at organizational conditions leads unavoidably to the discovery of at least some elements of uncertainty, confusion and contradiction. This discovery is of course a result of adopting an ambiguity perspective, but also – and this is my point here – of careful and detailed observation.

Ambiguity in organizational culture is thus the outcome of certain features in the world 'out there' but also of what one is looking for and how closely one looks. (So is the case with all phenomena and this is of course not to deny the 'influence of empirical reality' on these perception processes.) To look more closely – and less broadly – at organizations is often fruitful, and I certainly agree that much of the talk about unitary, unique, and harmonious 'corporate cultures' is the result of either brief glimpses or speculation without having looked carefully at all. Nevertheless, there are also problems with a move towards much closer observation, one of which is myopia.

There are, according to many authors, limits to ambiguity in cultural contexts, in a conceptual as well as a practical sense. Conceptually, even though ambiguity may well be an important aspect of culture, it is hardly the dominating one.

> If ambiguity and fragmentation are the essence of relationships, and if the feeble and transitory consensus that does form fluctuates constantly with various forces, there is no culture as most scholars ... define one. (Trice and Beyer, 1993: 14)

Practically, some modest degree of shared meanings is necessary for organizing processes being possible at all.

> What enables culture to arise in such situations is not the pervasive confusion and ambiguity, but the presence of a minimal degree of consensus and clarity about some issues. (Trice and Beyer, 1993: 14)

Advocates of an ambiguity view are definitively correct in pointing at an overemphasis on the degree of consensus and clarity in mainstream organizational culture thinking as well as, in some subculture thinking, a corresponding over-emphasis on strong group boundaries, internal consensus and conflict between groups. The challenge is to consider the frequently *simultaneous* existence of (a) relative clarity and common orientations associated with a degree of shared meanings across the organization, (b) diversity, conflict and multitude of overlapping group identifications, and (c) ambiguity and fragmentation on different levels. The next section will provide a modest proposal in this direction.

Multiplicity and bounded ambiguity

The diversity of groups and identifications with various communities means that there is considerable variation in what sets of meanings and values become salient in people's organizational life in different situations, also on an hour-to-hour basis. As one author comments, 'in the course of work, people walk out of one cultural enclosure and into another at different times of the day and periods of their lives' (Anthony, 1994: 31). This is partly related to the multiplicity of group distinctions, and identifications with associated ideas and values.

> ... the 'culture' of an organization is displayed through a huge variety of contested 'us' and 'them' claims. In some cases the organization will be 'us', but ideas about similarity and difference can call upon other sources as well. (Parker, 2000: 227)

The multitude of issues or areas that people in organizations must address clearly transgresses the idea of a single cultural framework offering sufficient guideline and shared orientation. Cultural ideas on gender and inequality have little connection with cultural ideas on how the targeted market of the company's product should be delimited and understood or which time perspective on performance evaluations are embraced. Of course, there are many issues which only a specific work group or department need to bother about at any depth, but there is also an endless area of issues to which a great many people, from various positions and for various reasons, must develop at least some understanding of in order to have some sense of overall direction and making cooperation across work groups possible.

When a person interacts with union representatives, an informal peer group, at a department meeting, a network of people with the same interest across various formal organizational boundaries, listens to a talk of a senior manager or acts as a representative of the company when meeting a major customer, different identities and work cultures become salient. As Ybema (1996) puts it, 'there are joint occurrences of unity and division in work relations' (p. 40), contingent upon 'the complexity of group membership, the ambiguity of rules and rituals and the coexistence of common and contrastive interests and identities' (p. 43). Experiences of variation, perhaps fragmentation and ambiguity are frequently pronounced, but there are also ideas and meanings binding people together, making various kinds of interactions possible, thus preventing a typical work day from being full of exotic and confusing experiences, calling for time-consuming sense-making in and after every interaction.

Themes like inconsistency and contradictions are important parts of organizational life, but frequently there are shared cultural understandings that regulate these. According to Jackall at least senior organizational participants are capable of dealing with this: 'adeptness at inconsistency, without moral uneasiness, is essential for executive success' (Jackall, 1988: 160). A strong selectivity of those reaching higher corporate office, in which the mastery and use of ambiguity – the capacity to avoid firm commitments in favour of flexibility – is central. There are shared ideas on taboos, hypocrisy, what kind of inconsistencies are 'natural' or 'tolerable' and what crosses a grey zone so that a person becomes perceived as too manipulative or confused and incompetent.

Sometimes there is a lot of acceptance of opportunistic behaviour and little of expectancy of people firmly and genuinely holding on to values and ideals, but still there are cultural rules that offer guidelines for how to relate to this. At least according to a senior manager in a US company interviewed by Jackall:

> The code is this: you milk the plants; rape the businesses; use other people and discard them; fuck any woman that is available in sight, and under your control; and exercise authoritative prerogatives at will with subordinates and other less mortals who are completely out of your league in money and status. *But you also don't play holier than thou.* (Jackall, 1988: 97, italics in original)

There are also, according to the same study, strong cultural ideas about people being loyal to and supportive of their superiors. What is 'right' is what the guy above you wants from you, as one cynical interviewee expressed it. In this kind of organization the formulations of corporate culture that we find in the (pop)management literature, characterized by a lot of nice-sounding values and ideals, is not that significant. It offers mostly a superficial set of guidelines, to be taken moderately seriously, perhaps mainly for junior and middle managers and other persons scrutinized by their superiors and eager to make a good impression for career and other reasons. But (other) cultural meanings still offer, for those being socialized well enough, frameworks and rules for how to deal with the ambiguous, arbitrary and political organizational life. Ybema (1996) notes that people in a company he studied 'were united on how to deal with their conflicts' (p. 56), which means that ambiguity is avoided without either consensus or differentiation dominating.

We can thus talk about *bounded ambiguity*, in which cultures do not necessarily establish clarity, shared orientations and consensus among broad groups of people, but still offer guidelines for coping with instances of ambiguity without too much anarchy or confusion. Bounded ambiguity may mean broadly shared rules and meanings for how to steer around tricky issues, e.g. avoid decision-making or involve as many people as possible in a difficult decision (Jackall, 1988). We can thus say that it offers 'meta-meanings' – clues for how to deal with tricky meanings. It may also mean a preference for vague, positive-sounding vocabulary, a tolerance for a certain, not to say considerable amount of inconsistency and even contradiction without reacting, the use of 'mediating myths' between a strong discrepancy between what is preached and what is practised (Abravanel, 1983). Bounded ambiguity may also take the form of rapid switches between different social identities legitimating various sets of ideas and meanings. A good example of bounded ambiguity is the way people dealt with the business concept in Enator, treated in Chapter 4.[8] The business concept and its meaning and role in the company were ascribed quite different meanings, but these were hardly confronted and implicitly negotiated in order to avoid confrontation. Obvious discrepancies between the espoused business concept and practised business were downplayed and explained away through references to the need to start with less optimal projects and then gradually realize the business concept fully through the cultivation of relationships with the client.

Bounded ambiguity does not mean that experiences of ambiguity are avoided, but that there are shared meanings and efforts to minimize the most disturbing experiences of confusion, contradiction and notorious uncertainty. One element here may be the development of a shared view of the specific issues of ambiguity – as in the case above where people seem to share the meaning and metaphor of circus and anarchy to make sense of the character of an organization, a cultural orientation that acknowledge but also reduce the ambiguity involved.

Summary

Some time ago there was great faith in the idea that whole organizations can have distinct cultures and that top management are central architects behind this; but this idea has lost its credibility. Still this view – sometimes referred to as an integration perspective – seems to dominate in popular and in a few academic management writings. It is often closely linked to an idealistic notion of culture in the sense that a set of overall meanings, ideas and values communicated by senior management will lead to a strong sense of direction and priorities shared broadly within the organization.

Against this idea of the top management-engineered, and organization-driven culture two alternative, but also complementary forms of critique have emerged. One emphasizes work context and everyday life that implies strong variation in complex organizations. It is argued that the specific tasks of work groups rather than the overall business of the company is decisive for the meanings and ideas of various groups. In line with this is also a focus on interaction processes and social identification, which frequently overlaps with work conditions and occupational belongingness. Work situation and group interaction lead to local cultures within organizations, which are differentiated from, sometimes even antagonistic against overall and abstract ideas associated with management rhetoric and other initiatives. The other critique of a unitary and unique, management-shaped organizational culture emphasize circumstances around the specific organization. Organizations are culturally shaped through inputs associated with macro forces and large groups widely distributed throughout various settings. These two approaches do not necessarily contradict, but may go hand in hand. Macro groups such as class, gender, profession, ethnic communities may account for the differentiation within organizations as various groups 'import' ideas, meanings and values into different parts of an organization. They certainly reduce the options for top management to have a strong say about the values, ideas and meanings people develop in their workplaces.

Although I have stressed the neglect of an interest in work – what people actually do in their everyday work situation – also in the interactionist thinking, from the middle of the 1980s onwards there has been a lot of interest in the cultural variation within organizations associated with position, background and interaction patterns. Martin and Meyerson call this a differentiation perspective.

Somewhat later, terms such as ambiguity and fragmentation became popular and any kind of distinct, stable patterns around the entire organization or specific groups or units within it, were disputed. Even more recently also a strong emphasis on ambiguity as a key feature of organizational cultures has attained a fair amount of critique (Parker, 2000; Trice and Beyer, 1993; Ybema, 1996). There seems to be some consensus that the multiplicity of cultural orientations in organizations need to be considered, implying a mix of broadly shared meanings, group-distinct meanings and ambiguity, but also an appreciation of individuals fluctuating between such experiences. Ambiguity and fragmentation are important aspects – of specific cultural manifestations such as symbols as well as of cultures as a whole – but at the same way as there are limits to management control there are also limits to ambiguity. Organizations unsuccessful in shaping even a moderate degree of common understandings on at least some issues and a shared understanding of variation and sources of dispute probably perform badly and may not, in a competitive context, survive. It is even possible to argue that if there is extreme ambiguity, then there is no organization, at least not in a cultural sense. Bounded ambiguity may be a useful concept here, drawing attention to ambiguity but also to the efforts to develop some shared meanings counteracting a stressful and unpractical level of confusion and uncertainty.

Notes

1   The distinction micro–macro is not unproblematic. It is sometimes used as indicating that there is an entity-like reality 'up there', above and outside specific actions and (micro-)actors. Macro entities like the state, the organization, the environment or the market then exercise power or produce constraints. But this is misleading. Macro is better seen as an economic way of trying to capture the myriad of micro events that make up social reality. When we refer to a green movement or environmental consciousness as a macro phenomena affecting at least some organizations, it is the aggregate of various people writing and talking about ecological problems, changes in legislation and changed behaviour – using public transport instead of cars, re-cycling material – that is referred to.

2   I use the term 'reality' with some hesitation, not wishing to suggest the existence of any 'objective' cultural reality. Organizational culture is not a simple mirror of social reality but a framework for understanding. It is, however, important to reflect carefully upon the ideas, beliefs, and values that are important as subjects in organizational life and to distinguish between 'key symbols' – symbols that play a vital role in terms of cognitive mapping, inspiring action, or summarizing emotions (Ortner, 1973) – and less significant ones. This can also be formulated as matter of the connectedness of cultural manifestations in a workplace. Arguably, some cultural manifestations are loosely connected to others.

3   In less 'entitative' terms this could be expressed as the use of a cultural perspective on organizations that should consider the significance of other, broader settings when exploring organizational-level cultural manifestations.

4   The expressions 'macro' and 'micro' are far from unproblematic. 'Micro' is often used to point to a rather detailed level, for example, the individual (Johansson, 1990), whereas the idea of culture applies to a collective rather than to the microscopic level. 'Macro' is used to indicate social phenomena above the individual level. Ouchi and Wilkins (1985), for example, talk about 'macro-analytic theories' and then refer only to the group and organizational levels. 'Macro' used in this way is not 'macro' enough for my purposes, for I want to draw attention to cultural aspects 'above' the organizational level. Talking about 'local' instead of micro culture helps avoiding a sharp distinction between macro and micro. The idea is that the macro and the local perspectives are different but complementary kinds of understandings of cultural phenomena in an organizational context.

5   This could be read as groups in the focal organization adapting the ideas, norms and practices common in other organizations and situations.

6   As pointed out in my previous notes, the societal level is not necessarily best treated as more 'reliable' or 'real' than any other object of analysis. To what extent society is a theoretically fruitful concept or a meaningful empirical entity is open to discussion (Ahrne, 1990). A recent critique of traditional understandings of macro-sociology makes the point that 'the macro appears no longer as a particular layer of social reality on top of micro episodes.... Rather it is seen to reside within these micro episodes where it results from *the structuring practices* of agents' (Knorr-Cetina, 1981: 34). My

position is that we must avoid reification of any of the various 'entities' or levels important for cultural studies of organizations. Drawing attention to macro-level entities such as society, industry, and class will allow us to understand local phenomena in a certain light but not to reduce them to reflections of more 'real' macro structures.

7   Total organizations are an exception to this; some organizations which have only or mainly an internal labour market, such as the police and the military, many Japanese industries, and, to some extent, certain Western industries recruiting mainly from within, are characterized by a rather low degree of cultural traffic, connected to the career trajectories of the employees, although cultural change in society certainly affects these organizations as well. Cultural traffic goes not only from 'society' (societal spheres outside the formal organization focused upon) to the organization but also in the opposite direction. Society is made up of organizations; as Perrow (1986) puts it, 'the major aspect of the environment of organizations is other organizations'. For the individual organization, its environment influences it more than the other way around; in other words, it is the environment (including the 'sum' of other organizations) rather than the (focal) organization that directs most of the traffic.

8   As with much else in contemporary business and organizations, efforts to utilize the business concept for a multitude of purposes – from providing a starting point for strategic management to a resource in market communication and a symbol for employee identification – means that it becomes the object of a multitude of sometimes incoherent and contradictory meanings. The vagueness and fluidity of the language use concerned allows for much flexibility, but parts of corporate practice is viewed as kicking back at the formulation of the business concept. The ambiguity of organizational life and multiple interpretations of corporate reality, partly fuelled by and fuelling this experienced ambiguity, means that the business concept – as other social-integrative means of management control – exists in an unclear social context. In this the dialectics between creating unity, coherence, direction, promise, pride and greatness, on the one hand, and contradiction, confusion, fragmentation, disappointment, conflict and cynicism on the other, easily become manifest.

8 Cultural Change and Conclusions

Reminder of the ambitions of this book

In this final chapter I will further explore and to some extent pull some of the themes addressed in earlier chapters together. The chapter also includes a few summaries of some core aspects of this book.

The overall purpose of this book is to suggest a framework for a sensitized thinking about organization. The concept of culture and in particular the idea of focusing on shared, but also contested meanings as a key dimension of management and organization are vital in such an enterprise. People may develop more or less of intellectual and practical skills in mastery and use of such a framework. A few people are intuitively good at this. Most of us benefit heavily from theoretical support to develop our capacity to interpret cultural phenomena and act in culturally sophisticated ways. This book of course contributes to the intellectual side of working with a cultural understanding. I have used many empirical examples to develop and illustrate ideas on how cultural thinking can be used in managerial and non-managerial organizational practice. I have refrained from suggesting technical rules for actions. On the whole, doing leadership in a culturally sensitive way calls for interpreting and acting in specific unique contexts; following recipes is seldom productive. Examples should be used to inspire learning and insight, rather than be copied.

Throughout the book I have emphasized some key themes in thinking culturally. Perhaps the basic one concerns the need to go beyond the level of the surface – behaviours and other 'external' aspects – and look at how people relate to seemingly objective, accessible and 'practical' matters. The crucial aspect of leadership is not to do things in any objectively 'correct' sense – what matters is how people interpret and relate to the actions.[1] A second basic theme is the dual nature of culture – on the one hand its usefulness for making complex interaction and coordination possible and on the other hand its constraining and repressive side. When providing guidelines and a sense of meaning and direction culture also freezes our world, prevents our imagination and reduces autonomy. A third vital theme concerns the dynamic and messy aspects of culture. Culture is anchored in tradition and frequently changes slowly, but there are many cultural manifestations and people in turbulent and multi-group situations move between them. Belongingness to a multiplicity of groups – organization, profession, age cohort, gender, ethnic community – forms a basis for movements between different sets of meanings in organizations. A fourth theme concerns the multiple levels of culture. Cultural meanings emerge, are shaped, maintained and change in specific interactions between people at the micro-level. But also larger forces – societal cultural traditions, changes of *Zeitgeist*, mass media impact – strongly affect cultural manifestations at the organizational level. Thinking culturally on a multitude of levels is thus called for; also when one is interested in workplace culture it is useful to bear in mind that this is not a cultural island.

This book addresses the advanced academic as well as the reflective practitioner – which of course is far from unproblematic. (The reflective practitioner does refer to a minority of all practitioners – obviously this book is not intended for the businessman wanting to kill a few hours on an airflight.) The specific needs and the time and space for 'deep thinking' are strongly different, but I still suspect that the four key themes just mentioned are valuable for both – for interpreting a wide range of issues in business and organizations as well as for acting upon these.

This chapter will mainly deal with organizational change as a theme for picking up some of the threads of this volume, but I will also address some related topics. First, I will further develop some ideas on the trivialization of 'managing culture' in the writings and teaching of the topic pretending to be management-friendly, in the light of the complexities addressed in Chapter 7. Then the area of organizational change will be discussed rather broadly. This is done in a way incorporating some of the ideas on leadership and management control with insights from critical theory and a multiplicity view on organizational cultures, treated in Chapters 5–7. The final parts summarize the overall approach for cultural thinking developed in the book and further develop the idea of cultural traffic, introduced in the previous chapter.

Against the trivialization of 'managing culture'

As elaborated above, most management-oriented approaches to organizational culture (frequently then labelled corporate culture) put forward a unitary and unique organizational culture that can be shaped by managerial intentions. We can label this the Managerially-led Unitary and Unique Culture (MUUC) view. The ingredients fit together: in order to be managerially led, the employees preferably should share similar characteristics. If not, all managerial interventions become more complicated. When different groups have different cultural orientations, they may respond differently on the same management talk, symbolic acts and material re-arrangements. In addition, a considerable amount of time and effort must be spent negotiating various opinions, dealing with confusions and conflicts emerging from cultural difference. The second U also has implications for the managerial possibilities in leading culture. If an organizational culture is not unique, but bears very strong imprints on meanings and values originating and anchored in families, regions, occupations, societies, etc. there will be considerable normative pressure from groups outside the specific organization, which may counteract and weaken the influence of management. Managers compete with other groups in defining what is correct and good. In organizations dominated by professionals – such as hospitals, accounting and law firms – management typically is relatively weak (Greenwood *et al.*, 1990; Parker, 2000; Winroth, 1999).

Taking differentiation and macro-externally grounded cultural orientations seriously thus make the case of managing culture more complicated. So at least is the case if the ambition is to manage entire organizations. This ambition is clearly dominant in most managerially oriented writings on organizational culture, not only in pop-management books, but also in academic texts. Here the reader is expected to prepare him- or herself for leading big organizations as a top figure. Empirical illustrations typically concern the intentions and actions of CEOs of very large corporations. In a chapter on 'understanding cultural change' in Brown (1995), for example, there are six cases, all with a focus on the top management perspective and initiatives; three of the cases are Ciba-Geigy, Nissan and British Airways while two others are less well-known companies but still employing thousands of employees. The exception is one school (focusing the principal).

This focus on the top management engaged in leading an entire organization is typically indicated to be written for managers and intended to be useful for this group. However, this is questionable, as very few people are or will ever become top managers and even fewer will become heads of very large companies. Of course, also less senior managers and some people in staff functions may benefit from being able to embrace a top management perspective in order to comply with and implement various strategies for cultural engineering. But typical top management activities as mass communication of frequently abstract and vague messages and initiating large-scale training programmes do not comprise the bulk of what most managers do. What is pretended to be a technical, practically oriented knowledge interest is really often an ideological one: the appeal lies in appealing to fantasies of being in the elite, of being grandiose and omnipotent. It is less narcissistically gratifying to imagine oneself as a subordinate or low-level manager. The overwhelming majority of managers and other practitioners are, however, not expected to manage entire cultures. Instead they manage *within* cultures and affect or negotiate the meanings and values of their subordinates, peers or immediate superiors. A useful approach for most managers calls for a more delimited focus than the (large) organization as a whole. The impact of most managers – including almost all that read management books – is typically restricted mainly to the people they interact directly with in everyday life. They have no or very little access to long-distance impact through videos, memos or for-public-consumption appearances, highly staged and prepared. They are not highly visible for large groups of people sensitive to what they signal, nor are they in control of a lot of resources through which a 'substantive' influence also affecting ideas and values can be accomplished. Given this more limited situation, the unrealistic claims about unitariness and uniqueness of organizations in the MUUC-literature and consultancy advices may be less relevant to consider. As a manager in charge of a sales force or a R & D unit, one often deals with relatively homogeneous groups and must respond to the occupational and other cultural orientations they bring with them to work.

Cases of cultural change in very large organizations often include other problems. To illuminate top management efforts to manage or change an organization of several thousand people, belonging to a large number of different groups, calls for a rather broad-brush approach. It is very difficult to say something of the effects of broadly targeted top management acts on how meanings are transformed as translation processes takes place in a variety of different specific contexts. Instead organizations are treated more or less as unitary wholes and almost exclusively from a top management perspective. The relationship between managerial initiatives and the reactions of subordinates is mainly external and mechanical. It is as if nothing active takes place in the minds of, and communication between, employees in interpreting managerial interventions. A simple stimuli-response thinking is common: management makes an intervention, the organization responds. It is acknowledged that there are sometimes inertia and resistance that account for some variation, but an overall standard response is typically emphasized. Brown (1995), for example, reports a mini-case of 'culture change at Nissan'. Nissan, one of the world's largest manufacturers of cars, ran into problems at the beginning of the 1980s, mainly due to economic causes, but to some extent also from deteriorating labour–management relations. A new CEO put forward the motto that 'management and the labour union should both discharge their duties properly'. He encouraged a downplaying of hierarchical relations and a stronger focus on the marketplace. He made attempts to improve communication and encouraged all employees to address each other as 'mister', regardless of rank, which was a break with an earlier practice to use titles in communication. He also removed pattern-maintaining symbols such as the wearing of uniforms by female employees and introduced flexible working hours.

From the brief account, nothing is said about how people reacted – how they interpreted and responded to the changes – and if these led to anything other than behavioural compliance. A cultural change is not that management tries to impose new behaviours, but a change of the ideas, values and meanings of large groups of people. Whether addressing other people as 'mister' led to a softening up of rank-related interactions and understandings or not, is impossible to say without carefully listening to various people encouraged – or forced to – adopt this new habit. Part of the problem is that trying to grasp cultural change in a heterogeneous company with 100 000 employees is difficult. The sheer size and heterogeneity of the object of study makes it difficult to avoid trivializing organizational culture.

A useful approach must have more depth and precision than most 'managing culture' talk: this is vague, positively biased and full of jargon. It tells the reader more of espoused managerial intentions and some highly visible acts than of the consequences on organizational culture. As top managers – in particular in their most spectacular acts and initiation of large scale programmes – must address broad groups with highly different circumstances, the messages become very vague and general in order to be understandable and perceived as positive by all.

Rather than a formula for the good overall organizational culture and a set of rules for how to create it or modify it, it is more interesting and practically valuable for managers to use cultural ideas in everyday interactions. This calls for local adaption and the case-by-case evaluation rather than blanket assessment of what is good and less good in shaping local ideas and meanings.

A strong argument against the use of vague and general talk seemingly favoured by top managers in their heroic efforts concerns the weak effect of words and symbolic acts that are used more broadly and thus are very familar to a particular group targeted for change. They are easily worn out and may lose appeal. Important is the use of talk, actions and material arrangements that appear to be coherent, i.e. back up each other, capture the imagination and appeal to what people see as important, meaningful and relevant. One can here talk about *symbolic effectiveness*, i.e. the degree to which an act, a statement or a physical object succeeds in condensing and expressing a rich content of meaning that appeals to the minds and hearts of a group. This calls for variation and novelty as well as careful targeting of local context. The first company that got rid of excessive status symbols – such as private parking space or big luxurious offices for executives – were probably more successful in bending people's minds and feelings towards feelings of community, while the fifty-eleventh company following this path may create limited responsiveness. Here the situation may rather be one of avoiding being seen as 'the stuffiest company in the business' and the ambition to minimize the evoking of a negative response rather than to influence people positively through community symbolism. For the individual manager mainly occupied by working with a group of ten or fifty people, high-powered symbolism such as big ceremonies, mission statements and spectacular acts are frequently less significant, as everyday communication around practical problems and the sense-making of the unit's direction, offer possibilities for a continuous influence of meaning. At this level, some trivialities pointed at here can more easily be avoided and the manager, given an interest and ability to listen, can get a feeling for how her or his words, deeds and arrangements actually are interpreted and how they interfere in the ongoing culture-shaping in the organization.

Managing culture

Change exaggerations

'Managing culture' is often equated with 'changing culture'. Culture is then frequently focused because existing ideas, beliefs, values and meanings are viewed as problematic and need to be transformed. The great interest in change may, however, be exaggerated. Inflation in the talk about a turbulent environment and about the pressing need for change may not correspond very well with careful analysis. There is a lot of talk in the mass media and the literature about drastic changes taking place at an accelerating speed. There is much reporting of the knowledge society, the new economy, the significance of e-commerce, rapidly changing tastes of customers, increasing global competition, the young generation being very different from the previous one, etc. which seems to imply a pressure for rapid changes. Old paradigms for management must be replaced by new ones, authors argue. That a bureaucratic ethos needs to give way for an entrepreneurial spirit, is a popular 'truth' (du Gay, 1996). More or less standardized scripts are regurgitated saying that companies move from discipline to learning, managers changing from administrators to leaders, hierarchies giving way to markets, the situation of organizational members changing from having been disempowered, to becoming empowered, and so on (e.g. Clegg *et al.*, 1996).

Change-talk is highly fashionable, but it may give a misleading picture of what is presently taking place (Grey, 1999). It is important to be sceptical to the messages of '... "policy entrepreneurs", management gurus and think-tankers who have a vested interest in the sweeping statement, popular slogan and digestible knowledge-gobbitt, regardless of how inconsistent with or embedded in existing bodies of knowledge' (Warhurst and Thompson, 1998: 20). A systematic study of 448 European firms during the 1992–96 period indicated some changes taking place (some degree of delayering, more decentralized operational decision-making, increased internal networking), but these were modest, not radical. Hierarchies still matter, so if companies grow they tend to add ladders; there is little of decentralized strategic decision-making and IT does not weaken hierarchy that much as there is more investment in vertical than horizontal networking (Ruigrok *et al.*, 1999).

That changes are less profound than said in the pop-management literature and that radical turnovers calling for heroic efforts of leaders described as charismatic put things straight again (e.g. Iacocca) are rather uncommon, do not of course prevent us from acknowledging that large-scale change sometimes is called for and does take place. Understanding culture and change, however, also calls for the appreciation of other types of cultural changes than intentional, large-scale, top-management led projects that lead to success.

The perhaps most influential idea, Lewin's refrigerator-model, is unfortunate as it tends to lock us into a rather odd view on changes. He suggests three stages in an intentional change project: unfreezing, change and refreezing. He imagines a frozen, i.e. fixed, social world, which can be heated up and then frozen again at will, through a correct intervention. As the world is constantly in change this is misleading. In organizations, people mature and get new impulses, they quit and are replaced, old customers leave, new ones enter. The gradual changes in society at large of ideas on authority, motives, sex roles, management ideas, the direction of attention to and from various phenomena (environmental problems, social and health care issues, geographical regions), means the ongoing changing of organizations. Organizations are part of a continuously changing social world and any effort to modify cultural orientations calls for a sense of these ongoing cultural changes.

There is often in talk about cultural change a strong focus on what is speculative, dramatic, engineered, supported by a group of actors wanting to 'market' the change efforts and possible results. Marketing the cultural change is, of course, a part of it. New ideas and values must be sold to groups supposed to take them on, but also to other audiences, such as external groups. 'Cultural change' frequently has an external side to it, e.g. when companies signal their new 'customer oriented culture' it is also a part of their marketing and image-production. Messages aimed for mass media and customers can, in their turn, facilitate cultural change through the company's personnel also noting these messages. They may pay more attention to and have greater confidence in what mass media report than what management communicates directly to them. The personnel can also be influenced through being affected by the expectations of customers and others, monitoring organizational personnel when interacting with and observing them. There is less talk about gradual cultural changes that cannot be connected with high-profile acts, actors or programmes. Such changes may, however, be profound and call for careful attention by managers. When such changes are portrayed, it is often done in a broad-brushed way (e.g. 'the new economy', 'knowledge society'), exaggerating the magnitude and speed of such changes and showing little interest in how they affect specific organizations.

Cultural change is often going in a 'negative' direction

Culture thus continuously changes and many changes are broadly seen as negative for those involved (a verdict that external observers may agree upon). Workplace climate, job and organizational commitment, a feeling for quality and responsibility, paying careful attention to and investing efforts in reading clues from the market, may for example deteriorate. We can talk about *cultural drifting*. This may be the outcome of new persons replacing others, people getting older, an effect of market changes or be unintentional effects of specific managerial interventions and systems. Downsizing is an obvious example. Also growth may affect culture. A senior manager in the consultancy business that I interviewed had observed that when companies grow and included more than 2–300 employees then the quality of the work detoriated in some respects. The organization then passed a point where it became impossible to maintain a close spirit and a good overview of people. In order to staff and run projects effectively, good personal knowledge of the people to use was necessary and at one point this knowledge was so limited that other mechanisms took over, leading to uncertainty, bureaucracy and limited trust. (In economic terms, the transaction costs increased.) Changes in size then seem to affect cultural orientations. In this case negatively, from the point of view of my informant, but in other cases in other ways. Growth in numbers of employed may be given meanings such as vitality, success, strength, etc., which is typically seen as positive. Often in relatively new companies growth seems to be perceived differently by different groups of people, thus creating some tension in the organization. The senior managers view growth as indicating the quality and success of the company while non-promoted groups sometimes view the increases in number being followed by weakened social relationship, a poorer workplace climate and a more distanced, hierarchical relationship to senior people which they earlier had a close contact with (Alvesson, 1995; Wilkins and Dyer, 1987).

Cultural changes thus frequently mean changes that are not necessarily seen as positive. They may also involve differentiation of meaning, so that a common understanding is disrupted making confusions and possibly conflicts more prevalent.

Reproduction of culture

One important task of managers – as well as of other people in organizations – is to reproduce or maintain culture. *Cultural maintenance* then means counteracting gradual change. Of course, in some situations ideas, values and meanings have drifted from what was perceived as an earlier and more positive state to such an extent that intended cultural change is needed to restore the situation. In such a case the situation calls for efforts to create change rather than just to reproduce what exists. Cultural maintenance is an integral part of most everyday activities, talk and structural arrangements in organizations. Sometimes managers and others may more systematically be oriented towards, for example:

- upholding virtues and morale and encouraging the continued dominance of a particular set of meanings informing how people perceive and relate to a specific issue;
- supporting organizational and departmental identity: in a complex and changing organizational world, identity-focused cultural maintenance work may counteract fragmentation through drawing attention to what may be seen as an essence or a core in what the organization or unit is doing, its coherence over time and space and its distinctiveness from other organizations or units;
- creating a cultural basis for image management: here maintenance is directed to recreating an internal basis for what is signalled as the organization's image or 'profile' to other external groups.

To continue with the example of changes associated with size of personnel force, implying a reduction of personal relations, organization-wide networking and a strong feeling of community and a shared project, cultural maintenance could involve more efforts to give the company a personal touch. This could be accomplished through being more careful about selective recruitment according to certain ideals and values, perhaps being prepared to slow down growth a bit (according to the rule 'when in doubt, don't employ'). Another option is to devote more attention to managerial action to connect people and spend more time and other resources to network-building rites, workshops, parties and think through carefully how these can be used, so they don't just strengthen further interaction within groups that already know each other. Such engineering efforts may only partly counteract the negative effects on overview and community following from expansion and growth in numbers. But only a modest impact may be sufficient to maintain at least some values and orientations that are deemed to be valuable. In cultural terms it is the meaning of size and personal relations that are of significance, not the precise amount of knowledge of other people that individuals have. A shared identification with the company producing a strong 'we' feeling may lead individuals to feel trust and positivity also towards persons they do not really know.

Organizational cultural change as a grand project, as organic movement or the re-framing of everyday life?

Moving on to the topic of ambitious cultural change, it can be fruitful to distinguish between three versions: the grand project; organic movement; and everyday life re-framing.

Change as a grand technocratic project

The most popular one in the literature and what most people probably have in mind when thinking about cultural change is the *grand technocratic project*. Most descriptive and even more normative models of large-scale cultural change are of this type (see reviews in e.g. Brown, 1995). It portrays or promises the possibility of an intentional large-scale transformation from a particular cultural situation to another, more superior and profitable one, although it is recognized that this is not easy and often takes place slowly.

The overall plan for accomplishing this is often a version of the following overall scheme:

Step 1: Evaluating the situation of the organization and determining the goals and strategic direction.
Step 2: Analysing the existing culture and sketching a desired culture.
Step 3: Analysing the gap between what exists and what is desired.
Step 4: Developing a plan for developing the culture.
Step 5: Implementing the plan.
Step 6: Evaluating the changes, making new efforts to go further and/or engaging in measures to sustain the cultural change.

The common means for accomplishing cultural change seem to be a combination of the following ingredients:

- New recruitment and selection procedures so that people expected to be supportive of a desired culture will be hired. Sometimes this is combined with laying off and/or replacing people perceived as not being of 'true grit'.
- New forms of socialization and training programmes to signal the desired values and beliefs.
- Performance appraisal systems in which the culturally correct ways of being and behaving are rewarded and encouraged.
- Promotion of people expressing and symbolizing the desired culture.
- Leadership which communicates cultural values in talk, actions and material arrangements, e.g. vision talk and for-public-consumption acts by the top manager.
- The use of organizational symbols – particular use of language (slogans, expressions, stories), actions (use of meetings in a ritual way, the visible use of managers' time to signal what is important) and material objects (corporate architecture, logotype, dress code).

According to this view culture change is a project emerging from and run from above. It is assumed that top management is the agent from which superior insight about the needed change emerges and also the chief architect behind the plan for change. Apart from planning and allocation of resources to change projects and making decisions in line with the wanted change, the dramaturgical acts of senior executives – public speeches, highly visible acts drawing attention to the ideals – also symbolize re-framing of how people should think, feel and act in accordance with new ideals and values. Consultants are frequently used to back-up senior managers in this kind of change project.

Cultural change as an organic social movement

Another way of thinking about cultural change is to see it as an *organic social movement*. Change is then mainly something emergent. There is no strong, uniform will acting as the centre in the change, neither is there that much of intentionality and a clear plan. Groups within the organization revise their thinking, valuing and giving meaning to phenomena 'spontaneously'. These new ideas may originate within the organizations as many people feel discontent with dominant ideas and practices and want to consider another set of ideas, but they may also originate outside the organization and then gradually take root there. It may be a matter of people in the organizations noticing changes in customers when interacting with them, calling for new responses and potentially involving reconsideration of important ideas and beliefs. It may also be broadly shared new ideas in society, e.g. on gender, a common European market or sustainable development, that affect people who then 'carry' and insert and express these ideas in the organization. Cultural change as an organic movement means that groups within an organization follow the flow of the new ideas gradually leading to organizational cultural change. A macho culture may then gradually be less masculinely oriented – military and sport jargon be less prevalent, or its masculine connotations weakened, females less strongly defined in domestic and sexualized ways, feelings and cooperation acknowledged more while fierce internal competition is seen as problematic. A company viewing itself as broadly international may define its geographical identity base as European. Adapting new ideas on the role of knowledge in business and management may mean that more attention is focused on sharing ideas and utilizing competence broadly. For organic movement changes to have a strong impact on organizations, senior managers need to share and support the new ideas and orientations. The senior managers are not, however, very central. They are not necessarily the initiators or those hardest pushing for the re-orientations. The characteristic of an organic movement change is: (1) the relatively broadly shared exposure to something implying a change in beliefs, ideas and values; and (2) the change implications of these already without top management or any other key actor being highly significant. Quite a lot of the 'agency' is then inherent in the availability of cultural changes originating in society at large or within specific groups significant for organizational members, e.g. customers, industry associations, major competitors, management consultancy companies, etc.

Sometimes broad societal or industry-level changes are so strong that individual organizations must respond to these. There is then an institutional pressure to adapt to new ideas – inability or unwillingness to do so leading to legitimacy problems (DiMaggio and Powell, 1983; Meyer and Rowan, 1977; Scott, 1995). Organizations, however, vary in what an external pressure leads to on the cultural level. The construction of norms and expectations differ, so does the values of them. The local dynamics and the acts of various individuals and groups are significant, e.g. in determining whether new ideas and values only lead to façade-changing responses or if meanings really change within the individual organization. The latter then is a matter of at least moderate cultural change. Façade-shifting arrangements do not call for any cultural change, even though it may trigger reactions in this direction, e.g. reinforce cynicism and opportunistic orientations among organizational members.

Cultural change is the re-framing of everyday life

A third view on cultural change is *everyday re-framing*. This connects to the view on leadership as management of meaning described in Chapter 5. As with organic movement there is less of a big, grand project in what is perceived as an inferior state is transformed to a superior one through the heroic acts of a top manage-ment, assisted by consultants and other managers. Quite different from organic movement, everyday re-framing does not presuppose some broadly shared collectively carried new understanding associated with broad trends in society. Everyday re-framing tends to be driven by one or a few senior actors, frequ-ently a manager but also informal authorities, and small groups of people may be central. It is most typically mainly incremental and informal, e.g. not clearly espoused or signalled as a project or a campaign with a set of distinct activities that are supposed to accomplish a pre-defined ideal. It is a matter of local cultural change; the actor(s) engaged in everyday re-framing mainly influences people he/she directly interacts with, although this may create wider effects as these people in the next instance may affect those they interact with. The impact of everyday re-framing may thus include more than a couple of dozen people, but nothing like in the broad macro-level cultural trends influencing organizations through social movement-like re-orientations among large groups of personnel or the long-range impact of grand technocratic projects through formally controlled techniques and allocation of large resources. Everyday re-framing is mainly an informal culture-shaping agenda, involving pedagogical leadership in which an actor exercises a subtle influence through the re-negotiation of meaning. A good illustration is the case of Gustaf, as described in Chapter 5, who gives space for his subordinates in the quarterly meeting in his division and sets the tone of this community-shaping event. He thus tries to reconstruct meanings around hierar-chy, differentiation and social distance and create a stronger identification with the unit.

Everyday re-framing is, in some ways, a weaker version of cultural change, as it is neither backed up by all the authority, formal power and resources in grand technocratic cultural changes, nor with the force of large collective cultural streams grounded in publicity, interest groups (outside the organization) and the pressure on organizations to be in harmony with its social environment and attain legitimacy. Local initiatives are also frequently constrained by broader organiza-tional culture as well as by relations of power. Everyday re-framing is, on the other hand, strongly anchored in interactions and 'natural' communication. It is also better adapted to the material work situations of people and has thus stronger action-implications. It means that there is good depth in terms of making clear the meanings and interpretations involved. Compared with the frequently rather lofty ambitions of efforts to transform an entire large organization, everyday re-framing has a potential 'realism' and a better connectedness to the level of meaning.

For the large majority of managers, not being at the top of large organizations, everyday re-framing is often the more relevant mode of cultural change, apart from being mobilized as implementers of grand projects. It calls for creativity, stamina, insights into one's own beliefs, values and ideas, communicative skills and some courage in making sacrifices, as drawing attention to and underscoring certain ideas may call for paying less attention to others, e.g. if one wants creativity and learning then one cannot emphasize quality very consistently and strongly, as new ideas and experimentations will involve some errors.

The grand technocratic project is a top-down cultural change, the organic movement change flows from the outside-inwards while the everyday re-framing change moves from the middle down and to some extent around.

The three types of change are not contradictory but may also go hand in hand. New ideas and values in society may 'soften up' an organization for change; top management may experience a combination of legitimacy problems and convictions that there are good 'internal' reasons for changes and therefore take initiatives to changes. Specific managers, without getting specific instructions to do something special but encouraged by societal changes and new signals from top management, may take initiatives to re-frame local thinking on the issue concerned. Within a specific domain, a division, department or a work group, the re-shaping of ideas, values and meaning then may be more drastic than in other parts of the organization, without necessary deviating from these in the direction of the change.

Working with change

Cultural change: preceding, following from or intertwined with 'substantive changes'

One important aspect of cultural change concerns whether this is a matter of primarily involving the level of values, ideas and beliefs or if it also, and perhaps mainly, involves more substantive matters, such as structural and material arrangements directly implying behavioural changes. One line of thought suggests that we must change people's ideas and values in order to make any 'real' change possible thus giving priority to a cultural level. Another would be that making people behave differently is what matters; cultural changes will follow from this. Re-allocation of resources and rewarding different behaviour then would then be sufficient. Most authors on organizational culture single out the cultural level as of main interest (e.g. Lundberg, 1985; Schein, 1985). Here, it is mainly idealistic means – articulation of visions, creating organizational rites, initiating training programmes, what leaders pay attention to, control, reward and teach – that are relied upon, although more substantive changes also clearly matter. Occasionally, the more material and substantive side of organizations is emphasized more strongly. Anthony (1994: 60), for example, argues that 'cultural change that is not reinforced by material change in structure, reward systems, precept and policy is likely to be seen as unreal and any adjustment to be temporary'.

I think this is partly a matter of the question concerned. If it is a matter of core business with direct perceived links to production, performances and performance measures, then a 'pure' cultural change appears unrealistic. But if we talk about something 'less material' like greater openness in the company or new ways of interacting with customers then the situation is different. If senior managers strongly favour this value, their personal example seems to have an effect on broader patterns in organizations (Hofstede *et al.*, 1990). There are various estimations whether a change towards knowledge sharing calls for structural measures, such as performance evaluations and incentives (as argued by e.g. Davenport and Prusak, 1998), or whether 'true' knowledge sharing presupposes value commitments (O'Dell and Grayson, 1998), that may be counteracted by formal control extrinsic rewards. Regarding gender issues, there is debate whether this can be accomplished through 'pure' cultural change or if it implies structural control. Many people argue that increased gender equality presupposes structural changes of the ratio men/women in particular in senior positions and that this calls for legislation and policy changes and sanctions/rewards to see to that the numbers become right. Greater representation by women then lead to cultural changes, it is assumed (Kanter, 1977; Ely, 1995). Another position assumes that the use of structural means – setting targets and then controlling that these are attained – to recruit or promote greater numbers of females in order to fill the quota does not imply a qualitative change and may backfire as those recruited/promoted will be negatively evaluated as the merits will be seen as less significant for their promotion and stereotypes be reinforced. It is argued that 'real change' calls for cultural redefinitions of gendered meanings and biases involving demasculinization of values and meanings (e.g. Alvesson and Billing, 1997).

I think it is fair to recognize the variety of different issues and the possibility of cultural change involving mainly a change of meaning and values without directly presupposing substantive changes. However, an interplay between the level of meaning and the level of behaviour, material and structural arrangement must often be considered in organizational change work. In order for behavioural change to be possible, it must be preceded by and accompanied by cultural re-orientations. Cultural change often calls for anchoring in labour processes and work conditions in order to communicate effectively. Efforts to accomplish change in meanings and values incoherent with substantive arrangements exercising behavioural control are often doomed. As pointed out in Chapter 7, the specific work situation is a powerful input in the development of sentiments and in sense-making processes at workplaces. New cultural messages must connect to this material level to be fully credible and to 'stick' in the minds and hearts of people.

When is cultural change necessary? Many changes in organizations do not necessarily imply radical changes in the beliefs, values and ideas of large groups of people. More radical organizational changes do, however, always involve cultural redefinitions of a substantial part of experienced reality. As pointed out throughout this book, there is a cultural dimension present in all social life calling for some degree of shared understanding. The downsizing situation during a recession at the computer consultancy Enator, earlier celebrating 'fun and profit', and tight social bonds at the workplace, was clearly not primarily a matter of cultural change. But also making people redundant and cutting costs takes place in a cultural context, which facilitates some joint understanding of the corporate situation and what is reasonable under harsh conditions. Without such an under-standing – which is often difficult to accomplish – there will be additional prob-lems in cooperating around the process of dismissal, and those dismissed as well as those that remain will develop highly varied and frequently negative and con-fused ideas of the meaning of the company and its relationships to the personnel.

The case of Hewlett-Packard during and after dismissing a number of people is of interest here. Many employees earlier assumed that HP was committed to lifetime employment, although this was never explicitly stated by the company. Decisions to 'downsize' and 'delayer', as it is called, upset some people and left scars on many. Although the belief in the company as strongly people-oriented was not left undamaged, the personnel on the whole still saw HP, after the event, as a good place to work and a survey showed higher levels of organizational commit-ment than in other companies in the study. Meanings such as the company 'moving from guaranteed employment to guaranteed employability', as a personnel offi-cer expressed it, probably contributed to create some understanding of the change (McGovern and Pope-Hailey, 1997).

The possibility of intended cultural change

Although cultures are always, at least in contemporary 'late capitalistic society', in motion, intentional and systematic organizational cultural change is a difficult project. In pop-management writings and talk, there is much optimism, but most reflective writers treating this topic downplay the chances of intended cultural change, i.e. of a grand technocratic type (Brown, 1995; Fitzgerald, 1988; Grey, 1999; Lundberg, 1985). Cultural manifestations shared by a larger collective com-prise a very heavy counterweight to the possibilities of a top figure exercising influence on people's thinking and feelings. Such a task is of course severely constrained by the rich variety of cultural manifestations and multitude of group identifications and commitments. There are also cultural constraints, held not only by a large part of the employees, but also by many top executives themselves, especially those promoted from within. Much reasoning on cultural changes take the position of how to change it (the organizational culture) or them (the masses), but rarely the question how should we change 'us', i.e. top management. The point with the concept of culture is that it refers to a whole collective of organi-zational participants, including those at the top. In situations deemed to call for radical change, top managers are sometimes seen as being 'outside corporate culture'. Frequently, the entrance of a new CEO is part of the plot in organiza-tional change initiatives, but also that person may share many of the values, beliefs and meanings of the organization targeted for cultural improvements. Even if top managers have some understanding of a needed redirection of cultural orientations, they may in vital respects be caught in taken for granted assumptions and develop blind spots for their own values and practices that reproduce what they think they are changing. In a research project we observed one senior manager giving a speech to his subordinates before a redesign of the organization. Values such as 'decentralization' and 'participation' were frequently mentioned – at the same time as he dominated the situation strongly and implicitly symbolized hierarchy and his own significance (Alvesson, 1996).

There are very few studies of cultural change initiatives. Frequently, studies do not follow these for more than a short time period and on a superficial level that is insufficient to draw any conclusions. An important exception is Pettigrew (1985). Siehl (1985) found that a new manager's efforts to change values in the organization studied had no major effects that could be registered, although they did influence the expression of values. Such an impact on the level of the espoused rather than on the 'deeper' level is probably the most common.

A more modest, but often difficult and important task not only for middle management, but also for top management is to maintain and/or modify – rather than radically change – certain values, ideals and virtues in the organization (Nord, 1985) or engage in more ambitious everyday re-framing of ideas, values and meanings in all kinds of interactions, as mentioned above.

The need for stamina in cultural change

One golden rule for intended cultural change is stamina. The ideal of quick fixes and the pressure on many companies to deliver good results in the short-term perspective runs directly against cultural change, as this normally takes time and calls for considerable skills, persistence and enthusiasm. One difficulty is that top managers frequently stay only a few years in their posts and the successor may have different ideas and/or want to try to put his or her own imprint on the business. This implies something other than ambitious cultural change, perhaps with the emphasis on other ideas, values or modes different from those favoured by the predecessor.

Another problem is associated with fashionability and the symbolism of appearing dynamic and change-oriented.

> The institutional premium is on new ideas, new perspectives, new definitions of catastrophe, new promises of salvation. Attention and consideration are not given to the glance backward at continuity-preserving traditions or to the contemplation of unifying dogmas, but to the hectic production of cultural goods. (Giesen and Schmid, 1989: 80–1)

According to Pfeffer (1994, Chapter 3), there is evidence that new employment practices evaluated as successful by companies that have adopted them are frequently not seriously implemented and/or have high mortality rates. Pfeffer suggests the need to be systematic and to have some overriding vision that supports implementation. Jackall (1988) argues that career prospects in the managerial world are contingent upon giving the impression of being dynamic and future-oriented and thus being capable of associating oneself with the latest ideas and dissociating oneself from less novel ideas and practices. This is at odds with sticking with a particular implementation plan and working through a new idea and a practice.

> A choice between securing one's own success by jumping on and off the bandwagon on the moment, or sacrificing oneself for the long-run good of a corporation by diverting resources and really seeing a program through is, for most managers, no choice at all. Ambitious managers see self-sacrificing loyalty to a company as foolhardy. (p. 143)

Watson (1994: 117) also notes that new management ideas 'are pushed through by managers trying to make a reputation and a career, who do not stay on to see them through'. We have here a fascinating paradox: the great value and hope placed on novelty and change undermine the chances of actually accomplishing significant change.

New ideas and practices are not necessarily focusing specifically on culture, but in order for new ideas and practices to have an impact they call for revisions of ideas and meanings so that they are anchored in and supported by people's thinking and values. Cultural support is needed also for 'anti-cultural' management practices such as rationalizations.

The lesson from efforts to install and make specific practices work thus is illustrative for the need for a long-term perspective and stamina in working with organizational change involving a significant cultural dimension. As disillusion, erosion of trust and resistance to change (change initiatives expected to lead to nowhere) are possible consequences of change programmes not carried through, there may be good reasons to be selective about these (Ramsay, 1996). A critical perspective on new fashions and the ability to do something ambitious with new ideas are vital here. To some extent critical thinking may facilitate an ability to: (1) carefully evaluate new concepts and the demands, problems and possibilities from all the grandiose promises and simplicities in the sales talk that are so common in management fashions; (2) attain a balance between jumping on the bandwagon and being a victim of fashion on the one hand and conservatism and rigidity on the other; and (3) to mobilize autonomy based on well-grounded convictions against the powers of conformism associated with either established wisdom-conservatism or fashionability. I am here thinking about adopting an intellectually well-grounded position. This is difficult in itself – it is easy to be persuaded by for example a 'new management paradigm' calling for 'entrepreneurship' against 'old' management based on 'bureaucracy' and then be eager to demonstrate for oneself and others that one really is of the true grit. Even if one is capable of withstanding the powers of new rhetoric in self-definition and view on the organization, it may be difficult to cope with the social pressure of a trend-sensitive social environment. The social and political costs for not complying may be high – as Jackall says, jumping on and off the bandwagon may be crucial for one's career opportunities.

Summary

Planned organizational cultural change is generally recognized as a difficult project. Cultures are in flux, but frequently slowly so and ongoing changes are something other than planned changes. Intended cultural changes call for creativity, insight, coherence, a combination of culture-focused and more substantive, material re-arrangements and considerable persistence. It also calls for luck. Much change talk and many initiatives are coupled with management fashions and hype, frequently leading to half-serious efforts seldom carried through. While these may lead to 'success' in terms of signalling the organizations' progressiveness and/or ability to live up to expectations of external audiences, the outcome in terms of the good of the organization in the long run is often less positive. Limited trust and cynicism among personnel may follow, making further, more ambitious change efforts more difficult. Amongst employees in one organization characterized by too frequent efforts to accomplish change statements such as 'We have got a new mission statement – once again', was common, indicating consider-able inattention and resistance to managerial change initiatives (Ramfelt, 1993).

A senior middle manager in a large high-tech company expressed her experi-ences of the possibilities of radical change as follows:

> I believe that change must come from both directions, i.e. there must be an organization that is mature, there must be people that are affirmative and open in their organization, there must be a clear will amongst managers. Only a will amongst the employees or only affirmation of the organization and the will amongst managers, is not sufficient.

This makes sense. Cultural change calls for receptiveness amongst the collective for new ideas, values and meanings. Without such an openness – which may be facilitated by cultural changes in the society, business or occupation or by a grow-ing awareness of fundamental problems in the organization – radical, intentional cultural change is very difficult.

A framework for thinking culturally of management and organization

The significance of culture in organizations and business of course depends on what the concept refers to; on the magnitude of the concept. It is important to avoid an all-embracing as well as a too narrow use of the term. If culture is seen as including all beliefs, ideas, values, norms, cognitions and feelings characterizing a collective, then of course it is crucial. If it is viewed as having nothing to do with management control, customers, politics, law, organizational structure, techno-logy, etc., then it appears as a less significant phenomenon. Culture is, however, as mentioned above, best utilized to interpret the dimension of meaning and sym-bols shared by a collective. As such it is more a way of understanding important aspects, a source of insights to virtually all areas of corporate life.

This book argues for the use of a more reflective concept of culture than is common in organization and management studies. Cultural interpretation then tries to avoid excessive temptations to simplify and trivialize and to appeal to practitioners and students wanting quick fixes and nurturing grandiose fantasies of becoming the top manager of a large company capable of managing and changing corporate culture through heroic deeds.

Traps in culture thinking

Drawing upon, but also further elaborating and in particular systematizing the argumentation throughout the book, I will point at some of the major fallacies in much culture thinking. These include strong tendencies to reify, essentialize, unify, idealize, consensualize, totalize and otherize. I will here very briefly com-ment upon these seven sins in (a)cultural thinking:

Reifying culture   To treat complex phenomena as things or thing-like is one way of controlling and economizing how we relate to and communicate around the phenomena. Culture becomes an 'it'. Expressions such as the corporate culture led to high performances, the different cultures prevented an integration process between the two companies after the merger, the new CEO changed the culture, the subcultures clashed ... are common. To treat culture as thing-like, similar to (physical) tools or obstacles, is misleading as meanings are not things. The apparent benefits in terms of the ease and straightforwardness of this kind of culture talk are deceptive as the phenomena are simply too poorly described and analysed. Sometimes reifying descriptions may be economical and can therefore be accepted; they are even to some extent unavoidable. The important thing is that the thinking should avoid or at least minimize cognitive reification (Johansson, 1990).

Essentializing culture   It is also common to describe culture in terms of a few essential traits. A culture may be said to be service-minded, adaptable, personnel-oriented, open, individualistic, performance-directed, etc. Such essentializing moves typically give a too strongly ordered and superficial view on culture. In particular in contemporary organizations, there is seldom a core of a few values and ideas putting their imprint on most significant areas of the organization. Defining culture through a few essential values and ideas easily also leads to people becoming caught in a few standard scripts for describing culture. To say something about what is behind a label such as 'a service-culture' calls for some careful interpretation as well as linguistic skills. Such an effort may well indicate that there are enormous variations in the precise meanings of 'service-orientation', within all the half or so of all companies in capitalist countries that present themselves with this label, and that the label says very little.

Unifying culture   Cultural orientations are often defined through easily accessible ways of defining groups or collectives. This can be highly misleading. In particular, it is important to avoid equating cultural boundaries with formal or legal ones, as implied by terms such as corporate culture or national culture. Sociological fact-sheet based principles for ordering social groups – such as age, class, gender or occupation – may be more relevant, but cultural orientations may not follow established *social* differentiation criteria. As pointed out above, and addressed also in the final section, the multiplicity of cultural groups and orientations in complex organizations need to be carefully considered and this goes against the temptation to treat organizations or groups as homogeneous.

Idealizing culture   To some extent the culture concept invites an idealizing understanding as it focus on the level of ideas, symbols and meanings. (Idealize here refers to a focus on meanings and ideas, not necessarily on ideals.) But a cultural understanding heavily emphasizing ideas in a social and material vacuum is not very helpful. From a top management perspective an emphasis on how leaders control culture through inexpensive means such as visions, rituals, symbolic acts and beliefs that the large masses will follow, is very satisfying. Ideas and meanings do not, however, just float around or become accepted outside a material context. People develop and (re-)shape cultural meanings in contexts in which material reality and labour processes are central, which motivates an interest not exclusively on 'pure' ideas and symbols but a focus also on how the material and behavioural levels are loaded with meaning and symbolism and affect cultural patterns and processes.

Consensualizing culture　It is common to assume that culture means unity and shared values within a company or another culture-bearing group. That cultural differentiation within an organization may be a source or reinforcer of conflicts is now broadly recognized. Shared meanings do not necessarily imply consensus and harmony. A common understanding does not mean shared values and harmony. An organization may be characterized by shared ideas and beliefs about the significance of self-interest, fierce internal competition and a view of corporate life as fairly harsh and jungle-like. Also in groups in which ideas on competition/ cooperation are less salient or pronounced people sharing the same cultural ideas and values may be competitors (cf. Bourdieu, 1979).

Totalizing culture　Totalizing culture has two meanings, both referring to the use of culture in a too all-embracing way. One concerns the tendency to use a very wide culture view incorporating almost everything, from assumptions and symbols to behaviours and social structures, i.e. how things are done in an organization. The response is, as said, to concentrate on meanings and symbols, but use this in relationship to behaviours and materia. The other totalizing tendency is to restrict oneself to values, ideas and meanings, but to claim that this can be captured once and for all, i.e. that the whole of how people think, feel and symbolize can be captured, as an integrated cultural system. But using the culture concept does not mean that all the meanings that a group share are addressed at the same time or can be summarized in a way that lead to good coverage. Rather it is the shared meanings on a specific topic that is of interest to pay attention to. Within a company the ideas on core competence, the future of the industry, sex roles, education and various informal social activities in and around work are loosely coupled. The study of cultural manifestations rather than cultural systems is thus to be preferred.

Otherizing culture　When we try to capture culture – like other ambiguous phenomena – we often use contrasts. Frequently these contrasts have a strong value-bias. We put up the good against the bad. When we set up something else as a contrast to what we want to illuminate we work according to the idea of the Other, the one that is not oneself or what one is propagating or really interested in. The Other is different, frequently inferior, and has the function of offering a good point of comparison. The Other is invoked in order to make an account or an understanding possible, it is uninteresting in itself, and its usefulness as a point of comparison makes a more nuanced description difficult. It is described in a way to produce a good effect in the description of the focal object of study. Otherizing culture means that differences are over-emphasized, simplistic descriptions are favoured, there is a strong selectivity in what is paid attention to and there is frequently a negative bias against it. Otherizing does not necessarily imply a clear value bias: the major problem is that treating something as a point of reference or comparison prevents nuances.

Having warned against these seven sins, I should add that my message is not that we should at all costs avoid inclinations to reify, essentialize, unify, idealize, consensualize, totalize and otherize culture. This is not possible and sometimes pragmatic reasons call for simplifications and the expression of something accessible – which often leads to some of the 'sins' above. Shortcuts may facilitate the expression of good points. At times, also, social reality may be in line with some of these 'sins', i.e. there 'are' organizations with a high level of consensus and harmony, which means that unifying and consensualizing are fully acceptable. My point is, however, that the traps and temptations should be handled with great care. Caution should be taken not to theorize culture in a way giving the seven sins privilege. Insightful cultural interpretation instead calls for a framework taking the complexity and fluid nature of meaning seriously. The next section will briefly summarize some ideas of relevance here.

Some principles for the productive use of the culture concept

In a sense, it is easier to point at the difficulties and pitfalls of culture thinking than give clear guidelines for its use. My conviction is that culture calls for an interpretive approach and there is no strong framework offering strict or detailed rules for that. Cultural thinking needs to be demonstrated. Such thinking, of course, is strongly facilitated by theoretical ideas on for example how metaphors work, the significance of meaning, social differentiation, symbolism, etc., as developed in this book. Here, I will only indicate some broad principles for how cultural analysis can be conducted as part of the summing up of the book. As in this text as a whole, these principles are relevant for researchers as well as practitioners – even though the level of intellectual ambition differs strongly; in a practitioner context this is typically subordinated to time pressure and instrumental concerns.

In order to get insightful ideas on culture the following pieces of advice seem relevant:

- The cultural aspect should be related to *specific events, situations, actions and processes* – we can 'find' culture through looking at the subtext of fairly representative or significant acts or arrangements. The careful investigating of something delimited – a carefully chosen and carved-out piece of organizational reality then forms a good entrance for the understanding of culture, making thick description possible.
- Culture should be treated as a *network of meaning* guiding feeling, thinking and acting rather than an external force – meaning then is an input or an element in feeling, thinking and acting with no determinate or mechanical effects. The network idea suggests that meanings may be loosely coupled. All this contrasts with the view of culture as an external mechanism working above the heads of people uniformly driving them in a particular way.
- Meanings should be viewed as *processual and situated* and not as a fixed essence – the meaning of concepts such as gender, leader, hierarchy, etc. are not static or take the same appearance in different situations. The meaning of being 'a woman' in a particular organizational culture differs due to specific

context. Even if sexuality, service and subordination are frequently ascribed to 'woman' in a patriarchical organization, different females may be 'caught' in or liberated from these meanings to different degrees and different ways contingent upon age, experience, self-esteem, type of work activity, social relations, etc. Different situations invoke various combinations of these elements and thus trigger processes in which cultural manifestations of gender appear.

- Cultural interpretation should also be sensitive to *variation and contradiction*, the action – and practice – related nature of cultural manifestations, and be reluctant to treat culture as an abstract system of values, presumed to have a general impact. The significance of differentiation and ambiguity means that organizations have many faces. All organizations, like other groups and communities, involve quite a lot of variation and contradictions. US society is frequently described as extremely individualistic, and many studies confirm this also at the organizational level (Hofstede, 1980; Tseng, 2000), but there are many (US) studies showing how people subordinate themselves to authorities (Milgram, etc.), and there seems to be considerable conformism and reluctance to take initiative in many US companies (Jackall, 1988; Carlzon, 1987). Individualism may be positively valued, but so is also team playing, loyalty and managerial prerogative, strongly circumscribing 'individualism' at the workplace.
- Any understanding of culture should also recognize how *power* operates in dominant meanings and the asymmetries of social relations work behind established cultural order. Cultural meanings do not develop freely or spontaneously, but bear the imprints of ideologies and actions of powerful agents. These agents also draw selectively upon cultural resources in political action, meaning that how social reality is shaped in specific situations is partly an outcome of the values and meanings that are invoked by actors reflecting sectional interests.

Summary

In order to facilitate cultural sensitive thinking on and in organizations the more common traps should be borne in mind, here summarized in the form of seven 'sins'. All tend to deny ambiguity and emphasize culture as order, clarity and the possibility of economical, straightforward and authoritative talk about culture. Against this an interpretative approach can be mobilized, in which the following virtues are expressed: a focus on specific cultural manifestations, in which meaning is seen as loosely coupled, complex, situated, bears the imprints of power and where cultural elements frequently vary and may even contradict each other.

Multiple cultural configurations and cultural traffic

The perspective I am proposing can be called a *multiple cultural configuration* view. It assumes that organizations can be understood as shaping local versions of broader societal and locally developed cultural manifestations in a multitude of ways. Organizational cultures are then best understood not as unitary wholes or as stable sets of subcultures but as mixtures of cultural manifestations of different levels and kinds. Even in seemingly homogeneous and stable organizations such as universities cultural configurations are multiple, complex and shifting (Alvesson, 1993a; Trowler, 1998). People are connected to different degrees with organization, suborganizational unit, profession, gender, class, ethnic group, nation, etc.; cultures overlap in an organizational setting and are rarely manifested in 'pure' form. Sometimes these variations and dynamics are created by changing external circumstances of organizations and in particular how these are constructed within an organization. Sometimes internal processes trigger reactions and social groupings bringing forward a particular cultural configuration, not earlier salient, e.g. awareness of the company spreading pollution may lead to some people in the organization to gather around and express strongly green values.

In the case of the Women's Bank, a bank run by women for female clients, a feminist ideology was broadly shared and had some influence, but on certain issues there were no broadly shared commitments, and ideologies which were not organization-specific informed different organizational members' understandings (Tom, referred to by Martin, 1987). Trainees, frequently from working-class backgrounds and being single mothers, sometimes did not turn up at work, thereby indicating that taking care of sick children was more important than work. Their trainers, frequently middle-class women, thought that this indicated that they were not serious about work. Different meanings of organizational loyalty and work commitment were salient here. Thus, cultural configurations vary according to the issue and the ideology to which they are related. Such is the case not only in average sized business companies employing a variety of occupational groups and characterized by far-reaching horizontal and vertical division of labour, but also within relatively small and, in many respects, less heterogeneous organizations, such as the Women's Bank. Variation is not only an outcome of local diversity, but also related to how macro-level, environmental and cultural diversity affect different segments of the organization.

Any specific cultural manifestation identified should be considered in the context of a multiple of cultural configurations, from local group interaction to occupational/industrial subfield orientations to macro cultural traditions and meaning patterns. Any specific manifestation is thus a possible source of insight on several levels. That is, several levels must be worked through in terms of interpretative powers before the researcher decides what is a reasonable interpretation pointing at a specific level of analysis. In the case of the Women's Bank, the feminist ideology broadly shared had some influence, but on certain issues ideologies which were not organization specific informed different members' understandings. Thus cultural configurations vary according to the issue and the ideology in question. The multiple cultural configuration view differs from the differentiation perspective and most talk of subcultures in three distinct ways: (1) it focuses partly on extra-organizational origins of local cultural manifestations, without reducing these local manifestations to mere reflections of broader patterns; (2) it pays attention to overlapping cultural configurations in the organization; and (3) it sees such configurations as changing, depending on the particular issue concerned.

It is especially important to note the existence of *cultural traffic*; that cultural patterns change with the flow of meanings and values in and around organizations.

The concept of cultural traffic underscores that values, ideas, meanings and understandings are affected by the societal level and have different kinds of origins and are clustered around different social categories depending on the issue concerned. There are several aspects to consider here.

There is a traffic associated with the distribution and changes in fashionable ideas driven by mass media, higher education, management books, consultants, green and feminist movements, and so on. Much of this is *media-carried* in the sense that there is not necessarily any personal interaction involved, but ideas and meaning can be transferred over long distances and reach wide audiences. It is important to recognize that these are not just an effect of groups and institutions 'outside' the organization communicating to people 'in' an organization that they, for example, should reduce pollution and waste, use new management buzz words and promote females to managerial tasks. People employed in an organization change with society and they organically bring 'in' new meanings and reinterpret or challenge existing ones.

There is also traffic associated with the moves of groups of people: organizations employ young people from schools, immigrants and people from new occupations. Between Taiwan and California there is, for example, a steady flow of Taiwanese people working for or founding Californian companies and then going back to Taiwan and/or forming steady links between the two places. In some areas, there is even talk about the 'Californization of (parts of) Taiwan' (Saxenian, 2000). Cultural traffic is then *group-carried*; ideas travel together with people's geographical and social mobility.

Related to these multiple 'cultural movements' where ideas and meanings originate in institutions and communities and then put imprints in a particular organization, but of great significance in itself, are the groupings and regroupings around various issues that trigger different social constellations and cultural orientations. We can thus talk about dynamic *cultural repositionings*, fuelled by the multitude and dynamics of social and ideational sources of meanings, ideas and identifications. Here we have a cultural traffic between the multitude of meanings and values made possible between the ideologies and discourses that are or can be made present in an organization.

The complexity, variation and tolerance for incoherence of cultural values, ideas and meanings matter here. Swidler (1986), looking upon culture as a 'tool kit', as symbolic resources, emphasizes how it can be used in various ways, i.e. for those with sufficient cultural competence. She notes how the Bible, for example, expresses a variety of messages and can, which has historically clearly been the case, be used to motivate and legitimate almost any position, objective or act. Within specific groups and communities, there are, however, limits to such variety.

I will give a brief illustration from my own experience. During one work-day in my department I first participated in a work group that was to propose improvements in the teaching of methodology. In the group we all agreed that this was important, that higher demands of students should be made and that the academic, research-connected nature of the education should be reinforced. I felt very pleased about this. After that I went to another meeting, with other, but not clearly dissimilar people present. Here the topic was how to recruit more students to a particular area. Here all the talk went almost in opposite direction from the first meeting and mainly was concerned with adapting to the expectations and wants of the students, emphasizing the vocational aspects of education, etc. Here academic values give way to 'customer-satisfaction' and other market-oriented ideas. I questioned this with little response, felt frustrated and left the meeting depressed. This example illustrates how a particular theme or issue led to the appearance of a set of ideas and meanings: in the first case it is intellectual, research-oriented, academic values that are salient; in the second case market values are brought forward. In similar ways, we have short-range dynamic cultural traffic in organizations where values, beliefs and meanings commute between centre and periphery, present and absent on different organizational scenes – scenes that can change rapidly. In order to nuance the picture – and avoid falling into the otherizing trap that I warned about above – I should add that the two settings also expressed some similarities: in the second case, the content and literature discussed still were within the limits of what is typically seen as suitable for academic studies.

Managing cultural change is partly a matter of trying to control or frame cultural traffic. Sometimes it takes the form of reinforcing or translating certain ideas and values that are espoused in media and thus are present in the awareness of groups in organizations. It can also be a matter of employing certain carriers of specific ideas and meanings, e.g. people of a particular sex, corporate background, age, from a specific school and/or with a particular cultural profile. Everyday re-framing may also be seen as managing cultural traffic; framing issues in a particular way or drawing attention to certain themes may be viewed as preventing certain meanings and values from being salient and calling upon others to take the stage. Rather than a source of meaning and value production, the leader then acts – and even more reacts – in the flow of cultural traffic, struggling to control and direct it.

Prospects

This book contributes to a more sensitive and reflective approach to organization theory and proposes a loosely integrated theoretical framework facilitating cultural interpretation and reflection on such interpretations. Organizational culture is a difficult field. Observations and analyses are very sensitive to the concepts and metaphors that inform them, and it is seldom self-evident how a given phenomenon is 'best' perceived and interpreted. It is tempting to stress complexities, and I may have succumbed to this temptation here, but I am also aware of the problems associated with demanding too much. A cultural framework for understanding management and organization can be used with different levels of sophistication and ambition. Intuition, personal knowledge and creativity are very important resources in deciphering and analysing culture, as well as using culture thinking in management and consultancy work.

Too much organizational culture thinking – among practitioners as well as popular and academic authors – has been grounded in functionalist assumptions about the potentially 'positive' consequences of culture. It has focused on founders and managers as prime movers and on instrumentally relevant cultural manifestations perceived as typical of the organization. Often the connection between culture, social practice, and the material aspects of people's organizational lives is neglected, which is partly a consequence of a top management, broad-brush view on what is presented as uniform corporate cultures.

The management-oriented literature draws attention to the generally fairly thin, or even very thin, line of understandings, meanings, values, and symbols shared by the majority of a company's personnel and managers, typically labelled corporate culture. As has been noted, there are exceptions. Sometimes the line is not so thin. Sometimes it is not even broadly shared, i.e. there are hardly any ideas, beliefs or values in common and distinct for those working in an organization. This focus on what is seen as common is sometimes appropriate, but overlooking all the cultural variation is sometimes counterproductive even from a management perspective. A pragmatic view of culture which can inform managerial action must to some extent consider culture's complexity; oversimplification may be persuasive but misleading. For most managers, however, organizational culture as a complex totality is not of primary interest. They work within and are constrained by a larger cultural context, but they mainly interact with a limited number of people and it is primarily the cultural dimensions of these interactions that is vital for them to consider in leadership and managerial work.

More important, defining organizational culture solely from a management/ technical cognitive interest precludes use of the culture concept to raise broader questions about cultural patterns in organizations, business, and working life and diverts attention from questioning of the status quo, for example in terms of dominant ideologies, political interests and self-constraining, taken-for-granted assumptions and beliefs.

The 'management-centric' interest in 'thin description' of corporate culture can be contrasted with the 'thick description' which examines complex layers of meanings in the anthropological tradition (Geertz, 1973). And, while recognizing the legitimacy and value of studies of corporate culture, it can rightly be argued that the use of culture studies to call into question taken-for-granted understandings and challenge parochialism has on the whole remained underdeveloped. One reason for this, apart from the technical preoccupation just mentioned, appears to be the widespread assumption that organizations are containers of cultures and researchers need not attend to anything outside them in cultural terms. (Cross-cultural management and institutional theory are in some respects exceptions.) Equating organization and culture easily leads to myopia. Organizational culture studies would benefit from taking organizations – as integrated entities – less seriously. Geertz (1973) suggests that anthropologists do not study villages, they study *in* villages. Organizational culture researchers might benefit from reconceptualizing their projects and beginning to study *in* organizations (bearing in mind that organizations are also part of society). Practitioners presumably already know that they manage in a particular local cultural context of the subordinates and closest colleagues and superiors. A concentrated interpretation of local meaning and values and idea-development based on this may, however, be supported by a cultural framework emphasizing this and not reinforcing broad-brushed and vague thought about mastering entire organizational cultures.

As I will never be tired of saying, a detailed understanding of organizational culture requires careful consideration of what 'culture' as a guiding concept draws attention to – and from – and what we better can capture through other vocabularies. There is a strong need for thinking through different, but complementary ways of using a cultural perspective. Culture is best perceived not simply as a provider of clues for understanding social integration and harmony and guiding behaviour, but also as a theoretical tool for developing sensitivity for differentiation, inconsistency, confusion, conflict, and contradiction. Organizational culture not only serves 'positive' functions such as fulfilling people's needs for meaning, guidance, and expressiveness but also leads to closure of mind and reduction of autonomy. Culture provides direction but also prevents us from 'seeing' and imagining. Culture reflects and reinforces not only (true) consensus but also domination. It is hardly possible to take all of these dimensions into account at one and the same time, but an awareness of the many faces and aspects of cultural manifestations in organizations makes possible a repertoire of ways of 'thinking culturally'. It is for example not impossible to consider culture as a guideline and a social glue as well as a set of blinders and a collective mental prison. Or as local manifestation as well as reflection of broader societal patterns. As we become increasingly aware of the way in which our conceptions create understandings of reality, explicit recognition of this seems appropriate. Showing how different approaches produce partial but instructive views of cultural manifestations in organizations will hardly tell the whole story, but it can encourage reflective thinking about how organizations function and how people live their organizational lives.

Note

1   I am here talking about leadership, i.e. action aiming at influencing people. The situation is different in 'less social' and more technical areas, e.g. doing financial investments or obeying legislation.

References

Abravanel, H. (1983) Mediatory myths in the service of organizational ideology. In Pondy, L.R. *et al.* (eds) *Organizational Symbolism.* Greenwich, CT: JAI Press.

Academy of Management Executive (1999) Comp USA's CEO James Halpin on technology, rewards, and commitment, 13, 2, 29–36.

Ahrne, G. (1990) *Agency and Organization.* London: Sage.

Allaire, Y. and Firsirotu, M. (1984) Theories of organizational culture. *Organization Studies,* 5, 193–226.

Allen, R. (1985) Four phases for bringing about cultural change. In Kilmann, R.H., Saxton, M., Serpa, R. *et al.* (eds) *Gaining Control of Corporate Culture.* San Francisco: Jossey-Bass.

Alvesson, M. (1987) *Organization Theory and Technocratic Consciousness.* Berlin/New York: de Gruyter.

Alvesson, M. (1990) Organizations: From substance to image? *Organization Studies,* 11, 373–394.

Alvesson, M. (1991) Organizational symbolism and ideology. *Journal of Management Studies,* 28, 3, 207–225.

Alvesson, M. (1993a) *Cultural Perspectives on Organizations.* Cambridge: Cambridge University Press.

Alvesson, M. (1993b) Cultural-ideological modes of management control. In Deetz, S. (ed.) *Communication Yearbook.* Vol. 16. Newbury Park: Sage.

Alvesson, M. (1993c) The play of metaphors. In Hassard, J. and Parker, M. (eds) *Postmodernism and Organizations.* London: Sage.

Alvesson, M. (1995) *Management of Knowledge-intensive Companies.* Berlin/New York: de Gruyter.

Alvesson, M. (1996) *Communication, Power and Organization.* Berlin/New York: de Gruyter.

Alvesson, M. (2000) Social identity and the problem of loyalty in knowledge-intensive companies. *Journal of Management Studies,* 37, 8, 1101–1123.

Alvesson, M. (2001) Knowledge work. Ambiguity, image and identity. *Human Relations,* 54, 7.

Alvesson, M. and Berg, P.O. (1992) *Corporate Culture and Organizational Symbolism.* Berlin/New York: de Gruyter.

Alvesson, M. and Billing, Y.D. (1997) *Understanding Gender and Organization.* London: Sage.

Alvesson, M. and Björkman, I. (1992) *Organisationsidentitet och organisationsbyggande. En studie av ett industriföretag* ('Organizational identity and organization building'). Lund: Studentlitteratur.

Alvesson, M. and Deetz, S. (2000) *Doing Critical Management Research.* London: Sage.

Alvesson, M. and Kärreman, D. (2001) Odd couple. Contradictions in knowledge management. *Journal of Management Studies* (forthcoming).

Alvesson, M. and Sandkull, B. (1988) The organizational melting-pot. An arena for different cultures. *Scandinavian Journal of Management,* 4, 135–145.

Alvesson, M. and Sköldberg, K. (2000) *Reflexive Methodology.* London: Sage.

Alvesson, M. and Willmott, H. (1996) *Making Sense of Management. A Critical Introduction.* London: Sage.

Anthony, P. (1994) *Managing Organizational Culture.* Buckinghamshire: Open University Press.

Ashforth, B. and Mael, F. (1996) Organizational identity and strategy as a context for the individual. *Advances in Strategic Management,* 13, 19–64.

Baker, E.L. (1980) Managing organizational culture. *Management Review,* June 1980, 8–13.

Bakka, J.F. and Fivelsdal, E. (1988) *Organisationsteori* ('Organization Theory'). Malmö: Liber.

Barley, S. and Kunda, G. (1992) Design and devotion: surges of rational and normative ideologies of control in managerial discourse. *Administrative Science Quarterly*, 37, 363–399.

Barney, J.B. (1986) Organizational culture: Can it be a source of sustained competitive advantage? *Academy of Management Review*, 11, 656–665.

Bartunek, J. and Spreitzer, G. (1999) The career of a popular construct: a pluralistic journey of understandings of empowerment. Paper presented at the annual meeting of the Academy of Management, August, Chicago.

Beck, B. and Moore, L. (1985) Linking the host culture to organizational variables. In Frost, P.J. *et al.* (eds) *Organizational Culture*. Beverly Hills: Sage.

Berg, P.O. (1982) 11 metaphors and their theoretical implications. In Berg, P.O. and Daudi, P. (eds) *Traditions and Trends in Organization Theory. Part II*. Lund: Studentlitteratur.

Berg, P.O. (1985a) Organization change as a symbolic transformation process. In Frost, P.J. *et al.* (eds) *Organizational Culture*. Beverly Hills: Sage.

Berg, P.O. (1985b) Techno-culture: The symbolic framing of technology in a Volvo plant. *Scandinavian Journal of Management Studies*, 1, 237–256.

Berg, P.O. (1986) Symbolic management of human resources. *Human Resource Management*, 25, 557–579.

Berg, P.O. and Kreiner, K. (1990) Corporate architecture. Turning physical settings into symbolic resources. In Gagliardi, P. (ed.) *Symbols and Artifacts: Views of the Corporate Landscape*. Berlin/New York: de Gruyter.

Berger, P. and Luckman, T. (1966) *The Social Construction of Reality; A Treatise on the Sociology of Knowledge*. New York: Doubleday.

Bernstein, R.J. (1983) *Beyond Objectivism and Relativism*. Oxford: Basil Blackwell.

Biggart, N.W. and Hamilton, G.G. (1987) An institutional theory of leadership. *Journal of Applied Behavioural Science*, 23, 429–441.

Billing, Y.D. and Alvesson, M. (1994) *Gender, Managers and Organizations*. Berlin/New York: de Gruyter.

Boje, D. (1991) The story-telling organization: a study of story performance in an office-supply firm. *Administrative Science Quarterly*, 36, 106–126.

Boorstin, D. (1960) *The Image*. New York: Athenum.

Borowsky, R. (ed.) (1994) *Assessing Cultural Anthropology*. New York: McGraw-Hill.

Bourdieu, P. (1979) *Outline of a Theory of Practice*. Cambridge: Cambridge University Press.

Boyacigiller, N. and Adler, N. (1991) The parochial dinosaur: The organizational sciences in a global context. *Academy of Management Review*, 16, 262–290.

Braverman, H. (1974) *Labour and Monopoly Capital*. New York Monthly Review Press.

Broms, H. and Gahmberg, H. (1983) Communication to self in organizations and cultures. *Administrative Science Quarterly*, 28, 482–495.

Broms, H. and Gahmberg, H. (1987) *Semiotics of Management*. Helsinki: Helsinki School of Economics.

Brown, A. (1995) *Organizational Culture*. London: Pitman.

Brown, A. and Starkey, K. (2000) Organizational identity and learning: A psychodynamic perspective. *Academy of Management Review*, 25, 1, 102–120.

Brown, R.H. (1976) Social theory as metaphor. *Theory and Society*, 3, 169–197.

Brulin, G. (1989) *Från den 'svenska modellen' till företagskorporativism?* ('From the Swedish model to managerial corporatism') Lund: Arkiv.

Bryman, A. (1993) Charismatic leadership in business organizations: Some neglected issues. *Leadership Quarterly*, 4, 289–304.

Burawoy, M. (1979) *Manufacturing Consent*. Chicago: University of Chicago Press.

Burrell, G. and Morgan, G. (1979) *Sociological Paradigms and Organizational Analysis*. London: Heinemann.

Burris, B. (1996) Technocracy, patriarchy and management. In Collinson, D. and Hearn, J. (eds) *Men as Managers, Managers as Men*. London: Sage.

Calás, M. and Smircich, L. (1987) Is the organizational culture literature dominant but dead? Paper presented at the 3rd International Conference on Organizational Symbolism and Corporate Culture, Milan, June 1987.

Calás, M. and Smircich, L. (1992a) Feminist theories and the social consequences of organizational research. In Mills, A. and Tancred, P. (eds) *Gendering Organizational Analysis*. London: Sage.

Calás, M. and Smircich, L. (1992b) Re-writing gender into organizational theorizing: Directions from feminist perspectives. In Reed, M. and Hughes, M. (eds) *Re-thinking Organization: New Directions in Organizational Theory and Analysis*. London: Sage.

Calori, R. and Sarnin, P. (1991) Corporate culture and economic performance. *Organization Studies*, 12, 49–74.

Carlzon, J. (1987) *Moments of Truth*. London: Ballinger.

Carter, P. and Jackson, N. (1987) Management, myth and metatheory – from scarcity to postscarcity. *International Studies of Management Organization*, 17, 3, 64–89.

Casey, C. (1996) Corporate transformations: Designer culture, designer employees and 'post-occupational solidarity'. *Organization*, 3, 3, 317–339.

Castoriadis, C. (1992) Power, politics, autonomy. In Honneth, A. *et al.* (eds) *Cultural-Political Interventions in the Unfinished Project of Enlightenment*. Cambridge, MA: MIT Press.

Chaffee, E. (1985) Three models of strategy. *Academy of Management Review*, 10, 89–98.

Clegg, S. (1987) The power of language, the language of power. *Organization Studies*, 8, 1, 60–70.

Clegg, S. (1989) *Frameworks of Power*. London: Sage.

Clegg, S. (1990) *Modern Organizations: Organization Studies in the Postmodern World*. London: Sage.

Clegg, S. and Hardy, C. (1996) Some dare call it power. In Clegg, S., Hardy, C. and Nord, W. (eds) *Handbook of Organization Studies*. London: Sage.

Clegg, S. *et al.* (1996) Management knowledge for the future: Innovation, embryos and new paradigms. In Clegg, S. and Palmer, G. (eds) *The Politics of Management Knowledge*. London: Sage.

Cockburn, C. (1991) *In the Way of Women*. London: Macmillan.

Cohen, A. (1974) *Two-Dimensional Man. An Essay in the Anthropology of Power and Symbolism in Complex Society*. London: Routledge & Kegan Paul.

Collinson, D. (1988) 'Engineering humour': Masculinity, joking and conflict in shop-floor relations. *Organization Studies*, 10, 181–200.

Cooper, R. and Burrell, G. (1988) Modernism, postmodernism and organizational analysis: An introduction. *Organization Studies*, 9, 91–112.

Covaleski, M. *et al.* (1998) The calculated and the avowed: Techniques of discipline and struggles over identity in big six public accounting firms. *Administrative Science Quarterly*, 43, 293–327.

Czarniawska-Joerges, B. (1992) *Exploring Complex Organizations*. Newbury Park: Sage.

Dahlström, E. (1982) Kan sociologin förtöja kulturanalysen? ('Can sociology anchor cultural analysis?') In Hannerz, U., Liljeström, R. and Löfgren, O. (eds) *Kultur och medvetande*. Stockholm: Akademilitteratur.

Dandridge, T.C. (1986) Ceremony as the integration of work and play. *Organization Studies*, 7, 159–170.

Dandridge, T.C., Mitroff, I.I. and Joyce, W.F. (1980) Organizational symbolism: A topic to expand organizational analysis. *Academy of Management Review*, 5, 77–82.

Davenport, T. and Prusak, L. (1998) *Working Knowledge*. Cambridge, MA: Harvard Business Press.

Davis, T. (1985) Managing culture at the bottom. In Kilmann, R.H., Saxton, M., Serpa, R. *et al.* (eds) (1985) *Gaining Control of Corporate Culture*. San Francisco: Jossey-Bass.

Deal, T.E. and Kennedy, A.A. (1982) *Corporate Culture*. Reading: Addison-Wesley.

Deetz, S. (1992) *Democracy in an Age of Corporate Colonization*. Albany: State University of New York Press.

Deetz, S. (1996) Describing differences in approaches to organizational science: Rethinking Burrell and Morgan and their legacy. *Organization Science*, 7, 191–207.

Deetz, S. (1997) Discursive formations, strategized subordination, and self-surveillance. In McKinley, A. and Starkey, K. (eds) *Foucault, Management and Organization Theory*. London: Sage.

Deetz, S. and Kersten, S. (1983) Critical models of interpretive research. In Putnam, L. and Pacanowsky, M. (eds) *Communication and Organizations*. Beverly Hills: Sage.

Deetz, S. and Mumby, D. (1986) Metaphors, information, and power. In Reuben, B. (ed.) *Information and Behavior*. New Brunswick, NJ: Transaction Books.

Denison, D. (1984) Bringing corporate culture to the bottom line. *Organizational Dynamics*, 13, 2, 4–22.

Dervin, B. (1990) Illusions of equality, reification of inequality: Problems in leadership research. Paper presented at International Communication Association, Dublin, June 1990.

Desphande, R. and Webster, F. (1989) Organizational culture and marketing: Defining the research agenda. *Journal of Marketing*, 53, Jan, 3–15.

DiMaggio, P. and Powell, W. (1983) The iron cage revisited: Institutional isomorphism and collective rationality in organizational fields. *American Sociological Review*, 48, 147–160.

Dougherty, D. and Kunda, G. (1990) Photograph analysis: A method to capture organizational belief systems. In Gagliardi, P. (ed.) *Symbols and Artifacts: Views of the Corporate Landscape*. Berlin/New York: de Gruyter.

du Gay, P. (1996) Making up managers: enterprise and the ethos of bureaucracy. In Clegg, S. and Palmer, G. (eds) *The Politics of Management Knowledge*. London: Sage.

du Gay, P. and Salaman, G. (1992) The cult(ure) of the consumer, *Journal of Management Studies*, 29, 5, 615–633.

Dunford, R. and Palmer, I. (1996) Metaphors in popular management discourse: The case of corporate restructuring. In Grant, D. and Oswick, C. (eds) *Metaphor and Organizations*. London: Sage.

Ebers, M. (1995) The framing of organizational cultures. *Research in the Sociology of Organizations*, 13, 129–170.

Ely, R. (1995) The power in demography: Women's social constructions of gender identity at work. *Academy of Management Journal*, 38, 3, 589–634.

Empson, L. (2001) Fear of exploitation and fear of contamination: Impediments to knowledge transfer in mergers between professional service firms. *Human Relations*, 54, 7.

Featherstone, M. (1988) In pursuit of the postmodern: An introduction. *Theory, Culture & Society*, 5, 195–215.

Feldman, J. (1991) The meaning of ambiguity: Learning from stories and metaphors. In Frost, P.J. et al. (eds) *Reframing Organizational Culture*. Newbury Park: Sage.

Feldman, J. and March, J. (1981) Information in organizations as signal and symbol. *Administrative Science Quarterly*, 26, 171, 186.

Filipo, J.-P. (1986) Service firms: Interdependence of external and internal marketing strategies. *European Journal of Marketing*, 20, 8.

Fineman, S. (1993) Organizations as emotional arenas. In Fineman, S. (ed.) *Emotion in Organizations*. London: Sage.

Fineman, S. (1998) The natural environment, organization and ethics. In Parker, M. (ed.) *Ethics & Organizations*. London: Sage.

Fitzgerald, T. (1988) Can change in organizational culture really be managed? *Organizational Dynamics*, 17, 2, 4–15.

Foley, D. (1989) Does the working class have a culture in the anthropological sense? *Cultural Anthropology*, 137–162.

Fombrun, C. (1986) Structural dynamics within and between organizations. *Administrative Science Quarterly*, 31, 403–421.

Fondas, N. (1997) Feminization unveiled: Management qualities in contemporary writings. *Academy of Management Review*, 22, 257–282.

Foucault, M. (1980) *Power/Knowledge*. New York: Pantheon.

Fromm, E. (1976) *To Have or To Be?* London: Abacus.

Frost, P.J. (1987) Power, politics, and influence. In Jablin, F. *et al.* (eds) *Handbook of Organizational Communication*. Newbury Park: Sage.

Frost, P.J. *et al.* (eds) (1985) *Organizational Culture*. Newbury Park: Sage.

Gagliardi, P. (1986) The creation and change of organizational cultures: A conceptual framework. *Organization Studies*, 7, 117–134.

Gagliardi, P. (1990) Artifacts as pathways and remains of organizational life. In Gagliardi, P. (ed.) *Symbols and Artifacts: Views of the Corporate Landscape*. Berlin/New York: de Gruyter.

Gardell, B. (1976) *Arbetsinnehåll och livskvalitet* ('Work content and quality of life'). Stockholm: Prisma.

Geertz, C. (1973) *The Interpretation of Culture*. New York: Basic Books.

Gherardi, S. (1995) *Gender, Symbolism and Organizational Cultures*. London: Sage.

Giddens, A. (1991) *Modernity and Self-Identity*. Cambridge: Polity Press.

Giesen, B. and Schmid, M. (1989) Symbolic, institutional, and social-structural differentiation: A selection-theoretical perspective. In Haferkamp, H. (ed.) *Social Structure and Culture*. Berlin/New York: de Gruyter.

Granovetter, M. (1985) Economic action and social structure: The problem of embeddedness. *American Journal of Sociology*, 91, 481–510.

Grant, D. and Oswick, C. (eds) (1996) *Metaphor and Organizations*. London: Sage.

Greenwood, R. *et al.* (1990) P2-form strategic management: Corporate practices in professional partnerships. *Academy of Management Journal*, 33, 4, 725–755.

Gregory, K.L. (1983) Native-view paradigms. Multiple cultures and culture conflicts in organizations. *Administrative Science Quarterly*, 28, 359–376.

Grey, C. (1999) Change in organizations? Working paper, Judge Institute of Management, Cambridge University,

Grönroos, C. (1983) Intern marknadsföring. In Arndt, J. and Friman, A. (eds) *Intern marknadsföring*. Malmö: Liber.

Gusfield, J. and Michalowicz, J. (1984) Secular symbolism: Studies of ritual, ceremony and the symbolic order in modern life. *Annual Review of Sociology*, 10, 417–435.

Habermas, J. (1972) *Knowledge and Human Interests*. London: Heinemann.

Hackman, J.R. *et al.* (1975) A new strategy for job enrichment. In Staw, B. (ed.) *Psychological Foundations of Organizational Behaviour*. Santa Monica: Goodyear.

Håkansson, H. and Snehota, I. (1989) No business is an island: The network concept of business strategy. *Scandinavian Journal of Management*, 5, 187–200.

Hall, E. (1993) Smiling, deferring and flirting. Doing gender by giving 'good service'. *Work and Occupations*, 20, 4, 452–471.

Hannerz, U. (1988) Culture between center and periphery: Toward a macroanthropology. Paper presented at symposion on Culture in Complex Societies, Stockholm, April 1988.

Hansen, K. (1996) The mentality of management: Self-images of American top executives. In Clegg, S. and Palmer, G. (eds) *The Politics of Management Knowledge*. London: Sage.

Hardy, C. (1994) Power and politics in organizations. In *Managing Strategic Action*. London: Sage.

Harris, L. and Ogbonna, E. (1999) Developing a market orientated culture: A critical evaluation. *Journal of Management Studies*, 36, 2, 177–196.

Hassard, J. and Parker, M. (eds) (1993) *Postmodernism and Organizations*. London: Sage.

Hedberg, B. and Jönsson, S. (1977) Strategy formulation as a discontinuous process. *International Studies of Management and Organisation*, 7, 2, 88–100.

Heilman, M., Block, C. and Stathatos, P. (1997) The affirmative action stigma of incompetence: Effects of performance information ambiguity. *Academy of Management Journal*, 40, 3, 603–625.

Helmers, S. (1991) Anthropological contributions to organizational culture. *SCOS Notework*, 10, 60–72.

Henriksson, K. (1999) *The Collective Dynamics of Organizational Learning*. Lund: Lund University Press.

Hentze, H. (1994) My greatest failure. In Adam-Smith, D. and Peacock, A. (eds) *Cases in Organizational Behaviour*. London: Pitman.

Hirsch, F. (1976) *Social Limits to Growth*. Cambridge, MA: Harvard University Press.

Hofstede, G. (1980) Motivation, leadership and organization: Do American theories apply abroad? *Organizational Dynamics*, Summer 1980, 42–63.

Hofstede, G. (1985) The interaction between national and organizational value systems. *Journal of Management Studies*, 22, 347–357.

Hofstede, G. *et al.* (1990) Measuring organizational cultures: A qualitative and quantitative study across twenty cases. *Administrative Science Quarterly*, 35, 286–316.

Horkheimer, M. and Adorno, T. (1947) *The Dialectics of Enlightenment*. London: Verso 1979.

House, R. and Aditay, R. (1997) The scientific study of leadership: Quo vadis? *Journal of Management*, 23, 409–473.

Inns, D. and Jones, P. (1996) Metaphor in organization theory: following in the footstep of the poet. In Grant, D. and Oswick, C. (eds) *Metaphor and Organizations*. London: Sage.

Jackall, R. (1988) *Moral Mazes. The World of Corporate Managers*. Oxford: Oxford University Press.

Jackson, N. and Willmott, H. (1987) Beyond epistemology and reflective conversation: Towards human relations. *Human Relations*, 40, 361–380.

Jaggar, A. (1989) Love and knowledge. *Critical Inquiry*, 32, 151–176.

Jeffcutt, P. (1993) From interpretation to representation. In Hassard, J. and Parker, M. (eds) *Postmodernism and Organizations*. London: Sage.

Johansson, O.L. (1990) *Organisationsbegrepp och begreppsmedvetenhet*. ('Concepts of organization and conceptual awareness') Goteborg: BAS.

Jones, G. (1983) Transaction costs, property rights and organizational culture: An exchange perspective. *Administrative Science Quarterly*, 28, 454–457.

Jönsson, S. and Lundin, R.A. (1977) Myths and wishful thinking as management tools. In Nystrom, P.C. and Starbuck, W.H. (eds) *Prescriptive Models of Organization*, Amsterdam: North-Holland.

Kanter, R.M. (1977) *Men and Women of the Corporation*. New York: Basic Books.

Kanter, R.M. (1983) *The Change Masters*. London: Unwin-Hyman.

Karasek, R.A. (1981) Job socialization and stress. In Gardell, B. and Johansson, G. (eds) *Working Life*. Chichester: Wiley.

Kärreman, D. (1996) *Det oväntades administration* ('The administration of the unexpected'). Stockholm: Nerenius & Santérus.

Kärreman, D. and Alvesson, M. (2000) Ethical closure in organizational settings – the case of media organizations. Working paper, Dept. of Business Administration, Lund University.

Kärreman, D. and Alvesson, M. (2001) Making newspapers. Conversational identity at work. *Organization Studies*, 22, 59–89.

Keesing, R. (1994) Theories of culture revisited. In Borofsky, R (ed.) *Assessing Cultural Anthropology*. New York: McGraw-Hill.

Kernberg, O. (1980) Organizational regression. In *Internal World and External Reality*. New York: Jason Aronson.

Kets de Vries, M. and Miller, D. (1984) *The Neurotic Organization*. San Francisco: Jossey-Bass

Kets de Vries, M. and Miller, D. (1986) Personality, culture and organization. *Academy of Management Review*, 11, 266–279.

Kilmann, R.H. (1985) Five steps to close the culture gap. In Kilmann, R.H., Saxton, M., Serpa, R. *et al.* (eds) *Gaining Control of Corporate Culture*. San Francisco: Jossey-Bass.

Kilmann, R.H., Saxton, M., Serpa, R. *et al.* (1985) *Gaining Control of Corporate Culture.* San Francisco: Jossey-Bass.

Kleppestø, S. (1993) *Kultur och identitet* ('Culture and identity'). Stockholm: Nerenius & Santérus.

Knights, D. and Morgan, G. (1991) Corporate strategy, organizations and subjectivity: A critique, *Organization Studies*, 12, 251–273.

Knights, D. and Willmott, H.C. (1987) Organizational culture as management strategy: A critique and illustration from the financial service industries. *International Studies of Management & Organization*, 17, 3, 40–63.

Knorr-Cetina, K. (1981) Introduction. The micro-sociological challenge of macro-sociology: Towards a reconstruction of social theory and methodology. In Knorr-Cetina, K. and Cicourel, A. (eds) *Advances in Social Theory and Methodology.* Boston: Routledge & Kegan Paul.

Kohn, M. (1980) Job complexity and adult personality. In Smelser, N. and Erikson, E.H. (eds) *Themes of Work and Love in Adulthood.* Cambridge, MA: Harvard University Press.

Kotter, J. (1985) *The Leadership Factor.* New York: The Free Press.

Krefting, L. and Frost, P.J. (1985) Untangling webs, surfing waves, and wildcatting: A multiple-metaphor perspective on managing organizational culture. In Frost, P.J. *et al.* (eds) *Organizational Culture.* Beverly Hills: Sage.

Kuhn, T.S. (1970) *The Structure of Scientific Revolutions.* Chicago: University of Chicago Press.

Kunda, G. (1992) *Engineering Culture: Control and Commitment in a High-Tech Corporation.* Philadelphia, PA: Temple University Press.

Kunda, G. and Barley, S.R. (1988) Designing devotion: Corporate culture and ideologies of workplace control. Paper presented at the American Sociological Association 83rd Annual Meeting, Atlanta, August 1988.

Lakoff, G. and Johnson, M. (1980) *Metaphors We Live By.* Chicago: University of Chicago Press.

Lasch, C. (1978) *The Culture of Narcissism.* New York: Norton.

Laurant, A. (1978) Managerial subordinancy: A neglected aspect of organizational hierarchy. *Academy of Management Review*, 3, 220–230.

Leach, E. (1982) *Social Anthropology.* Glasgow: Fontana.

Leidner, R. (1991) Serving hamburgers and selling insurance: Gender, work and identity in interactive service jobs. *Gender & Society*, 5, 2, 154–177.

Leiss, W. (1978) *The Limits to Satisfaction.* London: Marion Boyars.

Levy, D., Alvesson, M. and Willmott, H. (2001) Critical approaches to management. In Alvesson, M. and Willmott, H. (eds) *Critical Management Studies* (2nd edn) London: Sage.

Linstead, S. (1985) Symbolization and ambiguity in organizations: Induction, humour, and the symbolic process. *CEBES Journal*, 1, 2, 52–97.

Linstead, S. and Grafton-Small, R. (1990) Theory as artefact: Artefact as theory. In Gagliardi, P. (ed.) *Symbols and Artifacts: Views of the Corporate Landscape.* Berlin/New York: de Gruyter.

Lipman-Blumen, J. (1992) Connective leadership: Female leadership styles in the 21st-century workplace, *Sociological Perspectives*, 35, 1, 183–203.

Löfgren, O. (1982) Kulturbygge och kulturkonfrontation ('Culture building and culture confrontation'). In Hannerz, U., Liljeström, R. and Löfgren, O. (eds) *Kultur och medvetande.* Stockholm: Akademilitteratur.

Louis, M.R. (1981) A culture perspective on organizations: The need for and consequences of viewing organizations as cultural-bearing milieux. *Human Systems Management*, 2, 246–258.

Louis, M.R. (1985) An investigator's guide to workplace culture. In Frost, P.J. *et al.* (eds) *Organizational Culture.* Beverly Hills: Sage.

Lukes, S. (1978) Authority and power. In Bottomore, T. and Nisbet, R. (eds) *A History of Sociological Analysis.* London: Heinemann.

Lundberg, C.C. (1985) On the feasibility of cultural intervention in organizations. In Frost, P.J. *et al.* (eds) *Organizational Culture.* Beverly Hills: Sage.

Mangham, I. and Overington, M. (1987) *Organizations as Theatre*. Chichester: Wiley.

March, J. and Olsen, J. (1976) *Ambiguity and Choice in Organizations*. Bergen: Universitetsforlaget.

Marcus, G. and Fischer, M. (1986) *Anthropology as Cultural Critique*. Chicago: University of Chicago Press.

Marcuse, H. (1964) *One-dimensional Man*. Boston: Beacon Press.

Marshall, J. (1993) Viewing organizational communication from a feminist perspective: A critique and some offerings. *Communication Yearbook*, 16, 122–143.

Martin, J. (1987) The Black Hole. Ambiguity in organizational cultures. Paper presented to the 3rd International Conference on Organizational Symbolism and Corporate Culture, Milano, June 1987.

Martin, J. (1992) *The Culture of Organizations. Three Perspectives*. New York: Oxford University Press.

Martin, J. and Frost, P. (1996) The organizational culture wars: A struggle for intellectual dominance. In Clegg, S., Hardy, C. and Nord, W. (eds) *Handbook of Organization Studies*. London: Sage.

Martin, J. and Meyerson, D. (1988) Organizational cultures and the denial, channeling and acknowledgement of ambiguity. In Pondy, L.R. *et al.* (eds) *Managing Ambiguity and Change*. New York: Wiley.

Martin, J., Feldman, M.S., Hatch, M.J. and Sitkin, S.B. (1983) The uniqueness paradox in organizational stories. *Administrative Science Quarterly*, 28, 438–453.

Martin, J., Sitkin, S. and Boehm, M. (1985) Founders and the elusiveness of a cultural legacy. In Frost, P.J. *et al.* (eds) *Organizational Culture*. Beverly Hills: Sage.

Martin, J., Knopp, K. and Beckman, C. (1998) An alternative to bureaucratic impersonality and emotional labor: Bounded emotionality at the Body Shop. *Administrative Science Quarterly*, 43, 429–469.

McDermott, R. (1999) Why information technology inspired but cannot deliver knowledge management. *California Management Review*, 41, 4, 103–117.

McGovern, P. and Pope-Hailey, V. (1997) Inside Hewlett-Packard: Corporate culture and bureaucratic control. In Sackman, S. (ed.) *Cultural Complexity in Organizations*. Thousand Oaks: Sage.

Menzies, I. (1960) A case study in the functioning of social systems as a defence against anxiety. *Human Relations*, 13, 95–121.

Meyer, J. and Rowan, B. (1977) Institutionalized organizations: Formal structure as myth and ceremony. *American Journal of Sociology*, 83, 340–363.

Meyerson, D. and Martin, J. (1987) Cultural change: An integration of three different views. *Journal of Management Studies*, 24, 623–648.

Mills, A. (1988) Organization, gender and culture. *Organization Studies*, 9, 351–370.

Mintzberg, H. (1990) The design school: Reconsidering the basic premises of strategic management. *Strategic Management Journal*, 11, 171–195.

Morgan, G. (1980) Paradigms, metaphors, and puzzle solving in organizational analysis. *Administrative Science Quarterly*, 25, 606–622.

Morgan, G. (1983) More on metaphor: Why we cannot control tropes in administrative science. *Administrative Science Quarterly*, 28, 601–608.

Morgan, G. (1986) *Images of Organization*. Beverly Hills: Sage.

Morgan, G. (1996) An afterword: Is there anything more to be said about metaphors? In Grant, D. and Oswick, C. (eds) *Metaphor and Organizations*. London: Sage.

Mumby, D. (1988) *Communication and Power in Organizations: Discourse, Ideology and Domination*. Norwood, NJ: Ablex.

Narver, J. and Slater, S. (1990) The effect of a market orientation on business profitability. *Journal of Marketing*, 54, Oct., 20–35.

Nicholls, J. (1987) Leadership in organisations: Meta, macro and micro. *European Journal of Management*, 6, 16–25.

Nord, W. (1985) Can organizational culture be managed? A Synthesis. In Frost, P.J. *et al.* (eds) *Organizational Culture*. Beverly Hills: Sage.

Normann, R. (1977) *Management for Growth*. London: Wiley.

Normann, R. (1983) *Service Management*. London: Wiley.

O'Dell, C. and Grayson, J. (1998) If only we knew what we know: Identification and transfer of best practices. *California Management Review*, 40, 3, 154–173.

Olie, R. (1994) Shades of culture and institutions in international mergers. *Organization Studies*, 15, 381–405.

Ortner, S. (1973) On key symbols. *American Anthropologist*, 75, 1338–1346.

Ortner, S. (1984) Theory in anthropology since the sixties. *Comparative Studies in Society and History*, 26, 126–166.

Østerberg, D. (1971) *Makt och materiell* ('Power and materia'). Göteborg: Korpen.

Østerberg, D. (1985) Materiell och praxis ('Materia and praxis'). In Andersson, S. *et al.* (eds) *Mellan människor och ting*. Göteborg: Korpen.

Oswick, C. and Grant, D. (1996) The organization of metaphors and the metaphors of organization: Where are we and where do we go from here? In Grant, D. and Oswick, C. (eds) *Metaphor and Organizations*. London: Sage.

Ouchi, W.G. (1980) Markets, bureaucracies and clans. *Administrative Science Quarterly*, 25, 129–141.

Ouchi, W.G. (1981) *Theory Z*. Reading: Addison-Wesley.

Ouchi, W.G. and Wilkins, A.L. (1985) Organizational culture. *Annual Review of Sociology*, 11, 457–483.

Outhwaite, W. (1983) Toward a realist perspective. In Morgan, G. (ed.) *Beyond Method*. Beverly Hills: Sage.

Pacanowsky, M. and O'Donnel-Trujillo, N. (1983) Organizational communication as cultural performance. *Communication Monographs*, 50, 126–147.

Palmer, I. and Dunford, R. (1996) Interrogating reframing: Evaluating metaphor-based analysis of organizations. In Clegg, S. and Palmer, G. (eds) *The Politics of Management Knowledge*. London: Sage.

Palmer, I. and Hardy, C. (2000) *Thinking about Management*. London: Sage.

Parker, M. (2000) *Organizational Culture and Identity*. London: Sage.

Pennings, J. and Gresov, C. (1986) Technoeconomic and structural correlates of organizational culture: An integrative framework. *Organization Studies*, 7, 317–334.

Perrow, C. (1986) *Complex Organizations: A Critical Essay*. New York: Random House.

Peters, T.J. and Waterman, R.H. (1982) *In Search of Excellence*. New York: Harper & Row.

Pettigrew, A. (1979) On studying organizational cultures. *Administrative Science Quarterly*, 24, 570–581.

Pettigrew, A. (1985) Examining change in the long-term context of culture and politics. In Pennings, J. *et al.* (eds) *Organizational Strategy and Change*. San Francisco: Jossey-Bass.

Pfeffer, J. (1978) The ambiguity of leadership. In McCall, M. *et al.* (eds) *Leadership: Where Else Can We Go?* Durham: Duke University Press.

Pfeffer, J. (1981a) Management as symbolic action: The creation and maintenance of organizational paradigms. In Cummings, L.L. and Staw, B.M. (eds) *Research in Organizational Behaviour*. Vol. 3. Greenwich, CT: JAI Press.

Pfeffer, J. (1981b) *Power in Organizations*. Boston: Pitman.

Pfeffer, J. (1994) *Competitive Advantage Through People*. Boston: Harvard Business Press.

Pfeffer, J. and Salancik, G. (1978) *The External Control of Organizations*. New York: Harper & Row.

Pinder, C. and Bourgeois, V. (1982) Controlling tropes in administrative science. *Administrative Science Quarterly*, 27, 641–652.

Pondy, L.R. (1983) The role of metaphors and myths in organization and in the facilitation of change. In Pondy, L.R., Frost, P.J., Morgan, G. and Dandridge, T.C. (eds) *Organizational Symbolism*. Greenwich, CT: JAI Press Inc.

Power, M. (1990) Modernism, postmodernism and organization. In Hassard, J. and Pym, D. (eds) *The Theory and Philosophy of Organizations*. London: Routledge.

Prahalad, C. and Hamel, G. (1990) The core competence of the corporation. *Harvard Business Review*, 68, 3, 79–91.

Prasad, P. (1997) The protestant ethic and the myth of the frontier: Cultural imprints, organizational structuring and workplace diversity. In Prasad, P. *et al.* (eds) *Managing the Organizational Melting Pot*. Thousand Oaks: Sage.

Putnam, L. (1983) The interpretive perspective: An alternative to functionalism. In Putnam, L. and Pacanowsky, M. (eds) *Communication and Organization*. Beverly Hills: Sage.

Ramfelt, L. (1993) *Näringspolitiska samverkansprojekt ur ett organisationsperspektiv – Substanstiella och symboliska aspekter på organisatoriskt handlande* ('Industry policy cooperative projects from an organizational perspective'). PhD diss. Stockholm: Stockholm University.

Ramsay, H. (1996) Managing sceptically: A critique of organizational fashion. In Clegg, S. and Palmer, G. (eds) *The Politics of Management Knowledge*. London: Sage.

Ray, C.A. (1986) Corporate culture: The last frontier of control. *Journal of Management Studies*, 23, 3, 287–296.

Reed, M. (1990) From paradigms to images: The paradigm warrior turns post-modern guru. *Personnel Review*, 19, 3, 35–40.

Ricoeur, P. (1978) Metaphor and the main problem of hermeneutics. In *The Philosophy of Paul Ricoeur*. Boston: Beacon Press.

Riley, P. (1983) A structurationist account of political cultures. *Administrative Science Quarterly*, 28, 414–437.

Robertson, M. (1999) Sustaining knowledge creation within knowledge-intensive firms. Unpublished doctoral dissertation, Warwick Business School.

Rosen, M. (1985) Breakfast at Spiro's: Dramaturgy and dominance. *Journal of Management*, 11, 2, 31–48.

Ruigrok, W. *et al.* (1999) Corporate restructuring and new forms of organizing: Evidence from Europe. *Management International Review*, 39, 2, 41–64.

Saffold, G.S. (1988) Culture traits, strength, and organizational performance: Moving beyond 'strong' culture. *Academy of Management Review*, 13, 546–558.

Sathe, V. (1985) How to decipher and change organizational culture. In Kilmann, R.H. *et al.* (eds) *Gaining Control of the Corporate Culture*. San Francisco: Jossey-Bass.

Saxenian, A. (2000) Transnational entrepreneurs and regional industrialization: The Silicon Valley-Hsinchu connection. In Tzeng, R. and Uzzi, B, (eds) *Embeddedness and Corporate Change in a Global Economy*, New York: Peter Lang.

Schein, E.H. (1985) *Organizational Culture and Leadership*. San Francisco: Jossey-Bass.

Schneider, B. and Bowen, D. (1993) The service organization: Human resources management is crucial. *Organizational Dynamics*, 39–52.

Schneider, D. (1976) Notes toward a theory of culture. In Baso, K. and Selby, H. (eds) *Meaning in Anthropology*. Albuquerque: University of New Mexico Press.

Schön, D. (1979) Generative metaphor: A perspective on problem-setting in social policy. In Ortony, A. (ed.) *Metaphor*. Cambridge: Cambridge University Press.

Scott, R. (1995) *Institutions and Organizations*. Thousand Oakes: Sage.

Sculley, J. (1987) *Odyssey: Pepsi to Apple*. New York: Harper & Row.

Selznick, P. (1957) *Leadership in Administration: A Sociological Perspective*. New York: Harper & Row.

Sennett, R. (1980) *Authority*. New York: Vintage Books.

Sennett, R. (1998) *The Corrosion of Character*. New York: Norton.

Siehl, C. (1985) After the founder: An opportunity to manage culture. In Frost, P.J. *et al.* (eds) *Organizational Culture*. Beverly Hills: Sage.

Siehl, C. and Martin, J. (1990) Organizational culture: A key to financial performance? In Schneider, B. (ed.) *Organizational Culture and Climate*. San Francisco: Jossey-Bass.

Sköldberg, K. (1990) *Administrationens poetiska logik* ('The poetic logic of administration'). Lund: Studentlitteratur.

Smircich, L. (1983a) Concepts of culture and organizational analysis. *Administrative Science Quarterly*, 28, 339–358.

Smircich, L. (1983b) Studying organizations as cultures. In Morgan, G. (ed.) *Beyond Method Strategies for Social Research*. Beverly Hills: Sage.

Smircich, L. (1983c) Organizations as shared meanings. In Pondy, L.R. *et al*. (eds) *Organizational Symbolism*. Greenwich: JAI Press.

Smircich, L. (1985) Is organizational culture a paradigm for understanding organizations and ourselves? In Frost, P.J. *et al*. (eds) *Organizational Culture*. Beverly Hills: Sage.

Smircich, L. and Morgan, G. (1982) Leadership: The management of meaning. *Journal of Applied Behavioural Science*, 18, 257–273.

Smircich, L. and Stubbart, C. (1985) Strategic management in an enacted world. *Academy of Management Review*, 10, 724–736.

Stablein, R. and Nord, W. (1985) Practical and emancipatory interests in organizational symbolism. *Journal of Management*, 11, 2, 13–28.

Starbuck, B. (1993) Keeping a butterfly and an elephant in a house of cards: the elements of exceptional success. *Journal of Management Studies*, 30, 6, 885–921.

Sunesson, S. (1981) *När man inte lyckas* ('When you don't succeed'). Stockholm: AWE/Gebers.

Sveningsson, S. (2000) Strategy as a disciplinary technology. Working paper series 2000/5. Lund Institute of Economic Research. Lund University.

Swales, J. and Rogers, P. (1995) Discourse and the projection of corporate culture. The mission statement. *Discourse and Society*, 6, 223–242.

Swidler, A. (1986) Culture in action: Symbols and strategies. *American Sociological Review*, 273–286.

Sypher, B.D., Applegate, J. and Sypher, H. (1985) Culture and communication in organizational contexts. In Gudykunst, W. *et al*. (eds) *Communication, Culture and Organizational Processes*. Beverly Hills: Sage.

Tinker, T. (1986) Metaphor or reification: Are radical humanists really libertarian anarchists? *Journal of Management Studies*, 25, 363–384.

Tompkins, P. (1987) Translating organizational theory: Symbolism over substance. In Jablin, F. *et al*. (eds) *Handbook of Organizational Communication*. Newbury Park: Sage.

Trice, H.M. and Beyer, J.M. (1984) Studying organizational cultures through rites and ceremonies. *Academy of Management Review*, 9, 653–669.

Trice, H.M. and Beyer, J.M. (1985) Using six organizational rites to change culture. In Kilmann, R.H. *et al*., *Gaining Control of the Corporate Culture*. San Francisco: Jossey-Bass.

Trice, H.M. and Beyer, J.M. (1993) *The Culture of Work Organizations*. Englewood Cliffs, NJ: Prentice-Hall.

Trist, E. and Bamforth, K. (1951) Some social and psychological consequences of the longwall method of coal-getting. In Pugh, D. (ed.) *Organization Theory*. Harmondsworth: Penguin Books 1984.

Trowler, P. (1998) *Academics Responding to Change*. Buckingham: Open University Press.

Tseng, Y.-F. (1997) Immigration and transnational economic linkages: Chinese immigrants and internationalization of Los Angeles. Paper presented at conference 'Social structure and social change: International perspectives on business firms and economic life', Academia Sinica, Taipei, Taiwan, May 9–10, 1997.

Tsoukas, H. (1991) Analogical reasoning and knowledge generation in organization theory. *Organization Studies*, 14, 323–346.

Turner, B. (1971) *Exploring the Industrial Subculture*. London: Macmillan.

Tzeng, R. (2000) Under Taiwanese management: A case study in the United States. Paper. Academica Sinica. Taipei, Taiwan.

Van Maanen, J. (1991) The smile factory. In Frost, P.J. *et al.* (eds) *Reframing Organizational Culture*. Beverly Hills: Sage.

Van Maanen, J. and Barley, S.R. (1984) Occupational communities: Culture and control in organizations. In Staw, B.M. and Cummings, L.L. (eds) *Research in Organizational Behaviour*. Vol. 7. Greenwich: JAI Press.

Van Maanen, J. and Barley, S.R. (1985) Cultural organization. Fragments of a theory. In Frost, P.J. *et al.* (eds) *Organizational Culture*. Beverly Hills: Sage.

Van Maanen, J. and Kunda, G. (1989) Real feelings: Emotional expression and organizational culture. In Staw, B.M. and Cummings, L.L. (eds) *Research in Organizational Behaviour*. Vol. 11. Greenwich: JAI Press.

von Wright, G.H. (1986) *Vetenskapen och förnuftet* ('Science and reason'). Stockholm: Månpocket.

Warhurst, C. and Thompson, P. (1998) Hands, hearts and minds: Changing work and workers at the end of the century. In Thompson, P. and Warhurst, C. (eds) *Workplaces of the Future*. London: Macmillan.

Watson, T. (1994) *In Search of Management*. London: Routledge.

Weick, K.E. (1985) The significance of corporate culture. In Frost, P.J. *et al.* (eds) *Organizational Culture*. Beverly Hills: Sage.

Weick, K.E. (1987) Theorizing about organizational communication. In Jablin, F. *et al.* (eds) *Handbook of Organizational Communication*. Newbury Park: Sage.

Westlander, G. (1976) *Arbete och fritidssituation* ('The work and leisure situation'). Stockholm: PA-rådet.

Westley, F. and Jaeger, A. (1985) An examination of organizational culture: How is it linked to performance? Paper, Faculty of Management, McGill University, Montreal.

Whipp, R., Rosenfeld, R. and Pettigrew, A. (1989) Culture and competitiveness: Evidence from two mature industries. *Journal of Management Studies*, 26, 6, 561–585.

Wiener, Y. (1988) Forms of value systems: A focus on organizational effectiveness and cultural change and maintenance. *Academy of Management Review*, 13, 534–545.

Wikström, S. and Normann, R. *et al.* (1993) *Knowledge and Value*. London: Routledge.

Wilkins, A.L. and Dyer, W.G. (1987) Toward a theory of culture change: A dialectic and synthesis. Paper presented at the 3rd International Conference on Organizational Symbolism and Corporate Culture, Milan, June 1987.

Wilkins, A.L. and Ouchi, W.G. (1983) Efficient cultures: Exploring the relationship between culture and organizational performance. *Administrative Science Quarterly*, 28, 468–481.

Wilkins, A.L. and Patterson, K. (1985) You can't get there from here: What will make culture-change projects fail. In Kilmann, R.H., Saxton, M., Serpa, R. *et al.*, *Gaining Control of Corporate Culture*. San Francisco: Jossey-Bass.

Wilkinson, B. (1996) Culture, institutions and business in East Asia. *Organization Studies*, 17, 3, 421–447.

Willmott, H. (1993) Strength is ignorance; slavery is freedom: managing culture in modern organizations. *Journal of Management Studies*, 30, 4, 515–552.

Willmott, H. (1997) Management and organization studies as science? *Organization*, 4, 3, 309–344.

Winroth, K. (1999) *När management kom till advokatbyrån* ('When management came to the law firm'). Diss. Dept of Business Administration. Gothenburg University.

Wolf, E. (1994) Facing power: old insights, new questions. In Borofsky, R. (ed.) *Assessing Cultural Anthropology*. New York: McGraw-Hill.

Ybema, S. (1996) A duck-billed platypus in the theory and analysis of organizations: Combinations of consensus and dissensus. In Koot, W. *et al.* (eds) *Contradictions in Context: Puzzling over Paradoxes in Contemporary Organizations*. Amsterdam: VU University Press.

Young, E. (1989) On the naming of the rose: Interests and multiple meanings as elements of organizational culture. *Organization Studies*, 10, 187–206.

Yukl, G. (1989) Managerial leadership: A review of theory and research. *Journal of Management*, 15, 215–289.

Zaleznik, A. (1977) Managers and leaders: Are they different? *Harvard Business Review*, May–June, 67–68.

Zeithaml, V. *et al*. (1995) Problems and strategies in service marketing. *Journal of Marketing*, 49, Spring, 33–46.

Index

Page references in *italics* indicate figures or tables